MW01717339

Career Coaching: Fundamentals, Applications, and Future Directions

Heather N. Maietta

NCDA | National Career Development Association

National Career Development Association
A founding division of the American Counseling Association

305 North Beech Circle
Broken Arrow, OK 74012

Printed in the United States of America

NCDA opposes discrimination against any individual based on age, culture, disability, ethnicity, race, religion/spirituality, creed, gender, gender identity and expression, sexual orientation, marital/partnership status, language preference, socioeconomic status, or any other personal characteristic not specifically relevant to job performance.
(Approved by the NCDA Board – October 2016)

Library of Congress Cataloging-in-Publication Data

Names: Maietta, Heather N., author.
Title: Career coaching : fundamentals, applications and future directions / by Heather N. Maietta.
Description: Broken Arrow, OK : National Career Development Association, 2022. | Includes bibliographical references. | Summary: "This book is an overview of the practice of career coaching. It covers a brief history of career coaching and comparison of counseling and coaching. Techniques, ethics, theories and models, and assessments are shared to increase knowledge and proficiency in delivering career coaching services to diverse clientele groups. Themes for the future of career coaching related to workforce demands are included"-- Provided by publisher.
Identifiers: LCCN 2022008064 (print) | LCCN 2022008065 (ebook) | ISBN 9781885333650 (paperback) | ISBN 9781885333650 (adobe pdf)
Subjects: LCSH: Vocational guidance. | Career development. | Counseling. | Personal coaching.
Classification: LCC HF5381 .M27845 2022 (print) | LCC HF5381 (ebook) | DDC 331.702--dc23/eng/20220309
LC record available at https://lccn.loc.gov/2022008064
LC ebook record available at https://lccn.loc.gov/2022008065 3

TABLE OF CONTENTS

TABLE OF CONTENTS CONTINUED

TABLES AND FIGURES

Tables

Figures

TABLE OF CONTENTS CONTINUED

FOREWORD

Career coaching has been a much talked about concept in the world of career development for some time. I first learned about career coaching while serving adult learners in a higher education context in 2013. During this period, job seekers were still feeling the effects of the 2008 Great Recession and looking for help executing their career goals. In my pursuit of resources and knowledge to help drive the advancement of my clients, I stumbled upon career coaching. Since then, career coaching has become my go-to model for helping with career planning. As a newly forming extension of coaching, I have found that career coaching resources that uphold career development best practices are hard to locate.

This publication marks a significant moment in the career development industry as the National Career Development Association (NCDA) speaks to the benefits of career coaching, provides guidance on implementing career coaching and establishes an understanding between counseling, coaching, and advising. For over 100 years, NCDA has provided professional development, and publications are one key aspect of inspiring and empowering those in the field. This new monograph adds to the dozens of other NCDA books and monographs, covering significant areas such as teaching, assessment, ethics, group work, and more – many of which are referenced in this new monograph.

Career Coaching: Fundamentals, Applications, and Future Directions provides career professionals with a comprehensive overview of coaching as a methodology for administering career development interventions. The author, Dr. Heather Maietta, first walks the reader through the history of career coaching as an emergent career development method and then provides an overview of career coaching methods and models. She uses her extensive experience in coaching, researching, and consulting to provide readers with a road map for integrating coaching methods into their practice, including an abundance of resources found in the Appendix section.

Moreover, this publication is a welcome addition to the toolkit career professionals have available to help clients achieve their career goals. With an action-oriented framework, coaching is an added value to the career development process focusing on establishing rapport with clients, identifying goals, and facilitating action and client agency. This action-oriented focus of career coaching will help career development professionals address contemporary labor-market challenges such as the Great Resignation and COVID-19 pandemic. Whether you are a licensed counselor, career advisor, or career coach, you will find this publication useful for working with a diverse clientele in a post-pandemic world.

At The University of Baltimore, where I have the pleasure of serving as the Director of the Career & Internship Center, we utilize career coaching when working our students. I plan to use this monograph to enhance my skillset in coaching and expand my knowledge of action-oriented career planning. In addition to my own learning, this monograph will serve as a resource guide for training my team in effective coaching practice. Lastly, I will also utilize the resources from the Appendix in my private coaching business to help clients develop action-oriented plans for their career advancement. It is my hope, that this publication will open the door for coaching to be further integrated into the career development industry and used by career professionals around the globe.

Lakeisha Mathews, Ed.D, CCSP, GCDF, CPRW/CC
NCDA President-Elect, 2021-2022

CHAPTER 1
Career Coaching: An Introduction

"An average person taps only 10 percent of [their] potential."
– John Powell, *Fully Human, Fully Alive*

How can we help individuals better cope with adjustments during their working lives? Questions like this call for a new set of models, tools, and methods originating from society's diverse workforce clientele, creating a developing space for career coaches and career coaching as a helping profession. The workforce constantly calls upon its contributors to update their skills and competencies based on the rapid advances in technology and innovation. In addition, personal, relational, physiological, spiritual, and mental health issues impact career decision-making (Neuer Colburn & Jenkins, 2019), calling for career training in the preparation of any professional helper. Today's work environment remains competitive and ever-changing. Employers look for knowledgeable and skilled candidates who want to deliver value, solve problems, spark innovation, and increase productivity. Clients face these measurements in the hiring process, make decisions based on them, and seek support from career professionals to help navigate the frequently changing workplace.

Now more than ever, people are looking for support in creating a career path because they are ready to learn, identify and explore opportunities at a stage of their life that will enable them to grow towards their next exciting adventure. This monograph provides a deep dive into the world of career coaching, from career fundamentals to models to ethics and assessment administration. Whether you are just starting as a career coach or looking to update your knowledge and skills as a seasoned professional, this publication will support and challenge you, offer ways to deliver coaching with purpose, help you navigate the coaching process with confidence, and equip you with a toolkit full of possibilities.

What is Career Coaching?

There are many and varied definitions of coaching applied to a wide swath of disciplines, such as athletics, academics, leadership, organizations, life, and of course, career. Regardless of its application to a discipline, coaching is a human development process involving structured, focused interaction using appropriate strategies, tools, and techniques for desirable, sustainable change (Bachkirova et al., 2014). Apply this definition to career coaching, and you have work as the end goal. There are many reasons people seek career-related transitional support:

- Career decision-making (choosing a vocation)
- Promotion within a particular occupation or industry
- Relocation
- Voluntary job change
- In-voluntary job change
- Voluntary career change (redefining one's vocational choice)
- Shift from traditional employment to gig economy or vice versa
- Traditional to entrepreneur employment or vice versa
- Retirement to volunteer career
- Re-entering the workforce after a long stint of unemployment
- Stay-at-home family members and caregivers who are ready for employment outside the home
- Redefining one's career within the same organization

This list is not exhaustive, but it shows the link between career coaching and career transition.

Career coaches can also be supportive when exploring a sense of self and life design. Career coaching can help clients discover skills, values, interests, and strengths and connect these attributes to the world of work (Peiperl & Arthur, 2000). Career coaching can help clients build self-confidence and define their professional value proposition, which benefits job and other career advancement prospects. Finally, career coaching can help clear confusion and roadblocks as clients discern a professional roadmap.

Career Coaching Today

Career professionals will benefit from this monograph in various capacities across myriad industries. Its contents allow the reader to sample a broad array of topics needed to be knowledgeable and proficient to deliver career coaching services to a diverse clientele. The National Career Development Association (NCDA, 2015) defines career professionals as career counselors, career coaches, career consultants, career development facilitators, and other professionals who provide career counseling, career advice/advising, career coaching, career planning, job search assistance, and related services to others. Regardless of the title, career professionals wear many hats when supporting individuals in finding and maintaining employment and choosing their next career move. Therefore, the term career coach will represent all career professionals throughout this monograph, and career coaching will represent the act of providing career-related support.

Career Coaching and Career Counseling

In 1975, Super called for a re-examination of career education and highlighted the understanding and involvement of the individual in the performance of work-related roles. Super contended that career education should teach career development and help individuals control the unfolding of their careers as changing sequences and combinations of roles in education, home, community, occupations, and leisure as they go through life (Super, 1975). When viewing career progression from this lens, Savickas (2015) points out, "Career educators in the schools, and career coaches in organizations taught students and coached clients in making decisions, seeking information, managing time, overcoming barriers, and solving problems" (p. 136). Career coaching stems from multiple fields, such as psychology (positive, organizational, humanistic), management, education, and sociology (Peiperl & Arthur, 2000), and the discipline benefited from multiple viewpoints as it evolved to the present day. However, the language and practice within the career services profession are varied and often unclear when it comes to coaching, calling for new tools and resources for career coaches.

In 2010, the American Counseling Association (ACA) and 31 counseling organizations participating in *2020: A Vision for the Future of Counseling* (Kaplan & Gladding, 2011) crafted and adopted a shared definition of **counseling:** "a professional relationship that empowers diverse individuals, families, and groups to accomplish mental health, wellness, education, and career goals" (Kaplan et al., 2014, p. 368). Savickas (2011) posited that **career counseling** moves individuals from finding one's life work to constructing how to make one's life work. This counseling support requires a science of intervention that deals with designing a life and deciding how to use work in that life (Savickas, 2011). The NCDA (2015) *Code of Ethics* advances that career counselors provide career planning services to clients but are also able to offer a "deeper level of involvement with the client, based on the establishment of a professional counseling relationship and the potential for assisting clients with career and personal development concerns beyond those included in career planning" (p. 3).

The International Coaching Federation (ICF, 2021) defines **coaching** "as an act of partnering with clients in a thought-provoking and creative process, inspiring them to maximize their personal and professional potential, a process that is particularly important in today's uncertain and complex environment" (para 5). Hazen & Steckler (2010) classify **career coaching** "as one of the most focused, result-oriented forms of coaching" (p. 311). According to the NCDA (2015) *Code of Ethics* section A.1.b., "career planning" services are differentiated from "career counseling" services in the types of services provided to the client by the coach. NCDA (2015) further explains that career planning services include:

> an active provision of information designed to help a client with a specific need, such as review of a resumé; assistance in networking strategies; identification of occupations based on values, interests, skills, prior work experience, and/or other characteristics; support in the job-seeking process; and assessment by means of paper-based and/or online inventories of interest, abilities, personality, work-related values, and/or other characteristics. (p. 3)

All definitions presented in this chapter are grounded in developing a relationship with the client in a helping capacity to better the client's situation. Career coaches and career counselors help clients set career-related goals, although there are characteristic differences between the two (see Table 1). In career counseling, the origin of these discussions begins by reflecting on how past experiences have become barriers to current work challenges (Brown, 2016). A career counselor assesses a client's story and after that detangles confusion or addresses the emotional reasons why one may not progress in their career (Capuzzi & Stauffer, 2018). The desired result of both career coaching and career counseling are similar: to help the client move forward in setting and meeting their career goals, yet the path to achieving these desired results differ. Career coaches focus on the current situation and co-create goals and action plans to help clients move forward. They assess where clients are and encourage clients to set outcomes-driven direction grounded in the present yet future-focused. Career coaches can give advice, be highly directive, and have fewer professional boundaries than counselors. Counselors address mental health issues related to careers, cannot give advice, and tend to be much less directive (C. Luke, personal communication, November 26, 2021).

Table 1

Coaching and Counseling Characteristics

Coaching	Counseling
Present to Future	Past to Present
Collegial	Professional
Process Oriented	Exploratory & Process Oriented
Professional Training	State Licensure
Limited Confidentiality	Confidentiality

(Brown, 2016; Capuzzi & Stauffer, 2018; Duarte, 2018; Savickas, 2015)

Since the late 1990s to early 2000s, positive psychology has offered a more optimistic, forward-moving, strength-focused coaching model to draw from and put into practice. The coaching process lends itself to action-oriented techniques and information that can be applied effectively and efficiently in various contexts. In the words of Duarte (2018), "while considering the designations used by Savickas (2015), namely career educators and career coaches, it becomes clear that they [career counseling and career coaching] essentially do the same job, use similar methodologies, and have the same aims, although they work with different populations" (p. 86). Regardless of designation (see Table 2), all career professionals, whether engaging in basic career planning or deeper career counseling activities, should provide only services within the scope of their professional competence and qualifications (NCDA, 2015). Enhanced coverage of ethics related to the scope of services occurs in a later chapter.

Table 2
Career Coaching and Career Counseling

Both career coaching and career counseling tend to...	Coaching encourages...
assist clients	beginning the coaching process with the future in mind
set solution-based goals	the need to focus on 1-2 goals
have care at the core	a defined timeline of service
gather information through questioning	licensure (although not required)
practice based on foundational theories	action (by the client)
struggle with practitioner-client challenges	co-creating a relationship with the client
work with clients that desire change	decision-making power by the client to set the agenda, define goals and create action items
understand change occurs over time	

(Brown, 2016; Capuzzi & Stauffer, 2018; Duarte, 2018; Savickas, 2015)

Coaching Principles

Although coaching principles may vary from coach to coach depending on one's definition of coaching, coaching discipline, or the nuances of practicing coaching, each coach typically has a set of principles that guide their process. For example, in Canfield and Chee's (2013) book *Coaching for Breakthrough Success,* the authors explain how to draw out the skills and talents of clients through eight specific coaching principles:

1. The Coaching Spirit. Being a career coach means you believe all clients have potential. Coaching is a process that brings out the best in your clients because all individuals can thrive on challenges and flexibility. As we help our clients to grow, we also grow as coaches. However, new skills and knowledge are needed when we gain more responsibilities or pursue new roles. The coaching spirit posits that we are responsible for developing ourselves to better our clients.

2. Relationship and Trust. Building rapport with the client builds trust as we initiate and cultivate the coaching relationship (see Chapter 2). As trust increases, there is more opportunity for open, honest dialog, information sharing, and risk-taking. As a result, clients feel safe exploring their goals and co-creating a new future in whatever definition that future holds for them.

3. Asking Questions and Communicating Curiosity. Powerful questioning (see Chapter 2) is the cornerstone of effective career coaching. Asking powerful questions sparks curiosity in our clients, empowering them to discover future possibilities. This process creates buy-in. Questioning is an art – it requires practice, but if executed skillfully, it avoids judgment and advice-giving. A list of powerful questions can be found in Appendix A.

4. Listening. Listening is verbal and non-verbal. It is essential to hear what the client is saying and make meaning of the message. In addition to hearing the client, a coach is also responsible for deciphering body language. Being impartial and nonjudgmental and refraining from premature conclusions is important: a good motto to operate under is *right here, right now*.

5. Feedback and Awareness. Through feedback, awareness of a client's situation and career possibilities become more visible. It is at this stage that the client can take action towards goals.

6. Suggestions and Simplification. As the awareness level of the client's situation increases, conversation about responsibilities, change, and needs to execute the impending change to move forward must be discussed. It is essential (and fair) for the client to want and understand the implications of the change before the coach offers suggestions for the next steps. The client must be ready to move forward in their transformation.

7. Goals and Action Plans. Simply (yet not simple) setting into motion the desire for change. This motion entails establishing clear, realistic, time-bound goals with defined action steps. The coach's responsibility now is to execute a challenge and support technique. The goals are co-created between coach and client and guided by the coach.

8. Accountability and Accomplishments. Keeping a record of success and challenges is key to maintaining momentum. The coach and the client should keep score of goals and action steps because accountability drives accomplishments. A connected coach acknowledges the client's efforts and supports them as they progress towards their goal completion.

Employing the eight principles for effective coaching can benefit successful coaching outcomes, both for the client and the coach.

How Technology Impacts Careers and the Role of Career Coaching

Technology and artificial intelligence are changing the world of work at a dizzying pace as more and more roles are being re-tooled, re-imagined, and re-assigned with rapid advancements. Technological advancements have both positive and negative impacts. The use of technology in delivering career services has been evolving over the past several decades with subtle advances, and in more recent years at a rapid pace. Unfortunately, coaches and clients have had difficulty keeping up! The emerging trends of yesterday, such as résumé keyword search programs, virtual interviewing, and learning platforms to elevate skills, are now mainstream job searching and career advancement tools. Related to the workforce, job opportunities, career and life satisfaction, innovation, and automation have ups and downs. Here are a few of the many points to consider:

Positive Impact of Technology

- **Increased employment options.** In May 2021, Mercer found that 70% of companies said they planned to adopt the hybrid work model, which aligns with the desires of 97% of workers who desire some form of remote working arrangement (Pelta, 2021). As technology advances, lifestyles improve, which causes consumerism to increase, resulting in job creation. Technology advancement eliminates jobs in dying or slowing areas and increases job opportunities in other areas. Thus, jobs are replaced, not reduced.
- **Increased productivity.** Technology increases productivity, in many cases reducing the repetitiveness and other burdens on employees. Advancements also call for employees to stay active in their learning for increased skills development for the ever-changing marketplace.
- **Economic growth.** As companies advance their technology, the service range expands, creating more jobs. Economic growth will also come through tax revenue, creating more employment opportunities with better pay.

Challenges with Technology

- **Job loss.** The robots may not be coming to take our jobs, but innovation and artificial intelligence create redundancies in the workforce, eliminating some positions (in dying or slowing areas), occupations, or even employment sectors. In addition, reimagining a workplace, now driven by automation, will replace some jobs performed by people, many of whom are low-skilled workers. Consequently, income inequalities will further widen (see Chapter 6).

- **Employment gaps.** Technology changes more rapidly than most companies and people can adapt. Rapid changes often force individuals (voluntary or involuntary) to take employment gaps, and those that do may find it increasingly difficult to re-enter the workforce after a lag in employment.
- **Continued learning.** Changing and constantly improving technologies require all workforce sectors to continue advancing their skills and knowledge, often through additional coursework and certifications outside of working hours. Unfortunately, this can be too overwhelming for some to balance work and personal life.

Merisotis (2021) stated, "As artificial intelligence ultimately leads to automation of virtually all tasks that are repetitive and can be reduced to an algorithm, work does not go away but is transformed into the work of the future: human work – the work only people can do" (p. xi). Career coaches must continue to advance their skills and knowledge in coaching and workforce advancements in response to future work transformations. The coach's job is to be prepared to help clients find and perform jobs (most that do not yet exist) in a rapidly changing age of technology.

The Disruptive Forces of COVID-19

Career coaching calls for coaches to build close, interpersonal connections with clients, and in many ways, the pandemic made it more challenging to engage with clients using the preferred, tested methods. For years, career coaches have infused technology into their service delivery model in various ways; however, the pandemic challenged the career coaching industry to think about and incorporate technology-based delivery in new and innovative ways. Later chapters will discuss the use of technology as a mode of delivery and how coaches practice coaching techniques via technology; however, in brief, the following changes can be noted:

- **Communication clarity**. Most in-person, face-to-face coaching ceased during the pandemic, requiring coaching practices to pivot to virtual connection methods. Zoom, Google Chat, FaceTime, and other face-to-face virtual platforms are convenient connection alternatives. However, as with communicating via telephone, messages can be missed due to technological limitations or distractions. Increased verbal cues are ever-important as the virtual connection does not always provide the same benefits as in-person, where non-verbal communication cues can be detected simultaneously. Using built-in tools such as closed caption, chat functions, and video recordings to reduce errors in communications were necessary considerations.
- **New opportunities for group coaching**. Moving to a virtual coaching environment provided convenience, time, and space for more group work. Chapter 7 will highlight innovative group coaching techniques used with large and small groups in various settings.
- **In a word, pivot:** If you know anything about qualitative research, conducting open or semi-structured interviews is a standard and robust data collection method. The researcher always begins with some semblance of an interview protocol, the structure dependent on the discussion topic and the overarching research need. Likewise, the coach employs a structure in client sessions. However, coaches know that if barriers exist, progress stifles. On many occasions, the pandemic challenged coaches to throw away their protocol in place of providing a compassionate, listening ear. Throwing the session agenda to the wind in favor of discussing how the client made it through the week juggling the myriad of commitments may be necessary.

Social Responsibility

Many of the early career theories (see Chapter 3) that served as the foundation for the career coaching industry focused on the career development of white males. As our workforce has evolved, career theories have become more inclusive of gender, race, and sexual orientation. However, career-related assessments (see Chapter 5) still contain biases despite evolution. More than ever, career coaches must reach beyond their scope to offer services to those who have been economically discriminated against, marginalized, oppressed. Career professionals must continuously strive to examine their positionality regarding social justice issues, continue to seek knowledge and training in the area of social responsibility, and understand where the gaps and issues are in the current literature and resources and how to use various resources to serve their clients in the most effective, transparent way possible. Chapter 6 will discuss career coaching for diverse populations and coaching across cultures.

History and Evolution of Career Coaching

Career Coaching Beginnings

The word "career" comes from the Latin word "carrus" meaning cart; car; road; pathway (Online Etymology, n.d.). Of course, one rarely defines career as a cart or a car; analogies such as "defining one's professional path" or "developing a road to success" have been used to discuss career exploration and advancement. Over the last century, both significant and minor advancements have occurred in the areas of guidance and development in vocational behavior and career counseling. Career coaching stems from these advances. Although consensus has yet to exist regarding the correct development path, studies on career theories are still separated mainly into two subfields and guided by two different perspectives: vocational psychology (career choice, work adjustment, vocational behavior, career decision-making) and career psychology (career counseling, guidance) (Collin, 2009). Chapter 3 provides a variety of theoretical models applicable to career coaching birthed from the field of career counseling. For now, a historical overview of vocational guidance to the present day is presented.

In a Historical Nutshell

An influx of new immigrants created a need for vocational bureaus to help address the rapid growth in the industrial society of the late 1800s-early 1920s, a time known as the birth of vocational guidance. Frank Parsons's work, *Choosing a Vocation* (1909), which emphasized the significance of a methodical approach to vocational choice (Stephens, 1970), inspired these bureaus. The bureau's early work contributed to Parsons's book, which provided much of the foundation for vocational guidance for the next fifty years. Parsons believed individuals choose a vocation based on three factors: (1) an understanding of self (interests, abilities, aptitude, challenges), (2) knowledge of the occupational parameters (benefits, challenges, various employment options), and (3) being able to discern between knowledge of self and occupational decision-making (Parsons, 1909). In 1913, the National Vocational Guidance Association (NVGA) – the first professional organization for the industry – was established in Grand Rapids, Michigan, and is known today as the National Career Development Association (NCDA). Shortly following the establishment of NVGA was the Smith-Hughes Act of 1917, which funded vocational training in secondary schools and laid the foundation for land grant universities. In addition, the act earmarked federal funding to increase authenticity in curriculum and provide standards across vocational education programs (Moore, 2017).

The early 1900s also gave rise to early standardized testing, particularly aptitude. As World War I began, over 1.5 million soldiers were assessed for instruction and recruit classification within the armed services. Eventually, testing measures were made available to non-military counseling personnel. In 1927, Edward Strong developed an interest inventory the industry recognizes today as the Strong Interest Inventory (Capuzzi & Stauffer, 2018). Achievement and personality testing soon followed suit.

The 1930s-1940s saw much development in vocational guidance. With the onset of World War II, the Army produced the Army General Classification Test (AGCT), measuring general ability among its soldiers. When the war ended, the returning soldiers received counseling services through President Truman's Fair Deal Program to return veterans to previous employment. In 1944, the many Veteran's Administration Centers established at colleges and universities across the country resulted from the Fair Deal Program, later paving the way for developing college career centers. In 1946, Congress passed the George-Bardon Act, which established academic counselor training and vocational guidance programs.

The 1930s and 1940s were also a period of theory development. At this time, Parsons's (1909) model was the basis for vocational guidance, absent of testing and measurement. The notable outcome of this period was the 1939 Dictionary of Occupational Titles (DOT) – a classification of occupations based on traits, workplace setting, education requirements, and position specifics (Sharf, 2013). The DOT publication converted in 2001 to what is known as O*NET. Research and publications increased in the field of career development and vocational guidance (Earle, 1931; Edgerton, 1926; Fitch, 1935), and in 1936 Harper and Brothers published the first job-hunting book in America entitled, *Your Work Abilities: How to Express and Apply Them Through Man Power Specifications*, by A.W. Rahn. Shortly after that, in 1938, the oldest job search book still in existence was released, *Pick Your Job —And Land It!* by Sidney and Mary Edlund. Bernard Haldane of Bernard Haldane & Associates formed what is known to be the first executive career management firm in 1946.

The 1950s saw the passing of the GI Bill and the emphasis on job placement as a primary driver for filling workforce demand, which prompted the need for new job placement centers to support veterans' needs. In addition, the National Defense Education Act of 1957 increased the math and science curriculum and early efforts on advancing technology to compete globally. As a result, career development shifted focus and infused early technology efforts into career planning and assessment. Several key publications came out that continued to shape the profession, including Super's (1953) *A Theory of Vocational Development*, Roe's *Psychology of Occupations* (1956), and Holland's (1959) *A Theory of Vocational Guidance*.

The 1960s began what Neuer Colburn and Jenkins (2019) called the period of civil rights and the search for meaning in work. It was an idealistic time, when people sought employment that allowed them to change the world, rejecting the notion that work needed to be overly conforming and depersonalized. These ideals paved the way for the positive psychology movement (see Chapter 3). Driven by the growth and prosperity of the US economy, the 1960s and 1970s produced the most influential legislation shaping the career development profession. The Vocational Education Act of 1963 replaced the Smith-Hughes Act. Again, the concept of career education took hold, this time in the federal government, making funding sources accessible to school districts across the United States interested in piloting career education. The 1964 Economic Opportunity Act created many social programs, including Job Corps and the U.S. Employment Services Human Resource Development Program. In 1969, Opportunities Unlimited, the first nonprofit employment agency to assist employees and employers find each other, was developed by Tom Jackson, solidifying the role of outplacement firms. In 1970, Bolles published his job search book, *What Color is Your Parachute?* arguably the number one job search book of all time, in print for over 50 years.

Other notable legislation of the 1960s and 1970s included expansion of Vocational Rehabilitation Administration monies (1965), The Social Security Act (1967), the Elementary and

Secondary Education Act Amendment (1969), the Carl D. Perkins Vocational Education Act (1984, amended from 1978), and the Comprehensive Employment Training Act (1977). In addition, the Vocational Education Act strengthened career education information and communication between four federal agencies: the National Center for Education Statistics, the U.S. Bureau of Labor Statistics, the Employment and Training Commission, and the Education Commission. These legislative measures have, and continue to, directly or indirectly advance career education, job training, and employment opportunities for many individuals.

In terms of the US economy, the 1980s and 1990s did not experience the gains realized in the previous two decades, which prompted growth in career services support in counseling centers, schools, private practice, higher education, and government. These agencies provided career exploration and job search strategies to many students, graduates, underrepresented populations, and workforce returners. Technological advances and decreases in the industrial sector created a significant need as the unemployment rate rose and skilled labor declined. The government established Welfare to Work (1997) programs and various job training partnerships to encourage and, in some cases, force unemployed and subsidized aid recipients to seek employment. Career-related responses to these programs came in the One-Stop-Career Center Act (1994) and the School-to-Work Opportunities Act (1994). Simultaneously, the career services profession underwent notable changes, establishing vocational-career counseling competencies (1982) and creating the first certification in the profession: the National Certified Career Counselor (1983), and hosting the first (1987) and subsequent annual national conference devoted to career development (Brown, 2016). The federal government continued to advance the profession by passing the Americans with Disabilities Act (1990) and converting the Dictionary of Occupational Titles to O*NET occupational classification scheme by the U.S. Department of Labor.

The 1990s gave rise to outplacement agencies, as middle and senior-level executives experienced layoffs because of downsizing. In addition, vocational guidance in private practice amplified as the interest and need for tailored support for special populations increased. In 1990, the first professional association for résumé writers was formed, and in 2000 their name became the Professional Association of Résumé Writers and Career Coaches (PARWCC). It was also around this time that the concept of "career coaching" entered the literature. Whitmore's 2002 publication *Coaching for Change* referenced mentoring as being "one step removed [from coaching] and is concerned with the longer-term acquisition of skills in a developing career by a form of advising and counseling" (p. 24). Whitmore further stated "the beauty of coaching lies in its depth and impact" (p. 17). In a later article by Brooks (2005), career coaching was described as similar to career counseling in that both navigate career decision-making and planning, résumé writing, interviewing techniques, and more. Brooks goes on to explain "the career coach needs to have many of the same personality attributes as a counselor, including empathy, positive regard, and intuitive insights. However, career coaching is unique in its explicit emphasis on setting goals. It is outcome/solution-oriented rather than process/problem-oriented" (p. 33).

The economic downturn of 2008 devastated the economy in the United States and beyond, and the implications to unemployment were striking. Once again, career practitioners from every sector found themselves in demand which increased the interest in career-related certifications and credentials to educate and advance professionals entering and practicing in the profession. The National Career Development Association celebrated its 100th anniversary in 2013 and in 2017 created five new credentials. The information technology and social media revolution in the early 21st century also transformed government and college career centers into dynamic networking hubs connecting job seekers with hiring organizations.

With corporate America adopting more rigid organizational structures and varying opportunities, workforce needs grew, establishing new jobs and professions. The notion of matching an individual to work no longer applied in its simplistic form. The emergence of career models based on theory positioned career counseling as the support strategy as a developmental process to understand professional choice related to career (Super, 1957, 1990). Career education in schools and organizations became a popular support strategy. Varying schools of thought and methodologies were born to perform essentially the same job: coaching clients in making decisions, seeking information, managing time, overcoming barriers, and solving problems (Savickas et al., 2009).

Moving Forward

A 2021 report by Liu mentioned that 72% of employees said the COVID-19 pandemic caused them to rethink their skill sets. In addition, more than half of potential job-changers sought new training and skills development during the pandemic, and 1 in 4 workers considered quitting their jobs (Liu, 2021). Pre-pandemic careers look very different from today. A new era of career development continues to evolve, and the career services profession finds itself once again highly sought after to provide guidance and support (Niles, 2021). The impact of the COVID-19 pandemic will continue to redefine the career coaching landscape, raising questions about the value of advanced education, the stability of our health and communities, and the future of work. More than ever, employees are being asked to manage rapid change, remain nimble, apply a broad set of skills across the workplace of ever-changing demands based on unpredictable requirements, which calls for a deeply crafted but generic set of competencies (Maietta & Gardner, 2022).

For career development to be holistic, it must consider the individual within the life cycle and their various roles. Duarte (2018) noted, "What we are dealing with then are professional designations and not theoretical conceptualizations or differentiated interventions that use different models. Career educators and career coaches have the same mission: to help the individual climb up the career ladder" (p. 86). A career coach's role is not necessarily to help people climb "the ladder," as Duarte mentions. Counselors and coaches have similar roles in many respects, but the role of a coach far surpasses that of supporting job growth in the sense of upward mobility. Today, coaches help people make all kinds of changes. Therefore, career professionals who work with clients must integrate theory and practice from multiple disciplines: counseling, human resources, sociology, technology, and education, and consider an excessive number of factors when constructing a conversation about one's career path.

Brown (2016), Campone (2008), Dey and Cruzvergara (2014), Neuer Colburn and Jenkins (2019), and Pope (2000) present the evolution of career coaching from the same starting point to the present day, yet with varying perspectives based on social, political, and economic factors. However, many key historical points appear across all lenses regardless of how one views the developments leading to our present-day career coaching profession. To gain a more comprehensive snapshot of historical highlights of vocational guidance, career development, and career counseling in the United States, read Duane Brown's *Career Information, Career Counseling, and Career Development* (11th ed.; 2016).

Monograph Overview

This monograph will continue in Chapter 2 with a detailed account of the coaching relationship, coaching techniques, strategy, and execution, including the roles and responsibilities of the coach and client. Chapter 3 offers an overview of select theories and models related to the application of career coaching, including transition theory, career construction theory, positive psychology, theory of vocational choice, and the theory of planned happenstance. Models include the AIDA Model, Appreciative Inquiry, G.R.O.W, S.M.A.R.T., S.O.A.R., Job Crafting, Mind Mapping, Storytelling, and a few easy-to-use coaching tools. Chapter 4 discusses how career coaches adopt and apply sound ethical coaching practices in working with clients and maintaining a professional code of ethics. Chapter 5 highlights assessments for use in career coaching, beginning with a brief history of career assessment, type of assessment instruments, considerations in administering assessments, and the role technology plays in the assessment process. Next, the chapter presents ethical considerations in assessment use and options for formal and informal assessments. Chapter 6 discusses career coaching for diverse populations and being culturally and socially competent. Chapter 7 overviews the various ways that career coaches can work effectively and efficiently with groups. Finally, Chapter 8 raises questions and points of consideration on the growing practice of career coaching and the need for continued skills development to remain competitive as the next generation of career coaches leads the industry in growth and change.

COACH CORNER

Throughout the monograph, the reader will find boxes labeled, "Coach Corner", which will help solidify or apply the material being presented. The reader is encouraged to pause at each Coach Corner and look deeply at what is being presented.

References

Bachkirova, T., Cox, E., & Clutterbuck, D. (2014). Introduction. In E. Cox, T. Bachkirova, & D. Clutterbuck (Eds.), *The complete handbook of coaching* (2nd ed., pp. 1-18). Sage.

Brooks, K. C. (2005, Winter). "You would think...": Applying motivational interviewing and career coaching concepts with liberal arts students. *NACE Journal*. 28-36.

Brown, D. (2016). *Career information, career counseling, and career development* (11th ed.). Pearson Education.

Campone, F. (2008). Connecting the dots: Coaching research – Past, present and future. In D. B. Drake, D. Brennan, & K. Gortz (Eds.), *The philosophy and practice of coaching: Insights and issues for a new era* (pp. 91-109). Wiley & Sons.

Canfield, J., & Chee, P. (2013). *Coaching for breakthrough success: Proven techniques for making impossible dreams possible*. McGraw-Hill.

Capuzzi, D., & Stauffer, M. D. (2018). *Career counseling: Foundations, perspectives, and applications (3rd ed.)*. Routledge. https://doi.org/10.4324/9781315166797

Collin, A. (2009). One step towards realising the multidisciplinarity of career studies. In A. Collin & W. Patton (Eds.), *Vocational psychological and organisational perspectives on career* (pp. 3–18). Sense Publishers. https://doi.org/10.1163/9789087909178_002

Dey, F., & Cruzvergara, C. Y. (2014, Winter). Evolution of career services in higher education. *New Directions in Student Services, 148,* 5-18. http://doi.org/10.1002/ss.20105

Duarte, M. E. (2018). Career counseling and career coaching in working contexts: Learning from each other. In L. Nota & S. Soresi (Eds.), *Counseling and coaching in times of crisis and transition: From research to practice* (pp. 83–102). Routledge/Taylor & Francis Group.

Earle, F. M. (1931). *Methods of choosing a career.* G. G. Harrap & Company, Ltd.

Edgerton, A. H. (1926). *Vocational guidance and counseling: Including reports on preparation of school counselors.* Macmillan.

Fitch, J. A. (1935). Vocational guidance in action. *American Association of Social Workers* (Vol. 5). Columbia University Press. https://doi.org/10.7312/fitc94564

Hazen, B., & Steckler, N. (2010). Career coaching. In E. Cox, T. Bachkirova, & D. Clutterbuck (Eds.), *The complete handbook of coaching* (1st ed., pp. 311–323). Sage.

Holland, J. L. (1959). A theory of vocational choice. *Journal of Counseling Psychology, 6*(1), 35–45. https://doi.org/10.1037/h0040767

International Coaching Federation. (2021). *ICF code of ethics.* https://coachingfederation.org/ethics/code-of-ethics

Kaplan, D. M., & Gladding, S. T. (2011). A vision for the future of counseling: The 20/20 principles for unifying and strengthening the profession. *Journal of Counseling and Development, 89*(3), 367–372. https://doi.org/10.1002/j.1556-6678.2011.tb00101.x

Kaplan, D. M., Tarvydas, V. M., & Gladding, S. T. (2014). 20/20: A vision for the future of counseling: The new consensus definition of counseling. *Journal of Counseling and Development 92*(3), 366-372. http://doi.org/10.1002/j.1556-6676.2014.00164.x

Liu, J. (2021, April). 1 in 4 workers is considering quitting their job after the pandemic-here's why. *CNBC Make It.* https://www.cnbc.com/2021/04/19/1-in-4-workers-is-considering-quitting-their-job-after-the-pandemic.html

Maietta, H. N., & Gardner, P. (2022). *Ensuring success for students who transfer: The importance of career and professional development.* [Manuscript in Preparation]. University of South Carolina, National Resource Center for The First-Year Experience and Students in Transition.

Merisotis, J. (2021). *Human work.* Rosetta Books.

Moore, G. (2017). The Smith-Hughes Act: The road to it and what it accomplished. *Techniques Magazine, 92*(2), 17-21.

National Career Development Association. (2015). *2015 NCDA code of ethics.* https://www.ncda.org/aws/NCDA/asset_manager/get_file/3395

Neuer Colburn, A., & Jenkins, C. (2019). Historical influences on the practice of career counseling. In D. Capuzzi & M. D. Stauffer (Eds.), *Career counseling: Foundations, perspectives, and applications* (3rd ed.). Routledge.

Niles, S. G., (November 2021), Career development during a pandemic: Results of the NCDA Harris poll. National Career Development Association. https://www.ncda.org/aws/NCDA/asset_manager/get_file/631259?ver=2

Online Etymology. (n.d.). Career. In *Online Etymology Dictionary.* Retrieved January 10, 2022, from etymonline.com/word/career

Parsons, F. (1909). *Choosing a vocation.* Houghton-Mifflin.

Peiperl, M., & Arthur, M. (2000). Topics for conversation: Career themes old and new. In M. Peiperl, M. Arthur, R. Goffee, & T. Morris (Eds.), *Career frontiers: New conceptions of working lives* (pp. 1–19). Oxford University Press.

Pelta, R. (2021). Many workers have quit or plan to after employers revoke remote work. *FlexJobs.* https://www.flexjobs.com/blog/post/workers-quit-employers-revoke-remote-work/

Pope, M. (2000, March). A brief history of career counseling in the United States. *The Career Development Quarterly, 48,* 194-211.

Roe, A. (1956). *Psychology of occupations.* John Wiley & Sons.

Savickas, M. L. (2011). *Career counseling.* APA Books.

Savickas, M. (2015). Life designing with adults: Developmental individualization using biographical bricolage. In L. Nota & J. Rossier (Eds.), *Handbook of life design: From practice to theory and from theory to practice* (pp. 135–149). Hogrefe Publishing.

Savickas, M. L., Nota, L., Rossier, J., Dauwalder, J., Duarte, M. E., Guichard, J., Soresi, S., Van Esbroeck, R., & van Vianen, A. E. M. (2009). Life designing: A paradigm for career construction in the 21st century. *Journal of Vocational Behavior, 75*(3), 239-250. https://doi.org/10.1016/j.jvb.2009.04.004

Sharf, R. S. (2013). *Applying career development theory to counseling* (6th ed.). Cengage.

Stephens, W. R. (1970). *Social reform and the origins of vocational guidance.* National Vocational Guidance Association.

Super, D. E. (1953). A theory of vocational development. *American Psychologist, 8*(5), 185–190. https://doi.org/10.1037/h0056046

Super, D. E. (1957). *The psychology of careers: An introduction to vocational development.* Harper & Row.

Super, D. E. (1975). Career education and career guidance for the life span and for life roles. *Journal of Career Development, 2*(2), 27-42.

Super, D. E. (1990). A lifespan, life-space approach to career development. In D. Brown & L. Brooks (Eds.), *Career choice and development* (2nd ed., pp. 197–261). Jossey-Bass. https://doi.org/10.1016/0001-8791(80)90056-1

Whitmore, J. (2002). *Coaching for performance: Growing people, performance and purpose* (3rd ed.). Nicholas Brealey Publishing.

CHAPTER 2
The Fundamentals of Career Coaching

"Coaching is a partnership of equals whose aim is to achieve speedy, increased and sustainable effectiveness through focused learning in every aspect of the client's life. Coaching raises self-awareness and identifies choices. Working to the client's agenda, the coach and client have the sole aim of closing the gaps between potential and performance."

– Jenny Rogers, *Coaching Skills*

Chapter Highlights

This chapter will discuss a comprehensive overview of the coaching process, including the role of the coach and the client in the coaching relationship. In addition, it will offer information on the most effective coaching skills and techniques for career coaching. Finally, the chapter will explore the change process and strategies to overcoming barriers and resistance.

Learning Objectives

This chapter highlights the following:

1. Six principles that support the definition of coaching
2. Utilizing ingredients of a helping relationship in coaching
3. Application of the S.O.L.E.R. listening technique
4. Identify pitfalls to questioning and strategies to avoid during coaching
5. Analyze barriers to change and how to assist clients in overcoming obstacles

K – W - L

Now that you know what the chapter has to offer, take a few minutes to assess where you are in terms of your knowledge level and areas of learning using the K-W-L model. The first step in the K-W-L model is to self-assess what you already ***know*** about coaching strategy and execution. What coaching techniques have you applied to your practice that have helped you become more proficient in strategy and execution? Next, think about what you ***want*** to know about coaching in this chapter. Where do you feel are the gaps in your coaching knowledge and performance? Finally, to conclude this chapter, you will be asked to revisit the K-W-L model to assess whether this chapter provided you with information to fill some of your knowledge gaps. You will reflect on what you ***learned*** from this chapter and how it can apply to your coaching practice.

Overview of the Fundamentals

Chapter 1 discussed career coaching as a process involving structured, focused interaction using appropriate strategies, tools, and techniques for desirable, sustainable change to benefit the client (Bachkirova et al., 2014). A successful career coach motivates the client into action, helps the client close the gap between their goals and achievements, and increases the probability of success by sharing expertise, resources, and timely feedback. Rogers (2016) outlines six principles to support the above definition of coaching:

1. The client is resourceful. A coach does not resolve the client's issues but works with them to develop their resourcefulness.
2. The development of resourcefulness manifests through skillful questioning and a challenge and support philosophy. The role

of a coach is to discern what tools are needed for the client to achieve their set goals.

3. Coaching utilizes the client's past information only when necessary to support present and future growth and opportunity.
4. The client is instrumental in setting the coaching agenda.
5. Coach and client are equals. Career coaching is an interactive process between coach and client. The client sets the agenda and determines the best course of action with guidance from the coach.
6. Coaching is about change and action with an emphasis on doing. A coach does this by building foundations and creating pathways for the client's future.

Career coaching involves helping a client manage their relationship with work. This process is future-focused, goal and action-oriented, helping the client understand the many skills they have and how to apply them within different orientations and relationships (Rogers, 2016). The process recognizes the past as context for the present and future (Bennett & Bush, 2013). The coaching relationship is not indefinite, and therefore during the working timeframe, the coach needs to maximize independent strategies the client can implement over their working lifetime.

The coach/client relationship is important because it is client-centered (Stoltzfus, 2013), and the strength of the coaching relationship will predict coaching outcomes (Boyce et al., 2010; de Haan et al., 2011). A career coach is an objective participant who can often see situations more clearly than the client by listening carefully to the client, asking intentional questions to construct opportunities, and helping the client develop goals and action steps toward a future career path (Stolzfus, 2013).

The Role of the Coach

As Sir John Whitmore (2009) noted, "there are no quick fixes in business, and good coaching is a skill, an art perhaps, that requires a depth of understanding and plenty of practice if it is to deliver its astonishing potential" (p. 2). A career coach is a trained professional who listens, provides support and guidance, and offers resources to those who seek personal development, change, and career success. Career coaching is interactive and collaborative where the coach is patient, supportive, aware (as well as self-aware), and credible (Whitmore, 2009). Power is shared through the exploration process as the coach and client co-construct the client's goals and desired outcomes. The coach/client relationship "is central to coaching because it can often become the principal process vehicle from which its members' needs are expressed, and subsequently, goals are fulfilled" (Jowett et al., 2010, p. 20). The role of the coach is to:

- Create a safe environment
- Challenge opinions
- Focus on outcomes
- Ask purposeful questions
- Be open and honest
- Facilitate change
- Empower
- Exercise empathy
- Listen actively
- Build rapport
- Gain trust
- Promote positivity
- Respect diverse opinions
- Maintain confidentiality
- Remain present/future-focused

Coaches operate by the principle that all clients have the creativity and skills needed to reach their goals, and in order to reach goal attainment, the coach must build relational influence (de Haan 2008; Hargrove, 1995). Establishing a caring relationship, being a good listener, showing interest, acknowledging progress, and helping the client realize their strengths and application of talents all contribute to building relational influence.

The Role of the Client

Career coaching is a shared journey where the coach and client co-construct the client's goals and desired outcomes to support the client's relational power. Coaching from this lens feeds the client's hopes and puts the client's needs at the center of the coaching process (de Haan, 2008). This balance of power allows the client to assume responsibility and obligation for action. The client sets the coaching agenda and takes action because it is the client who assumes responsibility for achieving their goals under the direction of a coach. The coach's role is navigator and guide, empowering the client. The role of the client is to:

- Set the direction
- Be open to change
- Construct goals
- Take action
- Collaborate
- Share relational power
- Communicate
- Ask questions
- Use resources
- Focus on possibilities
- Believe in themselves
- Look to the future

As the coach and client build trust and rapport, the client can overcome barriers to forward movement. Advancing in one's goals is possible because the coach establishes an environment where the client is willing to be vulnerable based on the confidence that the coach is honest, open, reliable, and competent (Tschannen-Moran, 2004). The coach can guide the client to exercise action towards established goals when the client is ready for change and becomes a willing participant in the coaching process.

The Helping Relationship

Building a helping relationship is arguably the most crucial part of coaching. As exploration begins, the coach examines the client's situation and motivation to seek career support through exercising strong listening and questioning techniques. This interaction is key to building a helping relationship (Egan, 1975, 2010) and is necessary for successful coaching. A helping relationship is open and non-judgmental and built gradually as the coach encourages open and honest dialog and shows genuine interest and care in partnering with the client.

Acceptance, respect, understanding, empathy, trust, warmth, and genuineness comprise the helping relationship (Egan, 1975, 2010). The coach conveys *acceptance* when they relate to their client without judgment. They build *respect* when conveying genuine interest and concern for the client's needs. The coach shows *understanding* and *empathy* through practicing active listening and exercising non-verbal communication techniques, as the coach seeks clarification and feels the client's situation as if it were their own. *Warmth* and *genuineness* manifest via tone of voice, eye contact, body language, and a belief in a client's highest potential, communicated through encouraging language during the coaching process. Showing up on time and being prepared communicates *trust*, among other things. Eight behaviors are frequently present in a trusting environment and relationship: (1) recognition, (2) challenging yet attainable goals, (3) autonomy, (4) self-crafting work, (5) regular and robust communication, (6) relationship-building, (7) whole-person development, and (8) asking for help (Zak, 2017). Building a helping relationship is necessary for forward movement of the coaching process and understanding the client's needs (Egan, 1975, 2010).

Essential Coaching Skills

The coach builds a helping relationship through active listening, questioning, providing feedback, and reframing. Trained coaches understand that each skill has its time and place in the coaching process, and although the technique may vary from coach to coach, strong coaching can be instrumental in the client realizing their goals.

Listening

Listening is essential for effective communication and includes both words (verbal) and body language (non-verbal). Active listening allows the listener to decode underlying affective messages and then reflect back to the client the meaning of the message (Brew & Kottler, 2017). Active listening is necessary to promote deeper understanding and further exploration. Egan (1975, 2010) described the non-verbal aspects of how the coach listens using the acronym S.O.L.E.R.

S: face the client **S**quarely so that your body is positioned directly in front of the client. This posture communicates interest in the client (acceptance, genuineness)

O: maintain an **O**pen posture to communicate interest in the client (non-judgmental, empathy)

L: Lean towards the client and into the conversation as a way to convey understanding and interest in the discussion (warmth)

E: maintain **E**ye contact when it is culturally appropriate to do so (respect)

R: although not always possible, keep a relaxed demeanor. Maintain attentiveness, avoid fighting, overuse of questioning, or non-verbal gestures. If you are relaxed, the client is apt to be relaxed (trust).

Carefully listening to what the client is sharing helps the coach learn more about their background, strengths, interests, and why they seek coaching. When a coach fails to practice sound listening, barriers prohibit information gathering. Common barriers to listening include failure to pay attention to what the client is saying or non-verbally communicating. Pseudo-listening, a form of false listening where the listener only partially hears the speaker because the listener is focusing on other things (Murphy, 2020), can also be a common barrier. Some coaches have difficulty listening because they direct their efforts towards rehearsing or preparing to make their follow-up comments (Moore et al., 2016). Coaches who formulate thoughts on what to say next tend to interrupt to communicate their thought before it is lost or overlooked (Moore et al., 2016). Operational/structural tips to enhance listening include removing distractions, listening for content, suspending assumptions and judgment, remaining curious about the client's story, and observing body language. Listening is fundamental to the coach/client relationship, and practicing these tips can make all the difference.

Active Listening

Active listening is essential in all three stages of Egan's (1975, 2010) Skilled Helper model (discussed below), and the coach should employ active listening during each stage for various reasons. The coach listens to understand the essence of what the client is communicating verbally and non-verbally (tone of voice, body language, emotions) to hear the underlying concerns. Active listening helps the coach avoid the pitfalls discussed in the previous section and skillfully decide when to employ the different coaching questions. There are three common active listening techniques:

Paraphrasing. Paraphrasing is an active listening technique in which the coach repeats the client's words back to them, but not exactly as they were said. For example, a coach might reflect the whole sentence or select a few words or a single word from the client's statement. The coach uses this skill to match the tone, feeling of the client's words, facial expressions, and body language (Whitmore, 2017). For example, as a client is speaking, their non-verbal language might reflect a hunched body language as they say, "I was scared going into the job interview." The coach reflects back by mirroring their body language, paraphrasing, "It sounds like the job interview was a scary experience." Paraphrasing helps the coach succinctly understand the essence of what the client says without interpreting verbal and non-verbal cues. In addition, it helps clarify any gray areas of communication and creates clarification checkpoints during the coaching session.

Summarizing. Summarizing is another active listening technique in which the coach provides a brief overview of the client's story, repeating back what has been said but more briefly, without changing the substance or meaning (Whitmore, 2017). Summarizing can happen at the beginning of a coaching session, transitioning from one session to the next. It may also happen within the session to collect key points. Summarizing allows the client to hear an overview of the main points again, and sometimes this synopsis is a breakthrough moment for the client. Summarizing is similar to paraphrasing, except summarizing covers more information.

Challenging. Challenging is an active listening technique in which the coach uses powerful questioning (see Appendix A) to direct the client to look for answers through introspection. The technique aids the process of self-reflecting, allowing meaning-making to occur. It is said that the "client holds the answers and that the coach helps uncovering or discovering these answers through asking questions" (Askeland, 2009, p. 72). Challenging may involve seeking clarity, discovering blind spots, or testing assumptions.

Questioning

In Dale Carnegie's 1936 publication *How to Win Friends and Influence People,* he proposed that winning in the relationship game is to ask questions others will enjoy answering and listen attentively to their responses. Not everyone is born a strong listener, but strategies exist to enhance listening. One powerful strategy that increases understanding and draws people out of their comfort zone is questioning. Effective coaching is not about the answers provided by the clients; it is about the questions asked by the coach (Senge et al., 1999). Questioning is a skill that builds rapport and trust, spurs learning and exchanging ideas, and elicits necessary information to support clients' growth. Asking powerful questions (see examples in Appendix A) is arguably one of a coach's most frequently used skills, second only to listening. The International Coaching Federation (2021) defines powerful questioning as the "ability to ask questions that reveal the information needed for maximum benefit to the coaching relationship and the client" (p. 4). Bearwald (2011) posited that if coaches develop a question-driven methodology, it provides a richer, more relevant, and more meaningful partnership with their clients. In short, questioning improves interpersonal bonding.

Questioning is used in the career coaching process for many reasons, primarily to gather information and explore, understand, and help the client make sense of their experiences. Questioning also helps the client investigate their skills, interests, and values. In addition, questioning the client allows them to verbalize thoughts, feelings, concerns, or understanding. Finally, it holds the client accountable for their coaching progress because they can process information and experiences for themselves. Questions are not prescribed, right or wrong, or perfectly timed for use. Instead, coaches must use their professional judgment (i.e., evidence-based models or frameworks to guide and evaluate decisions and actions; Murphy, 2006) to tailor questions to the needs of each client. Here are four questioning types:

Closed-ended Questions

Closed questions can be practical in early career coaching conversations to make the client feel comfortable in the new environment and with coaching in general. Rock (2009) stated that the brain needs choice to function effectively. Closed-ended questions are usually easy to answer because the answers are limited and more prescribed, therefore, they convey safety in response. Closed-ended questions can be effectively used early in conversations to encourage participation and, for example, during fact-finding scenarios such as conducting research (Cox et al., 2014). They also serve a purpose when time with the client is limited because closed-ended questioning allows the coach to gather information quickly. Closed-ended questioning is particularly useful when seeking to elicit a specific piece of information or granular details. They allow much greater control than open questions.

It is important to remember that closed-ended questioning can limit the scope of the answer, so using this type of questioning skillfully and situationally is necessary. Closed-ended questions typically generate one-word or short-answer responses based on a list of options (provided or arbitrary), and if not asked at the appropriate time, they can stall a conversation or omit pertinent details. Examples of closed-ended questions include:

- Do you have a good relationship with your supervisor?
- When do you think you can execute action to reach your goal?
- Will your employer be amenable to this change?
- Have you conducted an informational interview in the past?
- When do you think you can complete your résumé?

Open-ended Questions

Open-ended questions invite the client to share information without leading them in a particular direction. This technique allows the coach to gain a deeper understanding and clarity, test gaps and perceptions, engage the client in more meaningful conversation, and hear client responses that often reveal unexpected information (Moore et al., 2016). Open questions allow for much longer responses and, therefore, potentially more creativity and information. The term open-ended suggests that many different answers are possible, and the response is not constrained (de Rivera et al., 2005; Hargreaves, 1984). Questions that begin with what, where, when, how, and who prompt reflection and lead to a fuller response. For example, instead of asking, "Did you like your last job" ask "What was it about the last job that you liked the most?" Phrases like: "Tell me more" or "Give me an example" are robust follow-up responses to keep the discussion active. Coaches are encouraged to use open-ended questions to engage and draw out details that help frame the problem.

Open-ended questions require the client to engage in more reflective thought, allowing the coach to practice attending and listening techniques. The coach may want to provide silent pauses in the dialog to allow the client to reflect, gather their thoughts and formulate a response. Also, it is helpful to use paraphrase and summarize techniques (see below) to clarify shared thoughts. Examples of open-ended questions include:

- How would you like things to be different in your job search?
- What do you think you will lose if you give up your current role?
- What have you tried before to make a change?
- What do you want to do next?

Leading

Leading questions sometimes call for a *yes* or *no* response, and when asked, the questioner tends to plug in descriptor words into the question (Mazzara, 2013). For example: "Would you describe your job search as discouraging?" or "Did you find the job search materials I sent you helpful?" When time is limited, when having difficulty drawing out specifics from the client, or when the conversation lacks focus, leading questions can serve the coach's interest because they can get the client to commit or steer a conversation toward an outcome (Swann et al., 1982). On the other hand, leading questions should be used with caution because they may be perceived as unjust and may influence the client's behavior or coerce the client into giving an incomplete or inaccurate response.

Inquiry

Inquiry questioning aims to augment knowledge, resolve doubt, or solve a problem. An inquiry question has several characteristics: (1) it is open to research, (2) it has multiple possible answers, (3) it has a clear focus, (4) the answer should be reasonably attainable, and (5) the answer matters to the conversation (Roy et al., 2003). An example of an inquiry-based question might be, "How would your life be different if you relocated to [new state] for this job opportunity?" In addition, a strong inquiry question focuses on a researchable issue, which data can support.

Tips for Questioning

Questioning is uniquely powerful for unlocking value, and coaches can hone questioning skills to make conversations more productive. McTighe and Wiggins (2013) posit that a conversation that contains good questioning is one that

- contains open-ended questions
- points towards important, transferable ideas within (and sometimes across) disciplines,
- requires support and justification; not just answers, and
- reoccurs over time - revisit questions and responses.

Regardless of the questioning type or stage in the coaching process, following a few general guidelines is important. First, the coach should craft questions with intention and ask background or foundational questions that elicit meaning to the topic. Getting the client to think about and open up to their situation is key to gathering helpful background information. Next, the coach should inquire into the client's current situation. What is currently going on that prompted coaching support? What professional desires does the client hold? This probing will draw out necessary or helpful information and encourage dialog (McTighe & Wiggins, 2013). Coaches will want to use questions purposefully, giving direction but leaving room for the client to answer the question without the coach supplying the solutions. When questioning the client, listen for understanding. Take a minute to process content – what did the client mean? Tune in to their body language – does it match their words? The coach should also pay attention to their reactions (physical and emotional) to what was said. These questioning tips can be the difference in building rapport and gathering the necessary information to set the client on a path forward.

Questioning Pitfalls

Although questions are the root of information gathering and play a critical role in rapport building, not all questions are well-judged or productive. This section identifies some common pitfalls of questioning and suggests ways to avoid them.

Solution-Focused Questions. The client is in charge of their journey and the coach's role is to serve as a guide without being overly directive or putting words in the client's mouth. Solution-focused questions direct the discussion suggestively. If the second word in the question is *you*, it is typically a solution-focused question. To avoid solution-focused questions, return to the original idea that prompted the question (Stoltzfus, 2013). For example, instead of saying, "Should you do research?" Try saying, "What research can you do that will help you gather additional information?" Turning a solution-focused question into an open-ended one can offer many possibilities instead of one (or no) solution.

Asking the Perfect Question. The perfect question is an impossibility – it does not exist. Just as every client differs, so too will each questioning script. Searching for the perfect question distracts from listening to the client and takes momentum away from the coaching conversation. Questioning is a skill that improves with practice.

Asking the Same Question. Repeating the question in multiple ways or rambling is distracting to the client. It also eats up valuable time in the coaching session. This pitfall occurs when a coach is uncomfortable with the silence caused by non-questioning or the client reflecting on a question. If the coach is unsure what question to ask next, it is helpful to pause, reflect on the client's response to the previous question, and proceed when it makes sense.

Coach's Interpretation. Reflecting techniques (discussed below) is a necessary skill for clarifying information. It is not the coach's responsibility to interpret the client's response to a question. Interpretation varies from individual to individual. For example, a client might say, "I am having difficulty interacting with my coworkers." A coach's interpretation of this response might be "You dislike your coworkers." or "You want to quit your job." Instead, the coach might respond by saying, "So what you are saying is you are experiencing some challenges communicating with your coworkers?" The client may be seeking support to increase communication strategies for improved interpersonal relations with their coworkers. However, the unhelpful interpretation of their statement (that the client is unhappy with their coworkers, therefore, they want a new job) can be avoided if, instead of assuming, the coach practices reflecting techniques.

Rhetorical. Rhetorical questions are not actually questions but statements posing as questions. They are asked to make some kind of claim or assertion (Koshik, 2005) and are, in tone and delivery, often judgmental and can be overly emotional, both for the giver and the receiver. Rhetorical questions have little use in a helping relationship. Examples include: "What were you thinking?" and "Did you really work on your job search this week?"

Feedback

Feedback is essential for maximizing the relationship and achieving successful outcomes. It should occur throughout the coaching relationship, in both verbal and written (contracts, supporting documents) ways. There are a variety of feedback types to consider. For instance, if a client is prepping for a job interview, it is essential to provide behavioral feedback on their presence. If the client asks for feedback on how to handle a workplace conflict, the coach will offer solicited feedback. If the client is crafting a résumé for a job application due by the end of the day, the coach may offer timely feedback. If the client needs specific, immediate critique to help understand areas of improvement, the coach may offer situational feedback. Regardless of the type of feedback, good feedback is timely, specific, and honest.

A coach should solicit feedback at the end of each coaching session for their learning and the client's growth. Asking questions, such as, "What was the most valuable part of today's session?" or "Is there anything you'd like to change about today's session?" can help identify a starting point for the next session and correct any mistakes from the session that may unnecessarily reoccur. Clients see themselves as others see them through the feedback process, but they also learn how the coach sees them (Williams & Thomas, 2005).

Principles of Effective Feedback

When offering the client feedback, the coach will want to be descriptive rather than judgmental or evaluative, and specific rather than general. The client will not alter behavior if feedback is vague or the message is not clearly understood. Time the feedback so that the client is open to receiving it. For instance, if the client has just received a job rejection, it may not be the right time to provide feedback on their poor interviewing skills. This feedback needs to be delivered, but timing matters if the feedback is to be helpful. It is also important to focus on what can be changed. For example, offering negative feedback on a client's attire the minute before they walk into a networking event will do nothing besides deflate their self-esteem. They cannot change their circumstances, so saying nothing at that moment is the best option.

Feedback is part of the helping relationship. If the coach established and continuously built a strong helping relationship (Egan, 1975, 2010), transparent, honest feedback will be possible in a safe and supportive environment. Feedback is a gift, and although it may not always be received as intended, the client will know – with the coach's reassurance – that their best interest is the coach's primary concern.

Reframing

Individual interpretation surrounds every situation, and this interpretation creates a frame. Looking at a situation through its frame provides one perspective on that situation. However, it is difficult for individuals to look outside a situation's frame differently. Because of this, individuals believe they are already aware of all the options available to them – the options they see in the situation's frame. Reframing is a coaching technique that helps the client see a current situation from a different perspective by changing or expanding the frame of the situation. When a coach helps a client reframe a situation, they help the client replace the existing framework with a new, more functional one. Reframing is especially helpful when a client seeks to make sense of a situation, discover new information, or develop strategies for action. (Bennett & Bush, 2013). The frame of reference can foster a different understanding of the situation and often opens up new ways of thinking and behaving (Watzlawick et al., 1974). Reframing a client's experiences in a positive light is known as positive reframing (Moore et al., 2016). Through this exercise, the client can see the situation with a new perspective, identify growth or choice options and better engage in problem-solving, decision-making, and learning.

Often, merely reframing one's perspective on a situation can also help people change how they feel about it. Not only do they see the situation from a different point of view, clients often feel differently about their choices after the reframing exercise. For example, a job loss can be devastating, but it can also be an opportunity to explore other careers, obtain additional education, or start a new business. The client may have been dreaming of a new business venture for quite some time but never seriously considered it until the job loss occurred. When the job loss happened, the only frame the client could view the situation through was a loss of employment. Reframing allowed the coach to expand the client's frame to view the job loss as an opportunity to pursue entrepreneurship.

Reframing is a two-step process. First, the coach and client frame the scenario. Framing the scenario is essentially giving a name to the issue. This first step provides an opportunity for the coach and client to be fully aware of the issues to address the next steps. The coach can now reframe scenarios that help the client develop and understand new perspectives. This exercise can help the client challenge previously held assumptions or beliefs, overcome fears, and shift the thought process. A client can draw from professional (i.e., education, work, volunteer, civic) or personal (i.e., hobbies, travel, interests, culture, family) experiences during the reframing exercises. See Table 3 for examples of questions a coach may use with various reframing strategies.

Table 3
Reframing Strategies

Reframing Strategy	Powerful, Positive Reframing Questions
Envisioning the Future	If you could fast forward one year from today, what role would you hold in your company?
Past Success	Remember a time when you felt successful. Envision that feeling of success applied to your current job. What would it look like?
Reflecting	Think of the last time you accomplished a win. What skill(s) did you exercise to make that win happen?

Reframing Tips

Change the Language. The language that career coaches use has a significant impact on client responses. A coach can use reframing to change the negative language to encourage a more open and positive client mindset. For example:

Client: "I am really shy and have never been confident in networking situations."

Coach: "Many people struggle to feel confident in networking situations, so you are not alone in feeling this way. Can you recall a positive networking experience? What was it about the experience that made it successful?"

Rule of Three. Since reframing is helping the client to move from a situation in which they feel stuck or confused, coaching with reframing requires three different ideas to begin, also known as the Rule of Three. The Latin phrase *omne trium perfectum* meaning "everything that comes in threes is perfect" is a general principle in which ideas presented in threes are inherently more interesting and more enjoyable (Dayan, 2019, para. 1). When engaging in a reframing exercise, encourage the client to brainstorm three alternatives to the current reality. Then, discuss the elements of each. Break elements of each alternative into sections of threes (for, neutral, against; or pro, neutral, con). Use the Rule of Three to repeat phrases, sentences, and words to emphasize key messages in each alternative.

Focus on Facts. Occasionally clients will get into a deficit-based mindset. Reframing can help edit this mindset, and one way to do that is to focus on factual language. For example, if a client declares they cannot accomplish a task, asking the client how they came to that conclusion can bring out the facts (or emotional responses) behind the statement. So often, the statement is based on a fixed mindset or the client feeling stuck in their current situation. Reframing can help the client understand a different path forward. Below are two examples illustrating how a coach can reframe a client's negative mindset by redirecting the discussion.

Example 1:

Client: "I really doubt that I can do anything about this."

Coach: "What is one small step that you might take to move forward?"

Example 2:

Client: "The job search has never worked for me,"

Coach: "If you envision a successful job search, what would that look like to you?"

In short, reframing an experience can offer a client more productive and positive thoughts, feelings and behaviors. It gives the client an increased sense of control and opens up more choices and possibilities (remember the Rule of Three). Reframing is most effective when a coach has established some rapport with the client and is extremely helpful in making decisions, learning, and problem-solving.

The Coaching Process

Coaching is a process. Every process consists of actions that lead to the desired result – in the case of career coaching, helping clients reach their goals and realize their full potential (Dietmar, 2021). Establishing a balanced partnership between the coach and the client is vital to the coaching process (Koppi, 2018). The goal of coaching is to move the client along the path of change, revealing underlying needs, strengths, and desires for change. These moments provide the coach and client new perspectives and opportunities to co-construct goals and actions for future growth. As Moore et al. (2016) posit, "There are few human endeavors that succeed without investing the time and effort to develop realistic and inspiring plans" (p. 125). Every coach approaches the coaching process differently depending on training, professional preference, business model, organizational objectives, or client needs. There is no right or wrong way to execute the coaching process, only suggested strategies for effective outcomes.

Egan's Skilled Helper

Egan (1975, 2010) presents a straightforward process for helping clients become active participants in their world, assigning meaning to action, exploring the problem, facing challenges, and establishing goals and new opportunities. Coaches implementing Egan's process walk the client through three stages: Exploration Stage (What is going on?), Understanding Stage (What do I want instead?), and Action Stage (How will I get there?). A brief overview of each stage follows.

Exploration Stage

What is going on? During the Exploration Stage, the coach investigates why the client is seeking coaching and probes deeper into the client's need to answer the question, "What is going on?" During this stage, the coach defines the purpose of the coaching intervention and begins gathering and analyzing data and information pertinent to the situation (Dietmar, 2021). The Exploration Stage is time for the coach and client to begin building a relationship with one another, which will extend for the duration of the coaching process. They establish rapport, a foundational component of a collaborative, working relationship. The coach also practices active listening and attending skills, which increases the client's trust (Smaby & Maddux, 2011). Common actions during the Exploration Stage are the pre-coaching questionnaire, the intake, and early coaching sessions, including formal and informal assessment administration.

Understanding Stage

What do I want instead? The coach's main objectives in the Understanding Stage are to develop a more in-depth and objective understanding of the client's situations and assist them in exploring options and achievable goals (Nelson, 2007). The Understanding Stage is where intense coaching conversations take place. The coach gathers and analyzes data while the coach and client explore options and set goals. Reframing will be most helpful during the Exploration and Understanding stages (Egan, 1975, 2010) of the career coaching process where gathering and making sense of information is crucial. The helping relationship grows. Common actions during the Understanding Stage are continued coaching sessions, assessment debriefing, occupational research, informational interviewing, and other knowledge-based activities.

Acting Stage

How will I get there? This final stage includes the client and coach co-creating strategies to achieve their goals (Riggall, 2011). Strategies and action for change through realistic goal setting are primary components of the action stage. The coach and client work through issues incorporating problem-solving and decision-making methods as needed (Nelson, 2007). The Acting Stage is also a time of accountability, where the coach ensures follow-up, progress review, and reflection and evaluation of goals (Dietmar, 2021). Common actions during the Acting Stage are submitting applications, interviewing, setting long-term goals and action steps, and salary negotiations.

Having a collaborative relationship with the client will help the overall coaching process, for the client will be more open, and the coach will be able to identify areas that need attention. Nelson (2007) indicated that the helper should remain non-judgmental and empathetic throughout the entire coaching process while encouraging the client to stick to relevant topics. Professionals employ Egan's model in a wide range of helping professions, from coaching to social work, counseling, and teachers who work with willing clients focusing on clients' choices (Riggall, 2016). At each stage in the model, key developments occur in the coaching process, such as conducting an intake and goal setting. Here is a review of some of the key developments that help the coach execute the coaching process more effectively and successfully.

Pre-Coaching Questionnaire

Before the initial coaching session (intake), it is helpful to gather basic information from the client through a pre-coaching questionnaire. Disseminating a pre-coaching questionnaire is also key component of the Exploration Stage because it helps the coach enter the initial coaching session with a baseline sense of client characteristics and why they seek support (Egan, 1975, 2010). Specifically, the coach learns why the client desires career coaching and can gather relevant background (demographics, employment history, education/training) and other pertinent information outside of the initial coaching session. A pre-coaching questionnaire can also help the coach determine the initial coaching session direction and offer opportunities for personal connection, which helps build rapport. Pre-coaching questionnaires also help the coach gather information about the client quickly. A coach can send a simple pre-coaching questionnaire via email or post using a survey platform (e.g., Survey Monkey, Qualtrix), then review the results before the initial coaching session. In addition to basic demographics, sample pre-coaching questions might include:

- What do you hope to gain from working with a career coach?
- What coaching approaches motivate / demotivate you?
- How do you prefer to connect with your career coach (in-person, virtually, email, phone)?
- How will you know when you are receiving value from the coaching process?
- What major changes have you been faced with over the last year?
- On a scale of 1 - 5, how stressed do you feel right now – what are your key stressors?

In addition to gathering relevant background and other pertinent information, the coach will also need to review consent and administrative logistics prior to the initial coaching session. Finally, aside from a pre-coaching questionnaire, a coach may use informal assessments, such as a mind-mapping exercise or a Wheel of Life activity (Mind Tools Content Team, n.d.). See Chapter 3 to generate insight into the client's wants and desired coaching outcomes.

Intake

The coach/client partnership begins during the initial coaching session or intake (see Appendix B for a sample intake form) when the coach and client spend time "taking in" information from each other (Kimsey-House et al., 2018). The intake is a key component of the Exploration Stage as it allows the coach to answer the question, "What is going on?" (Egan 1975, 2010). There are three main goals of the intake. First, the coach and client establish trust and rapport (Brown & Grant, 2010), setting the tone for the entire coaching relationship. Second, the intake is a time for the coach to set the foundation for future work. Setting the foundation includes framing the roles of the coach, client, the coaching sessions, expectations, and processes. This conversation supplies the client with expectations about the coaching process and the client's role. Setting the foundation also includes the communication loop, precisely how the coach and client will connect for the duration of the coaching relationship. Finally, the intake clarifies the client's main coaching topic: Why does the client seek coaching support? If the coach conducted a pre-coaching questionnaire, they likely have a broad idea of why the client is seeking services. The coach probes deeper into the details during the intake. From these details, the coach and client create the vision and goals the client will work on for weeks and possibly months to come (Moore et al., 2016). Information gathering around these three goals: establishing rapport, designating roles, and identifying the coaching topics will ensure a match between the coach and the client and lay the foundation for the working relationship that is to come.

The pre-coaching questionnaire and intake are essential because each client is unique: their goals for coaching are different, the reasons for seeking support vary, the time and financial situations differ, and their personal and professional aspirations are distinctive. One client's needs might call for the coach to start with a battery of self-exploration activities; another might require job search support; yet another might need promotional growth. Where the coaching process begins depends on the client. It is impossible to script the perfect coaching session. The overall purpose of the pre-coaching questionnaire and intake are to gather early information about the client, communicate and come to a mutual understanding of the coaching process, and cement the basics of the helping relationship (Kimsey-House et al., 2018). A skilled coach can mold subsequent coaching sessions to the client's needs based on the pre-coaching questionnaire and intake information.

Establishing a Coaching Plan – Sample Client Session

Every client session is different. The pre-coaching questionnaire and intake will determine the course of the coaching plan and the strategy that the coach employs. However, most coaching sessions follow a similar pattern.

Recap

Begin every coaching session with a recap of the previous session. Assess client wellbeing and connectedness to the day's coaching process.

Progress

Check-in on progress between sessions (including homework), discuss wins and areas of opportunity. Make a note of the client's verbal and non-verbal cues, any items to follow up on at a later date, and resources that might be helpful to share.

Agenda

Give the client time to set the agenda for the coaching session. Work with the client to set clear goals for the coaching session to maximize session efficiency and ensure clear, measurable outcomes. At first, the client may have difficulty setting the agenda. Goals may be unclear or arbitrary. After the first session, the client will become more versed in setting the agenda. Goals will become more apparent and more concrete.

Execute

Discuss the agenda, explore topics, and help clients create options and action plans around their session goals. Here, coaching strategies (see Chapter 3) are most effective. For example, the G.R.O.W. model (**G**oals, **R**eality, **O**ptions, **W**ay; Whitmore, 2009/2017) is an accessible, session-by-session format to follow:

- **G** The client indicates where they want to be (shares and sets **G**oals)
- **R** The coach uses powerful questioning (see Appendix A) to understand where the client is now (their current **R**eality)
- **O** Together the coach and the client brainstorm **O**ptions to reach the goals that have been identified (goal attainment)
- **W** Together the coach and the client decide on the best course of action to execute the **W**ay (forward)

Follow-Up

Near the end of each coaching session, conclude by highlighting the main points covered, clarifying any misunderstood or gray areas, and outlining and agreeing on the next steps. Assign homework activities to anchor session to session and schedule the next meeting. Although the discussion points and exploration activities will change depending on the client's agenda and the coach's execution strategy, it is helpful to follow a similar session format for each client meeting.

Goal Setting

Every client meeting should incorporate a discussion on goals, and following a session format will ensure goals are discussed and reviewed from session to session. Setting goals in the career development process is one of the most challenging aspects of coaching (Capuzzi & Stauffer, 2018). However, goal setting is an essential first step in the client taking ownership of their career development. Thousands of books, articles, and resources exist on setting goals, including well-known strategies for goal setting. During Egan's (1975, 2010) Understanding Stage, the coach and the client explore the fundamental question, "What do I want?" Exploring this question helps the coach develop knowledge of the client's situation, which is critical for goal setting. The coach and the client share roles and responsibilities in the goal-setting process.

Coach's Role in Goal Setting

During the Exploration Stage (Egan, 1975, 2010), the coach gathers information on the client's past and desired outcomes for coaching through the pre-coaching questionnaire and intake. This information is essential for establishing goals with the client that address concerns and major areas for learning and development. The coach and client create a plan with attainable, measurable, specific results and target dates with this information. Chapter 3 outlines additional strategies for clients of various ages and stages. Regardless of the chosen strategy, the coach should make adjustments as needed, whether due to pauses in coaching (e.g., unplanned vacation) or changes in the client's situation (e.g., a job offer that unexpectedly materializes). The coach should be clear with the client that goals are fluid and modifications can be made to their plan at any time in the coaching process.

The coach also helps the client identify and access different resources relevant to set goals (e.g., books, connecting with professionals). However, the coach should not provide these resources as a substitute for coaching but as an additional resource to work done together.

Client's Role in Goal Setting

The client is responsible for setting their goals. As much as the client might want the coach to set goals, they must fully own this portion of the career development journey. Otherwise, the goals will not be the client's goals; they will be the coach's goals. The client is also responsible for completing activities related to the set goals. If the client cannot meet an action, the coach and the client should revisit the goals and discuss modification (and reasons for the modifications).

Sample Goal Setting Questions

Many resources offer lists of questions for every coaching scenario: powerful questions, probing questions, motivational questions, dream job questions, and of course, goal setting questions. A well-known coaching resource is Stoltzfus's (2013) *Coaching Questions: A Coaches Guide to Powerful Asking Skills.* Here are a few common goal-setting questions to consider:

- In what ways can you envision achieving that goal?
- What is holding you back from achieving your goal?
- What can you do in the following (day, week) to move your goal forward?
- Of the goals we have outlined in today's session, which are you most interested in pursuing?

Appendix A is a list of powerful questions for various scenarios, many of which relate to goal setting.

Problem-Solving

The art of problem-solving is integral to the career coaching process and deeply connected to goal setting and action planning. One of the reasons clients seek out career coaching is to gain a trusted partner to help them solve their problems. Thus, problem-solving becomes central to the coaching process. As a coach identifies and sets goals with the client, the problem-solving process kicks into gear. The coach's role in problem-solving is to turn problem statements into solution-oriented questions (Dietmar, 2021).

As the coach works with the client in defining goals and generating strategies to accomplish those goals, problems may arise, whether surfaced by the client or materialized through goal execution. The coach's job is to set a strategy to remove the roadblock. A simple reflection exercise can help. For example:

Step 1: (coach and client) Identify the problem

Step 2: (client) Identify 2-3 questions that might help reframe the problem

Step 3: (coach and client) Discuss the questions for solution-focused resolution

The coach helps the client set an action plan associated with the forward movement of goal attainment, including securing alternatives if a future pivot is needed. As in goal setting, coaches should encourage the client to gather information to help the decision instead of deciding for the client. Naturally, the client will look to the coach for advice and confirmation; however, they are more likely to follow through on decisions that they make for themselves.

Building a Supportive Network

Helping the client build a supportive network may reduce their dependency on the coach and enable them to function more effectively when the coaching process concludes. As the client explores possibilities, develops action plans, or establishes partners for accountability, a coach helps the client identify individuals or groups to access information, resources, and feedback. Building a supportive network also includes identifying role models, mentors, or other influential partners the client can lean on or tap for support and accountability. Building a supportive network helps the client develop independence from the coach and interdependence with others (Del Corso & Briddick, 2015). Here are several questions to help the client build a supportive network:

- What is important to you in an accountability partner?
- From whom could you seek that information?
- Who in your network may have had a similar challenge and would be willing to provide you with information about their experiences?
- How might you ask someone to work with you?
- How can you improve upon what you are doing right now by developing a new partnership?

Assessments

It is important that the coach has a working knowledge of various assessment tools and is skilled at selecting and interpreting them to best support their client's goals and needs. See Chapter 5 for an in-depth look at assessments for use in career support.

Transitioning the Relationship

Coaching is time-bound. While some clients may find comfort in working together, the coaching relationship should have a clear beginning and ending. Seasoned career coaches recognize this and communicate the terms of engagement to the client upfront.

Recapping the Coaching Process

Conduct a Pre-Coaching Questionnaire

Conducting a pre-coaching questionnaire will provide background information and relevant demographics.

Conduct an Intake Session

Clarifying the coaching process, including providing consent details in an informed consent

COACH CORNER

When I first began my coach training, Dick Knowdell said to me: "You should be able to give the client what they need in eight sessions, including a framework to continue long-term growth and development without you once your work with them is done" (D. Knowdell, personal communications, July 28, 2008).

form (see Appendix C), discussing the contract and coaching process, gathering pertinent information on the client's situation, and beginning relationship building.

Execute Coaching Sessions

Crafting an action plan for working together will ensure the helping relationship gets off to a good start. An action plan is typically initiated in the first session. Continue relationship building, exploration, and goal setting in subsequent sessions and administer career assessments if needed.

Discuss and Set Session Agenda

Always remember that the client sets the session agenda.

Set Short and Long-Term Goals and Action Items

As with the session agenda, the client sets coaching goals based on desired outcomes. The coach provides activities (homework) that hold the client's motivation from session to session.

Review Goals and Action Items

From session to session, review the homework with the client. This process supports client progress and increases motivation.

End a Coaching Session

Together the coach and client decide how client progress will be monitored and build this monitoring into the client's action plan.

Conclude Coaching Role

The coach must be prepared to effectively conclude an active coaching role based on the terms of the coaching agreement.

Resistance and Readiness for Change

A client's forward movement in the career coaching process heavily depends on their readiness for change. Reluctance to change can happen anytime in the coaching process, yet working with a client reluctant to change is more challenging at some points in the coaching process than at others. Understanding the components for change can help coaches navigate the change process with their clients more effectively and efficiently.

Types of Change

Miller & Rollnick (2013) suggest that a coach must first understand the various components of change (types, levels, and readiness) to execute change interventions. Various types of change impact a coaching process that may or may not be within the client's control.

Natural Change

Natural change is change due to commonplace occurrences. Natural change occurs without the assistance of a coach. For example, approaching retirement as part of the normal aging process or the reorganization of a company under new ownership. These are active decisions on the client's part and part of the natural change process.

Brief Intervention

Brief intervention holds that a relatively short occurrence, such as a networking meeting or attending a professional workshop, can bring about change.

Dose Effects

More is not always better. For example, submitting quality job applications may be better than submitting a quantity of job applications. The coach can help the client differentiate between applications that are worth the extra time and those that can be passed over because they are not an ideal match.

Faith and Hope (Placebo Effect)

If the client believes they can do something, they are more likely to try to succeed.

Coach Effect (Pygmalion Effect)

If the client believes the coach genuinely understands their situations and cares, they are more motivated.

Waiting List Effect

Initiate change by keeping the client active in their career development journey between appointments. It helps the client progress and feel in control.

Change Talk Effect

Listening to the client's statements that imply a greater willingness and interest in changing and focusing on these statements in more detail is an example of the change talk effect. If the coach hears the client mention something that implies a willingness to change, the coach can be ready to assist.

Levels of Change

In addition to types of change, there are various reasons that clients resist change and on varying levels. Resistance is usually a reaction to how one perceives change or misconception around the change. However, if a coach can help the client find the root cause of their resistance, change can usually be overcome. Change management expert Rick Maurer (1996) outlined the three levels of change resistance that include:

Level 1 - I Don't Get It

Information in facts, figures, and ideas comprises a level 1 resistance to change. A space where knowing the *why* of change is necessary for moving forward (Maurer, 1996). A career coach can be instrumental in supporting the client's willingness to change through conversations that include visual data (e.g., labor market) presented in a clear, straightforward way relevant to their goals.

Level 2 – I Don't Like It

Change is emotional, triggering the fight or flight response in level 2 resistance to change (Maurer, 1996). The client will either be preoccupied with stress induced by the change or retreat caused by the change. A career coach's role is to normalize the change process, create excitement (motivational interviewing works well here), and maintain a helping relationship's ingredients: understanding, empathy, warmth, and genuineness (Egan, 1975, 2010).

Level 3 – I Don't Like You

Reassurance is key during level 3 as resistance is usually deeply entrenched (Maurer, 1996). The client may display a feeling of distrust towards the individuals presenting the change, primarily because the idea of change is uncomfortable or frightening. When a client is resistant to change, mending damaged relationships and maintaining the ingredients of a helping relationship such as acceptance, respect, and trust is the goal (Egan, 1975, 2010). Reaching this goal rebuilds the excitement needed for the client to embrace the change they are trying to implement towards their career growth.

Readiness for Change

The transtheoretical model (TTM) or readiness for change model (Prochaska et al., 1994) helps the coach understand a client's positioning within the change process and where the coach can most impact progress. The TTM comprises six stages of change and assumes that people do not change behaviors quickly and decisively. Instead, they move continuously through a cyclical process (Prochaska & Velicer, 1997; Liu et al., 2018). Different coaching strategies are most effective for each stage of change, and as movement occurs, the client's perception of change transforms over time. For example, in earlier stages, the client assumes more negative than positive thoughts and actions towards change, but the balance shifts as the client realizes increased opportunities related to the change process. Prochaska and Velicer (1997) and Prochaska et al. (2001) highlight the six stages of change (see Figure 1) as:

Pre-contemplation

During pre-contemplation, a client has not yet considered making a change because the client is often unaware of a need for or does not possess a desire for change, which is often the result of a lack of information or misinformation.

Contemplation

During contemplation, a client has intentions of beginning the change process and is considering the pros and cons of changing their behaviors to initiate the process of change.

Preparation

The client is ready to take action and is determined to change. The client makes small steps towards behavior change, believing change is possible. Therefore, the momentum to move is high.

Action

The client takes ownership of the change process during the action stage. The coach and client identify and implement a plan, and the client intends to keep moving forward with that behavior change.

Figure 1
Stages of Change

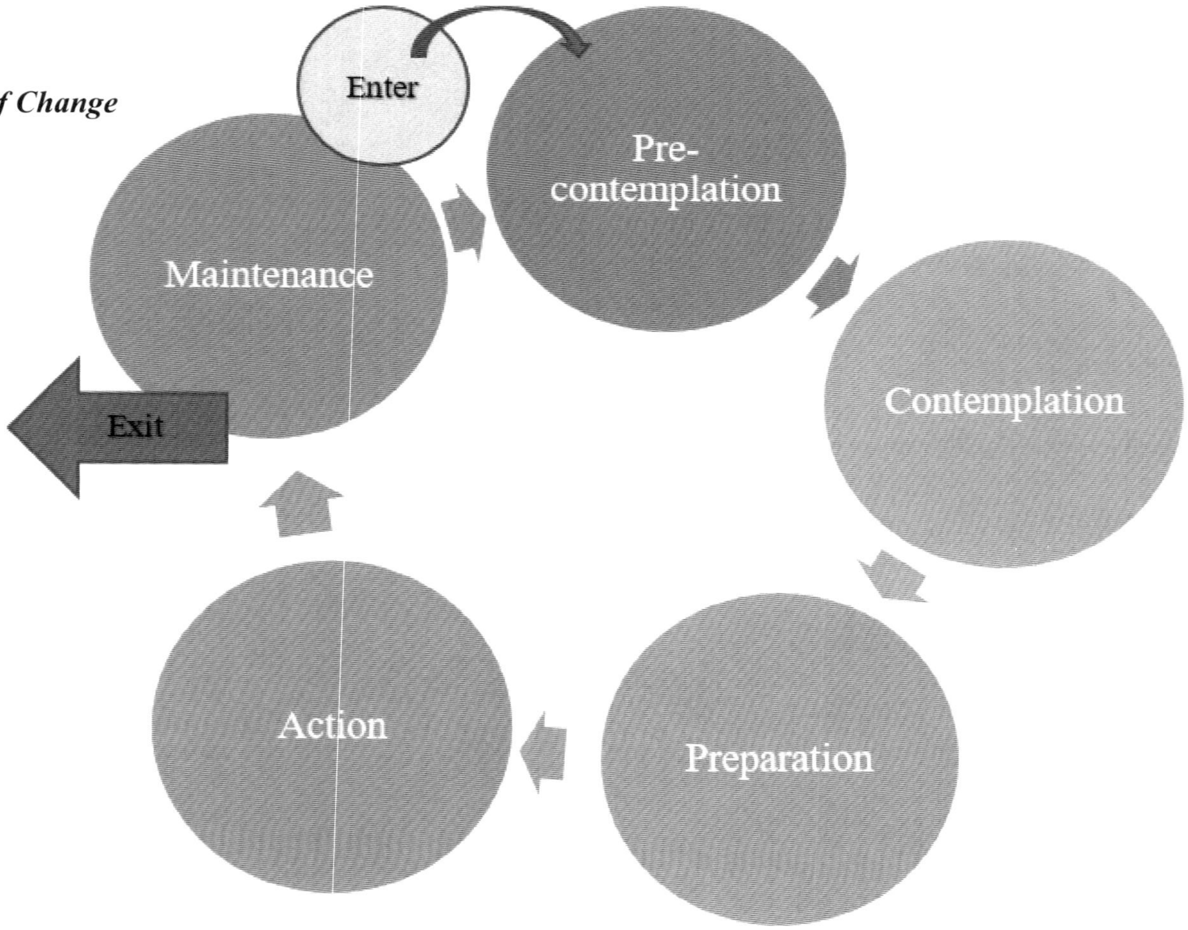

Maintenance

Sustaining change for a period of time (defined as more than six months) and maintaining the behavior change going forward allow for long-term impact. People in the maintenance stage work to prevent relapse to earlier stages, become independent of their coach, and realize an independent life with their new goals. The coach exits the coaching process during maintenance.

Termination

Although not all clients enter termination, the client has no desire or need to return to their unhealthy situation in this stage. In career development, reaching termination is a case-by-case situation dependent on the individual and career-related concerns (Prochaska & Velicer, 1997; Prochaska et al., 2001).

Limitations of the Transtheoretical Model

TTM offers a baseline analysis for readiness for change and offers broad intervention strategies to address various stages of the decision-making process; however, one should consider the limitations of this model.

- The stages do not consider the social context of change, such as socioeconomic status and income.
- The lines between the stages can be arbitrary, with no set criteria for determining a person's stage of change.
- There is no clear sense of how much time one needs for each stage or how long a person can remain in a stage.

Clients do not always make coherent and logical plans when navigating stages of change; however, the TTM is one tool a coach can use to support a client's forward movement in the decision-making process.

Navigating Change

During each stage of change, a client can rationalize excellent reasons to move forward and stay complacent. This push/pull is called ambivalence or simultaneous conflicting feelings about moving on to the next stage of change. According to Miller and Rollnick (2013), ambivalence is a form of approach-avoidance and is the core of a resistant client. A coach's role is to work with the client to mitigate the ambivalence that challenges each stage of the change process - to help the client move out of the state of ambivalence so they do not remain stuck between change stages.

Motivational Interviewing

Originally developed to support substance abuse patients (Miller & Rollnick, 2013; Manuel & Moyers, 2016), motivational interviewing (MI) is a therapeutic method designed explicitly for ambivalent clients about behavior change. It includes four core elements: (1) collaboration (an equal partnership between coach and client), (2) support of autonomy (emphasizing choice and control), (3) evoking rather than installing, and (4) accurate empathy (Miller & Rollnick, 2013). The premise of MI is that ambivalence is a normal part of behavioral change (Moyers, 2014), and if coaches are to work with clients in a change process, they will encounter clients with bouts of ambivalence. The technique is now widely used to support behavioral change for hygiene care (Weinstein et al., 2004), confidence (Kuerbis et al., 2019), health (Lundahl & Burke, 2009), and career (Rice et al., 2017), among many professions.

The coach works with the client through MI to enhance inherent motivation towards specific client goals by resolving ambivalence. Because ambivalence is considered a normal reaction to the change process, a coach should expect to encounter ambivalence at some point in the coaching process. An example of an ambivalent statement might sound like one of these, "I know I need to look for a new job, but the job search

COACH CORNER

How does readiness impact the coaching process?

What factors should be considered when working with a reluctant client?

process is daunting" or "I want to go to grad school, but the time commitment and cost won't allow me to do all the traveling I love to do!" MI is primarily interested in helping clients decide to change rather than helping clients make change because the coaching focuses on why change should occur (Moyers, 2014). The coach places value on the client's choice, agency, and autonomy in the change process (Deci & Ryan, 2012).

Motivational interviewing requires two critical elements for success. The first is the relational component between the coach and the client. Understanding, congruence, and unconditional positive regard are critical to creating a safe, accepting environment where clients can explore change (Rogers, 1959; Gordon, 1970). The second emphasizes language in the coaching sessions: change talk or the spontaneous speech from the client that favors the desired change (Miller & Rose, 2009). Change talk focuses on understanding the client's perspectives through reflective listening and evoking clients' concerns. The coach takes special care to focus on the client's verbalized motivations for change, which counteracts their ambivalence or "resistance to change." As commitment language emerges, behavior change is more likely because the change talk evokes a more substantial commitment to change (Miller & Rose, 2009). The change talk is only successful if the first element is present – understanding. The coach responds to the ambivalence with empathy, evoking a positive response.

Resistance to change is natural, but it impacts the coaching relationship. Whether it is a coach-to-client mismatch or a reluctant client who lacks follow-through or has low motivation, the coaching process cannot move ahead without the client's openness to change. A client needs to be willing, able, and ready to change. The coach's responsibility is to work with the client to mitigate the resistance. Because change is a process that happens at varying levels, stages, and for various reasons, a coach's job is to move a client into new territory, stretching their boundaries and helping them find new resourcefulness. Dweck (2006) believes that building resourcefulness contributes to building a growth mindset. A growth mindset is developing resiliencies and building solid motivation to take on challenges and overcome difficulties, whereas a fixed mindset considers human attributes such as intelligence and creativity to be fixed at birth (Yeager & Dweck, 2012). Erasing a client's limiting beliefs towards change is a step towards building this resourcefulness.

The Coaching Process: In Conclusion

A successful coach collaborates with the client to identify relevant goals and create action items around these goals. The coach can then support the client's resourcefulness through motivating and challenging the client, fostering a sense of accountability for the goals while celebrating wins along the change continuum. Being confident in moving clients through stages of change can positively impact career decision-making, providing greater assurance that coaches are offering the most effective services possible. When clients are ready to embark on career exploration, the coaching process can be powerful and satisfying. Although a coach cannot script a perfect coaching session, they can follow a process. The next chapter provides a way to implement the coaching process learned in this chapter, including applying career theory and models for coaching success.

Knowledge Check

1. What are the six principles that support the definition of coaching?
2. How can you utilize ingredients of a helping relationship in coaching?
3. Reflect on the questioning pitfalls discussed in this chapter. How have you overcome these pitfalls in your coaching role?
4. Identify barriers to change and strategies to help clients overcome these barriers.
5. Discuss the application of the S.O.L.E.R. listening technique for effective coaching.

K-W-L Model – What Have I Learned?

To conclude this chapter, revisit the K-W-L model to assess whether this chapter provided you with information to fill some of your knowledge gaps. Finally, reflect on what you ***learned*** from this chapter and how to apply it to your coaching practice.

References

Askeland, M. (2009). A reflexive inquiry into the ideologies and theoretical assumptions of coaching. *Coaching, 2*(1), 65-75.

Bachkirova, T., Cox, E., & Clutterbuck, D. (2014). Introduction. In E. Cox, T. Bachkirova, & D. Clutterbuck (Eds.), *The complete handbook of coaching* (2nd ed., pp. 1-18). Sage.

Bearwald, R. (2011). It's about the questions. *Educational Leadership, 69*(2), 74-77.

Bennett, J. L., & Bush, M. W. (2013). *Coaching for change.* Routledge.

Boyce, L. A., Jackson, J. R., & Neal, L. J. (2010). Building successful leadership coaching relationships. *Journal of Management Development, 29*, 914–931. http://doi.org/10.1108/02621711011084231

Brew, L., & Kottler, J. A. (2017). *Applied helping skills: Transforming lives* (2nd ed.). Sage.

Brown, S. W., & Grant, A. M. (2010). From GROW to GROUP: Theoretical issues and a practical model for group coaching in organisations. *Coaching: An International Journal of Theory, Research and Practice, 3*(1), 30–45. http://doi.org/10.1080/17521880903559697

Capuzzi, D., & Stauffer, M. D. (2018). *Career counseling: Foundations, perspectives, and applications (3rd ed.).* Routledge. https://doi.org/10.4324/9781315166797

Carnegie, D. (1936). *How to win friends and influence people*. Cardinal Edition.

Cox, E., Bachkirova, T., & Clutterbuck, D. (Eds.). (2014). *The complete handbook of coaching* (2nd ed.). Sage Publications.

Dayan, S. (2019, July/August). Omne trium perfectum. *Modern Aesthetics.* https://assets.bmctoday.net/modernaesthetics/pdfs/MA0819_CF_Threes.pdf

de Haan, E. (2008). *Relational coaching: Journeys towards mastering one-to-one learning*. Wiley Publications.

de Haan, E., Culpin, V., & Curd, J. (2011). Executive coaching in practice: What determines helpfulness for clients of coaching. *Personnel Review*, 40, 24–44. http://doi.org/10.1108/00483481111095500

de Rivera, C., Girolametto, L., Greenberg, J., & Weitzman, E. (2005). Children's responses to educators' questions in day care play groups. *American Journal of Speech Language Pathology, 14*(14-26). https://doi.org/10.1044/1058-0360(2005/004)

Deci, E. L., & Ryan, R. M. (2012). Motivation, personality, and development within embedded social contexts: An overview of self-determination theory. In R. M. Ryan (Ed.), *Oxford handbook of human motivation* (pp. 85–107). Oxford University Press.

Del Corso, J. J., & Briddick, H. S. (2015). Using audience to foster self-narrative construction and career adaptability. In P. J. Hartung, M. L. Savickas, & W. B. Walsh (Eds.), *APA handbook of career intervention: Vol. 2. Applications* (pp. 255–268). American Psychological Association.

Dietmar, S. (2021). *Developing coaching skills: A concise introduction.* Concise publishing.

Dweck, C. S. (2006). *Mindset: The new psychology of success.* Random House.

Egan, G. (1975). *The skilled helper: A model for systematic helping and interpersonal relating*. Brooks/Cole Publishing Company.

Egan, G. (2010). *The skilled helper: A problem management and opportunity development approach to helping* (9th ed.). Brooks/Cole Publishing Company.

Gordon, T. (1970). *Parent effectiveness training*. Wyden.

Hargreaves, D. H. (1984). Teachers' questions: Open, closed and half-open. *Educational Research, 26*(1), 46-51. https://doi.org/10.1080/0013188840260108

Hargrove, R. (1995). *Masterful coaching*. Jossey Bass.

International Coaching Federation. (2021). *Current ICF Core Competencies*. https://coachingfederation.org/app/uploads/2021/05/Current-ICF-Core-Competencies_Brand-Updated.pdf

Jowett, S., O'Broin, A., & Palmer, S. (2010). On understanding the role and significance of a key two-person relationship in sport and executive coaching. *Sport & Exercise Psychology Review, 6*(2), 19-30.

Kimsey-House, K., Kimsey-House, H., Sandhal, P., & Whitworth, L. (2018). *Co-active coaching: The proven framework for transformative conversations at work* (4th ed.). Nicholas Brealey.

Koppi, S. (2018). Career coaching: A new paradigm for student-centered career services. *NACE Journal*. https://www.naceweb.org/career-development/organizational-structure/career-coaching-a-new-paradigm-for-student-centered-career-services/

Koshik, I. (2005). *Beyond rhetorical questions*. John Benjamins.

Kuerbis, A., Lynch, K. G., Shao, S., & Morgenstern, J. (2019). Examining motivational interviewing's effect on confidence and commitment using daily data. *Drug and Alcohol Dependence, 204*. https://www.ncbi.nlm.nih.gov/pmc/articles/PMC6924511/

Liu, J. (2021, April, 21). 1 in 4 workers is considering quitting their job after the pandemic-here's why. *CNBC Make It*. https://www.cnbc.com/2021/04/19/1-in-4-workers-is-considering-quitting-their-job-after-the-pandemic.html

Liu, K. T., Kueh, Y. C., Arifin, W. N., Kim, Y., & Kuan, G. (2018). Application of transtheoretical model on behavioral changes, and amount of physical activity among university's students. *Frontiers in Psychology, 9*. https://doi.org/10.3389/fpsyg.2018.02402

Lundahl, B., & Burke, B. L. (2009). The effectiveness and applicability of motivational interviewing: A practice-friendly review of four meta-analyses. *Journal of Clinical Psychology, 65*(11), 1232–1245. https://doi.org/10.1002/jclp.20638

Manuel, J. K., & Moyers, T. B. (2016). The role of ambivalence in behavior change. *Society of Addiction, 111*, 1910-1911. https://doi.org/10.1111/add.13378

Maurer, R. (1996). Using resistance to build support for change. *The Journal for Quality and Participation, 19*(3), 56-66.

Mazzara, J. J. (2013, March). Leading questions on direct and cross-examination. *Michigan Bar Journal 92*(5), 36-39.

McTighe, J., & Wiggins, G. (2013). *Essential questions: Opening doors to student understanding*. ASCD.

Miller, W. R., & Rollnick, S. (2013). *Motivational interviewing: Helping people change* (3rd ed.). The Guildford Press.

Miller, W. R., & Rose, G. S. (2009). Toward a theory of motivational interviewing. *American Psychologist, 64*(6), 527-537. http://doi.org/10.1037/a0016830

Mind Tools Content Team. (n.d.). *Wheel of life*. https://www.mindtools.com/pages/article/newHTE_93.htm

Moore, M., Jackson, E., & Tschannen-Moran, B. (2016). *Coaching psychology manual*. (2nd ed.) Wellcoaches Corporation.

Moyers, T. B. (2014). The relationship in motivational interviewing. *Psychotherapy, 51*(3), 358-363. https://doi.org/10.1037/a0036910

Murphy, K. (2020). *You're not listening: What you're missing and why it matters*. Celedon Books.

Murphy, T. P. (2006). Judgment: The foundation of professional success. *Consulting Psychology Journal: Practice and Research, 58*(4), 185-194. https://psycnet.apa.org/doi/10.1037/1065-9293.58.4.185

Nelson, P. J. M. (2007). *An easy introduction to Egan's skilled helper solution focused counselling approach* [PDF]. http://highgatecounselling.org.uk/members/certificate/CT1W3%20Paper%202.pdf

Prochaska, J. O., Norcross, J. C., & DiClemente, C. C. (1994). *Changing for good: The revolutionary program that explains the six stages of change and teaches you how to free yourself from bad habits*. W. Morrow.

Prochaska, J. O., & Velicer, W. F. (1997). The transtheoretical model of health behavior change. *American Journal of Health Promotion, 12*(1), 38-48. https://doi.org/10.4278/0890-1171-12.1.38

Prochaska, J., Velicer, W., Fava, J., Rossi, J., & Tsoh, J. (2001). Evaluating a population-based recruitment approach and a stage-based expert system intervention for smoking cessation. *Addictive Behaviors, 26*(4), 583-602. http://doi.org/10.1016/S0306-4603(00)00151-9

Rice, S. L., Hagler, K. J., Martinez-Papponi, B. L., Connors, G. J., & Delaney, H. D. (2017). Ambivalence about behavior change: Utilizing motivational interviewing network of trainers' perspectives to operationalize the construct. *Addiction Research and Theory, 25*(2), 154-162. http://doi.org/10.1080/16066359.2016.1236191

Riggall, S. (2011). Social work students' experiences of using the Egan skilled helper model. *The Journal of Practice Teaching and Learning, 11*(1), 37-53. https://doi.org/10.1921/jpts.v11i1.262

Riggall, S. (2016). The sustainability of Egan's skilled helper model in students' social work practice. *Journal of Social Work Practice, 31*(1), 81-93. https://doi.org/10.1080/02650533.2015.1082465

Rock, D. (2009). *Your brain at work*. HarperCollins.

Rogers, C. R. (1959). A theory of therapy, personality, and interpersonal relationships as developed in the client-centered framework. In S. Koch (Ed.), *Psychology: The study of a science. Vol. 3: Formulations of the person and the social context* (pp. 184 –256). McGraw-Hill.

Rogers, J. (2016). *Coaching skills: A definitive guide to being a coach* (4th ed.). Open University Press.

Roy, D., Kustra, E., & Borin, P. (2003). *What's unique about inquiry?* Centre for Leadership in Learning, McMaster University. http://cll.mcmaster.ca/resources/misc/whats_unique_about_inquiry.html

Senge, P., Kleiner, A., Roberts, C., Ross, R., Roth, G., Smith, B., & Guman, E. C. (1999). The dance of change: The challenges to sustaining momentum in learning organizations. *Performance Improvement, 38*(5), 55-58. https://doi.org/10.1002/pfi.4140380511

Smaby, M. H., & Maddux, D. D. (2011). *Basic and advanced counseling skills: The skilled counselor training model.* Brooks/Cole.

Stoltzfus, T. (2013). *Coaching questions: A coach's guide to powerful asking skills* [Kindle Edition]. Coach 22.

Swann, Jr., W. B., Giuliano, T., & Wegner, D. M. (1982). Where leading questions can lead: The power of conjecture in social interaction. *Journal of Personality and Social Psychology, 42*(6), 1025-1035. http://doi.org/10.1037/0022-3514.42.6.1025

Tschannen-Moran, M. (2004). *Trust matters: Leadership for successful schools*. Jossey-Bass.

Watzlawick, P., Weakland, J., & Fisch, R. (1974). *Change: Principles of problem formation and problem resolution.* Norton & Co.

Weinstein, P., Harrison, R., & Benton, T. (2004). Motivating parents to prevent caries in their young children: One year findings. *Journal of the American Dental Association, 135*(6), 731–738. https://doi.org/10.14219/jada.archive.2004.0299

Whitmore, J. (2009). *Coaching for performance.* Nicholas Brealey Publishing.

Whitmore, J. (2017). *Coaching for performance* (2nd ed.). Nicholas Brealey Publishing.

Williams, P., & Thomas, L. (2005). *Total life coaching.* Norton Publishing

Yeager, D. S., & Dweck, C. S. (2012). Mindsets that promote resilience: When students believe that personal characteristics can be developed, *Educational Psychologist, 47(*4), 302-314, http://doi.org/10.1080/00461520.2012.722805

Zak, P. J. (2017). Trust factor: *The science of creating high-performance companies.* AMACOM.

CHAPTER 3
Theories and Models in Application

"As for the future, it remains unwritten. Anything can happen, and often we are wrong. The best we can do with the future is prepare and savor the possibilities of what can be done in the present."

– Todd Kashdan, *Curious? Discover the Missing Ingredient to a Fulfilling Life*

Chapter Highlights

Chapter 1 highlighted scholars and historical legislative milestones that shaped career services. Historical developments in the field were heavily influenced by theory–from psychology to education to business–guiding and shaping career coaching practice. Long-standing theories have evolved over the years, and new theories are being developed that provide a foundation for career guidance and decision-making. Career coaches may choose one or more theories to guide their approach to coaching and not all coaches choose the same theories when practicing. This chapter will discuss the application of coaching theories and models. Each section will offer a detailed description of various models with accompanying graphs or charts, including AIDA Model, Appreciative Inquiry, Behavioral Interviewing, G.R.O.W., S.M.A.R.T., S.O.A.R. Model, Job Crafting, Mind Mapping, and Storytelling, and conclude with a few easy-to-use coaching tools.

Learning Objectives

This chapter highlights the following:

1. One or more theories that guide a coach's approach to career coaching
2. Application of coaching models to the practice of career coaching
3. How to combine models when needed

K – W – L

Now that you know what the chapter has to offer, take a few minutes to assess your knowledge level and areas of learning using the K-W-L model. The first step in the K-W-L model is to self-assess what you already ***know*** about applying coaching models to the career coaching process. Next, think about what you ***want*** to know about applying a specific model or two to your practice. Where do you feel are the gaps in your coaching knowledge and performance? Finally, to conclude this chapter, you will be asked to revisit the K-W-L model to assess whether this chapter provided you with information to fill some of your knowledge gaps. You will reflect on what you ***learned*** from this chapter and how it can apply to your coaching practice.

Theory's Role in Career Coaching

In his book *Flourish*, Martin Seligman (2011) posited:

> As coaching stands now .... its scope of practice is without limits.... It also uses an almost limitless array of techniques... The right to call oneself a coach is unregulated, and this is why scientific and theoretical backbones are urgent... For this transformation of coaching, you first need the theory; next, the science; and then the applications. (p. 70)

Career coaching has birthed from the field of career counseling which has, itself, advanced into a multifaceted discipline with various discourses that structure distinct interventions and services, including vocational guidance, academic advising, career education, job placement, career development, career coaching, vocational rehabilitation, career construction, and life designing (Savickas, 2015). The work of career coaching is rooted in many career development theories, both historical and modern. The goal of this monograph is not to provide a detailed history of career theory as there are complete texts that offer in-depth analysis, such as Sharf's (2013) *Applying Career Development Theory to Counseling*; however, several theories from the career development world and other industries are practically applicable and highlighted in this chapter. Theories applied to career development directly impact career coaching, guiding strategies in working with clients in various settings. Krumboltz (1996) contends, "The purpose of theory is to help us understand a complex domain to take more useful and intelligent actions. A theory enables us to step back from the nitty-gritty details and see the big picture. A good theory is a simplified representation of reality, identifying relationships among the most crucial characteristics and ignoring the rest" (Krumboltz, 1996, p. 56). On a practical level, theoretical knowledge can aid coaching in better understanding the clients' decision-making and increase the coach's confidence in the approach.

The Learning Process

There is a wide swath of research dedicated to the study of focusing on strengths as a way to yield more favorable results in one's life. For example, Donald Clifton believed that talents or natural reoccurring patterns of thought, feeling, and behavior, productively applied, are the most significant opportunities for success (Cameron et al., 2003). Likewise, career coaching is naturally strength-based, relying on the assumption that more progress is made by focusing on an individual's strengths rather than weaknesses, and in doing this, coaches help the clients manage deficits rather than ignoring them (Biswas-Diener, 2010).

Chapter 2 detailed the coaching process and looked into how career coaches work with clients from pre-evaluation through completion. Individuals seek career coaching because they desire change. The desired change may be subtle or significant depending on the client's goals. During the change process, clients will encounter barriers. A client will come to the coaching process with pre-existing barriers, and barriers will present themselves as the client works to achieve the goals they set towards their career aspirations. There will be barriers the client is aware of, while others go unnoticed. The coaching process itself may be a barrier. For example, a client's unwillingness to change or fear of failure may be unknown barriers. Working with the client to overcome barriers is part of the teaching and learning process.

In the 1970s, Noel Burch from Gordon Training International developed a theory called the Four Stages of Learning Any New Skill (Reilly, 2012). Often referred to as the competency ladder or the four stages of competence (see Figure 2), this learning theory is important for career coaches to be aware of when working with clients. The four stages are unconscious incompetence, conscious incompetence, conscious competence, and unconscious competence (Broadwell, 1969; Curtiss & Warren, 1974; Adams, 2011; Reilly, 2012).

Unconscious Incompetence (UI)

Individuals do not understand or know how to do something and do not recognize their deficit in this area. They are unaware of how little they know and are unfazed by what they do not know. They tend to remain in this stage until prompted to learn in their deficit area (Reilly, 2012).

Conscious Incompetence (CI)

Though individuals do not understand or know how to do something, they are aware of their deficit in that area and the value of learning or possessing knowledge in their deficit area (Reilly, 2012). They have learned enough to understand how little they know and how little they know bothers them (Curtiss & Warren, 1974).

Conscious Competence (CC)

Individuals understand how to do something; however, demonstrating the skill or conveying the knowledge requires concentration and effort. They have learned a good deal and are beginning to master an area or subject, but the mental concentration level is high (Reilly, 2012).

Unconscious Competence (UC)

Individuals have had much practice where the area or subject becomes second nature. In certain circumstances, the individual has become proficient to a point where they can teach the area or subject to others (Adams, 2011). Their area or subject has become almost a habit, and mastery is assumed (Reilly, 2012).

Figure 2
Stages of Learning

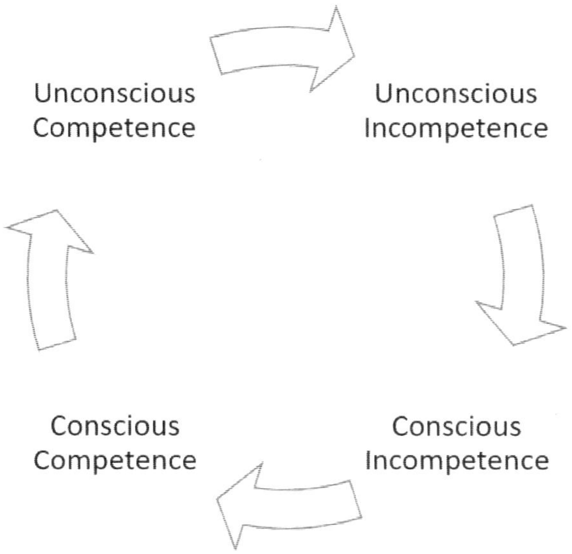

Figure 2 can be applied to an example related to career coaching. In this example, Heather was recently let go from ABC Engineering. Unhappy about this development as it was not her choice to leave, Heather immediately began her job search. She feels confident that her education and experience will land her a new role within a week or two. Heather applies to a couple of jobs at competing firms and plans to enjoy the week off until the offers begin pouring in. Heather is currently in the **unconscious incompetence** stage because she believes she understands the job market and her ease with obtaining a position, given her qualifications, but she is unaware of the challenges.

Several weeks pass. Heather receives no calls for job interviews, and her motivation to search for employment decreases as the days pass. Heather feels less and less confident in her skills, abilities, and job prospects. Last week she began looking at job boards every day, only to be more discouraged by the lack of opportunities. Finally, during a parent-teacher meeting, one of the moms mentioned working with a career coach during her job search last year. At that moment, Heather realized she needed help with her job search and asked the mom for the coach's contact information. Heather is currently in a state of **conscious incompetence.**

Two days later, Heather met with the career coach. The career coach worked with Heather to introduce concepts, resources, and data related to the job search. The coach connects Heather's knowledge and skills to current openings, helps Heather expand her search range, and pursue creative ways to search for opportunities, such as using her broad and deep network. Heather receives help from the coach with enthusiasm and works hard to tweak her search productively. The work with the career coach moves Heather from a state of conscious incompetence to **conscious competence.** Heather feels ready to implement what she has learned related to her search; however, she is not ready to do this alone. She wants to continue working with her coach because she is still unsure about her abilities related to deeper parts of the search, like interviewing or salary negotiation – things she has not done in a long time.

After a short time, Heather receives several invitations to interview. These invitations give her and her coach a chance to practice interviewing. Together, they practice, refine, and practice more until it feels like a natural process. At this point, Heather has entered a state of **unconscious competence.** At this stage of the learning process, Heather's career coach can step away from their work, and Heather can feel confident in her abilities to continue and succeed in the job search independently.

Coaching Theories and Models

Coaches can use knowledge of the learning process to evaluate where clients are in their career transition in the coaching process. However, clients may not fully ascribe to the coaching process until they understand that coaching holds value. Coaching theories and models are an extraordinary way to demonstrate value on various aspects of the coaching process: strengths, skills, abilities, personality, and how to apply information about the self to all aspects of the career exploration process. Next, various coaching theories and models and their applications are covered.

Schlossberg's Transition Theory

Whether expected or not, transitions are turning points that shape relationships, routines, assumptions, and roles, and the effect of a transition is dependent on the individual's perception of the transition, which could be positive or negative depending on their coping mechanisms. Schlossberg (1984) originally defined transition as an "event or nonevent resulting in change" (p. 43).

Transition Types

Schlossberg and colleagues identified three types of transitions: anticipated, unanticipated, and nonevent (Schlossberg et al., 1995) and assigned definitions and examples to each. Anticipated transitions are relatively common and allow individuals to predict change, anticipate options, and plan. For instance, graduating from high school, transitioning from one job to another, and retiring from the workforce are anticipated transitions. Unanticipated transitions are nonscheduled, unpredicted events, often resulting in chaos. Examples of unanticipated transition might be a forced transfer resulting from a college closure (Maietta, 2022), job loss due to company closure, or the need to seek an alternative career path due to an accident or health reasons. Finally, when the anticipated transition does not occur, this non-event can also alter a life trajectory. Non-event examples include a promotion or job offer that never materializes or a work relocation that falls through.

When an individual experiences transition, they move through two phases: approaching transition and taking stock of coping resources. Approaching transition includes identifying the transition type (anticipated, unanticipated, nonevent), context, and impact. Taking stock of coping resources helps one understand the transition itself (Goodman et al., 2006; Schlossberg, 1984; Schlossberg et al., 1995). Reflecting and responding to change impacts how individuals experience, relate to, and adequately manage a transition.

Context and Impact of Transition

Understanding the context and impact of a transition is as essential to supporting a client through a transition as is identifying the transition type. Context is the "relationship of a person to the transition (personal, interpersonal, community); and the setting of transition (family, work, health, friends)" (Schlossberg, 1984, p. 47), all of which play a role in career decision-making and potential difficulties that may arise (Amir & Gati, 2006; Gati et al., 1996; Gati, 1993; Osipow, 1999; Osipow et al., 1976). The impact of a transition is the "degree to which a transition alters daily life" (Schlossberg, 1984, p. 52) – essentially, how much psychological, emotional, and chronological energy the transition drains. The more significant the impact of the transition, the higher the need for complex coping methods and diverse resources (Schlossberg, 1984). Understanding context and impact helps clients gain perspective and confidence when approaching a transition and navigating through the transition. Add a clear identification of type (anticipated, unanticipated, or nonevent), and the transition can be met with a stronger sense of confidence and ability.

Approaching transitions is the first phase of Schlossberg's transition theory. In this phase, one must identify the transition by type, context, and impact. Schlossberg (1984) maintains that if one's approach to transitions is comprehensive and systematic, the likelihood of a successful transition increases.

Coping with Transition

Phase two, taking stock of coping resources (TSCR) or the 4 S System, influences how individuals experience transitions and react to or cope with those experiences through the lens of situation, self, support, and strategies (Schlossberg, 1984; Schlossberg et al., 1995). The 4 S system is a useful way for coaches to help clients navigate transition by helping them utilize existing resources and drawing on internal resiliencies.

Situation. Situation includes the trigger event(s) that caused the transition, the timing of the transition in the larger context of life-plan, the sense of control over the situation caused by the transition, role changes that the transition may have prompted, the transition time frame, previous experience with similar transition(s), parallel stressors, and the appraisal of the transition as positive, negative, or nonthreatening (Goodman et al., 2006). For example, in a job search, situational awareness would refer to how the coach and client understand the impact of the job search related to the client's life circumstances. If a client is interested in accepting a role they aspire to but doing so requires them to relocate their family across the country, exploring the impact of such transition would be necessary for positive forward movement.

Self. Self includes personal and demographic characteristics, socioeconomic status, sex, gender, age, health, ethnicity/culture, psychological resources, values, and resiliency (Goodman et al., 2006). In transitions, the self refers to those unique characteristics, experiences, perceptions, and worldviews shaping or reshaping how a person transitions from one life phase to another. Self-efficacy plays a role in transition related to self and career search, specifically an individual's confidence to perform important career selection and search activities (Solberg et al., 1994). Self also considers a client's career maturity and adaptability or an individual's degree of career decision-making and readiness to make occupational choices (Savickas, 1997; Savickas & Porfeli, 2012). Many clients seek career support to help navigate career change in various forms. A client's readiness for change, such as preparing for and participating in a new work role or navigating unpredictable adjustments prompted by changes in work and working conditions, can impact and be impacted by one's self-concept (Goodman et al., 2006; Savickas, 1997).

Supports. Supports include friends, family, mentors, and available community structures (Goodman et al., 2006). Access to and awareness of community resources designed to facilitate a transitional event can impact how supported an individual feels, particularly for individuals without personal and professional support systems necessary for healthy career decision-making. For example, the LinkedIn 2018 Workplace Learning Report (Lefkowitz & Pate, 2018) revealed that 94% of respondents would stay employed at a company longer if the company invested in their career development. Furthermore, 56% would spend more time learning if their managers suggested a course to improve their skills. Supports are also essential for clients from varied underrepresented populations (see Chapter 6), as discrimination in the workplace and the career search process are well-documented (Baldwin & Johnson, 1992; Fassinger, 2008; U.S. Equal Employment Opportunity Commission, 2020; Phelps & Constantine, 2001; Terrell, 2021). Supports help clients combat and navigate career-related transitions and impacting obstacles.

Strategies. Strategies involve coping choices and behaviors, which may modify the situation caused by the transition, control the meaning of the situation, and manage stress resulting from the situation (Goodman et al., 2006). Lazarus (1966) undertook robust research on stress and coping, later expanded by Lazarus and Folkman (1984), which argued that stress consists of three processes. When an individual experiences stress, there is a primary appraisal or process of perceiving the threat to oneself. After that, the individual undergoes secondary appraisal, bringing a potential response to the threat to mind. Only then can the individual cope or execute a response to the stressor. Lazarus and Folkman (1984) posit that coping is context-specific. Thus, individuals seek different coping strategies depending on situational factors. These coping strategies help individuals redefine and identify actions to mitigate the transition. In addition, strategies allow individuals to manage pressure and appropriately respond while navigating the transition. Clients can benefit from discussing strategies for navigating the transition and how those strategies impact goal attainment.

In short, a transition is a dynamic change occurring over time, in reasonably identifiable stages, with positive and negative associations. A transition affects and is affected by our identities, relationships, values, behaviors, and contexts. Schlossberg's transition theory (1984) holds two key assumptions for career coaches who work with individuals in transition. First, individuals in transition are often confused by multiple decision points and stressors, but effective coaching can help focus attention, solve problems and move the client towards success. Second, family, friends, and coworkers are supportive persons who help individuals through various transitioning phases. These assumptions make this theory particularly appropriate when working with individuals in transition: a time of potentially great confusion but with the potential to work with many helpers and many resources.

Holland's Theory of Vocational Choice

John Holland was a seminal scholar and prolific author on the typology work choice. Holland authored numerous books and articles introducing and refining psychological theories related to vocational preference, resulting in two widely used inventories: the Vocational Preference Inventory (VPI; Holland, 1985) and the Self Directed Search (SDS; Holland et al., 1994), both measuring self-assessed competencies and interests connecting personality and occupational preference. As a result of his life's work, Holland's (1997) theory of vocational choice is one of the most widely researched and applied career development theories (Rayman & Gottfredson, 2020). Holland argued that human behavior is a function of interactions between individuals and environments. The theory incorporates personality psychology, vocational behavior, and social psychology, including self-perception theory and social stereotyping. Career coaches should note that some researchers have noted limitations of the theory related to age, gender, class, education, and general cognitive function (Sharf, 2013). Nevertheless, career development professionals primarily use Holland's theory of vocational choice to orient clients to the world of work, provide a methodical mechanism for career exploration, and, ultimately, facilitate career decision-making and planning (Swanson & Gore, 2000).

A tenet of Holland's theory focuses on the interaction or fit between individuals and their environments. Holland's theory centers on the notion that most people fit into one of six personality types: Realistic, Investigative, Artistic, Social, Enterprising, or Conventional (RIASEC), typically depicted as a hexagon (see

Figure 3; Holland, 1997). The theory matches work environments and six personality types, including expected behaviors related to each type (Gottfredson & Richards, 1999). The theory links person-environment interactions, providing explanations for questions such as: "What personal and environmental characteristics lead to satisfying career decisions?" or "What personal and environmental characteristics lead to stability and change in the kind and level of work a person performs over time?" or "What are the most effective methods for assisting people with career challenges?" Included here is a brief overview of each type:

Realistic

A realistic work environment is demanding and requires technical expertise, and calls for physical ability and exertion. Occupational examples may include commercial farming, horticulture, construction, or manufacturing. A realistic personality enjoys a practical approach to problem-solving, with a lower tolerance for the abstract. These individuals are the doers who have a higher appreciation for money, power, and status than some other personality types. These individuals have a high need for practical advice and expect tangible outcomes from a coaching environment.

Investigative

An investigative environment is solution-focused, with many problem-solving opportunities in which individuals are encouraged to use complex, abstract thinking. Occupational examples may include veterinarian, statistician, physician, or computer programmer. Investigative personalities enjoy exercising their intellect–they are the thinkers. These individuals love learning for the sake of learning, solving puzzles, mathematical equations, or searching for solutions to unknown problems. Investigative clients are intrigued with solving the question of what is next in their career journey and may approach their exploration through an analytical lens, taking charge of their search.

Artistic

An artistic environment is free and expressive, where creativity is encouraged. This workplace encourages artistic expression and seeks employees with original thought and independent mindset. Artistic types provide and welcome less-structured workspaces for personal and emotional expression. Occupations may include working in a photography studio, art gallery, museum, or design firm. An artistic personality enjoys space to express themselves to be free and open to creative possibilities–these individuals are the creators. Artistic personalities are satisfied in art, music, or literature-related occupations and see themselves as expressive and independent individuals. Mind mapping or guided imagery exercises might appeal to an artistic personality type in the career exploration process.

Social

A social environment is responsive to others in a humanitarian way, in that members support and encourage one another. There are similar ideals among members in the social environment, yet flexibility in acceptance. Occupational examples may include teaching, counseling, social work, or some aspects of health care. A social personality enjoys resolving conflict and seeking consensus through discussion. Social personalities are the helpers, preferring to resolve conflict quickly and formidably. Social personalities are interested in the coaching process from a coaching lens. They are generally participatory in the coaching process while understanding and appreciating the benefits of coaching.

Enterprising

Management and persuasion are the hallmarks of the enterprising environment, and an enterprising personality typically possesses both competencies. As natural risk-takers, enterprising personalities are confident, social, and assertive, and the enterprising environment demands these characteristics of its people as the environment typically involves selling and persuading.

Figure 3
Holland's Hexagon: The relationship among Holland's types

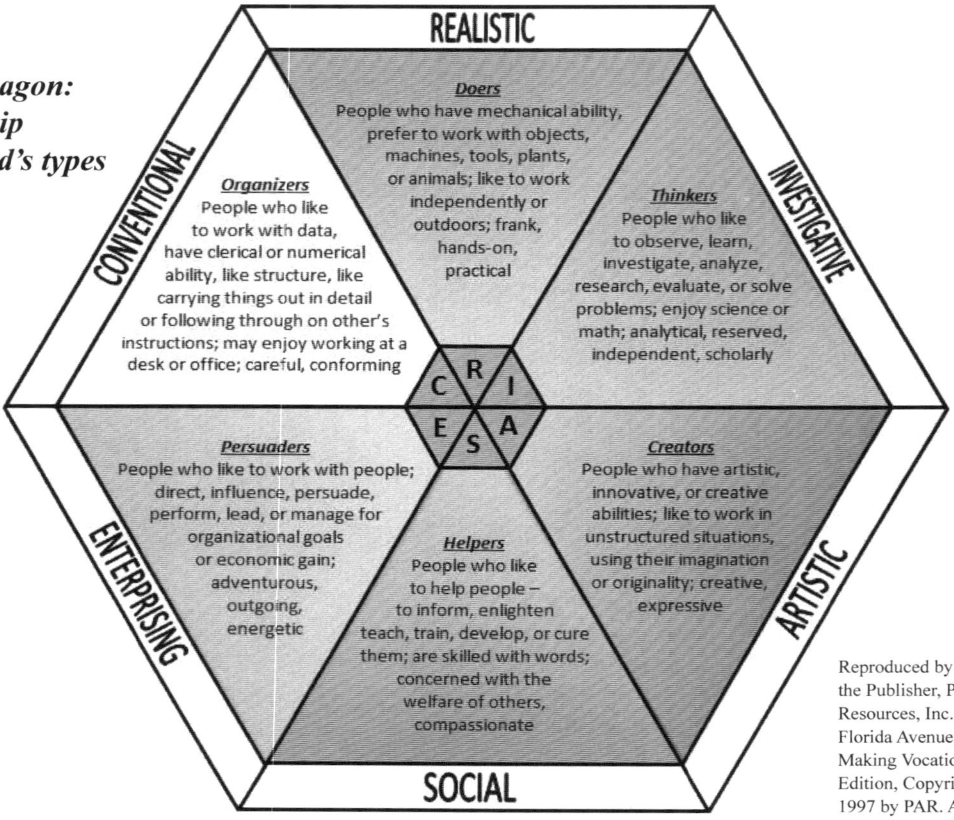

Occupational examples may include stockbroker, financial advisor, insurance broker, or realtor. These individuals present themselves as confident and self-assured and participate in the career coaching process; however, this can sometimes cover deeper insecurities or uncertainties about change or career decision-making.

Conventional

Conventional environments are traditional and systematic, with strict processes and record keeping. Office settings are commonly conventional environments, and typical occupations include accountant, lawyer, government official, and bookkeeper. Conventional personalities are the organizers of the group. Conventional personalities enjoy routine, order, dependability, organization, and an environment that feels valued for accomplishments. A conventional client will appreciate an organized approach to the career decision-making process and expect the coach to be dependable and systematic in their approach to coaching.

Holland's (1959, 1997) theory assumes all individuals possess a combination of all six types in varying degrees and, at some point, work in environments that call for or utilize type preferences in multiple ways. However, the three most dominant types are an individual's preferred type or Holland code. For example, if a client completes the Self-Directed Search (Holland, 1997) and the top three scores were artistic, investigative, and social, their 3-letter Holland code would be AIS.

Holland's theory of vocational choice is a seminal theory in career development that has stood the fluctuations of the workforce and constant change in client needs. Many clients, particularly college students, place a high value on learning about things that interest them (Eagan et al., 2017). Moreover, bridging the gap between pursuing career decision-making based on overlapping interests and other competencies is a touchstone for a coach's work (Koppi, 2018). As a result, Holland's theory of vocational choice is useful for career coaches, supported by a considerable body of research, and used in several valid assessment instruments. Moreover, the theory is relatively straightforward and the assessments are uncomplicated to administer.

HEROIC Narrative

Career and life roles go through cycles of stability and change, with few adhering to a linear work and life planning model referred to in *Three Boxes of Life* (Bolles, 1978). Narrative assessment and storytelling help clients self-advocate because meaning-making happens through storytelling (Feller, 2017). A HEROIC mindset embraces **H**ope, self-**E**fficacy, **R**esilience, **O**ptimism, **I**ntentional exploration, **C**uriosity, and **C**larity. Feller and Franklin (2020) posited that a HEROIC mindset helps clients develop a more profound knowledge of their skills and abilities and how these work across systems. Learning comes through failure, and understanding the perspectives of others is essential to navigating a lifetime of transition.

The HEROIC Narrative Assessment System

The HEROIC Narrative Assessment System (HNAS) guides users through a narrative career and life clarification process rooted in life stories, directed exploration of promising occupational possibilities and integrating experiences into a holistic picture. Figure 4 offers a visual of the client's journey. First, it is necessary to recognize that the client's past story needs to be honored, and

Figure 4
HEROIC Narrative Assessment System (HNAS)

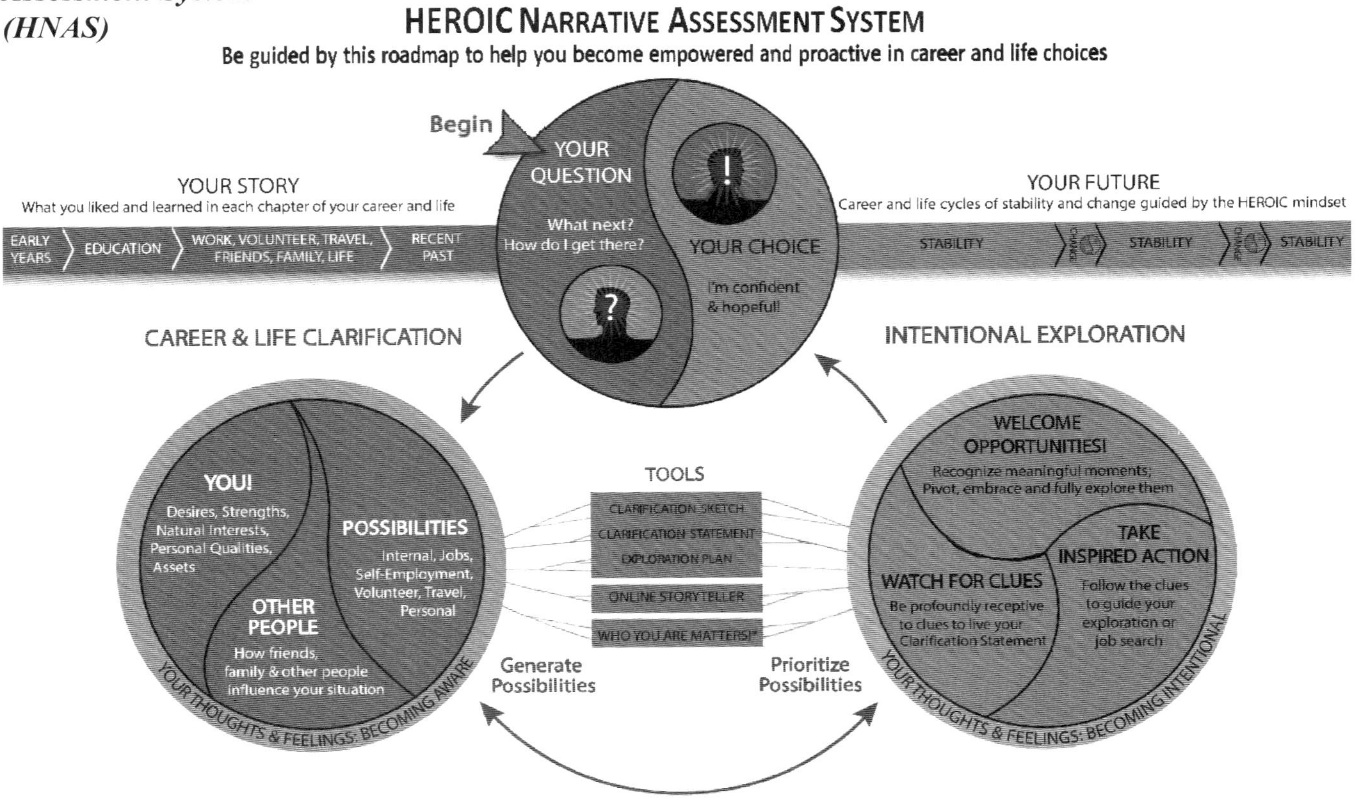

Adopted from "The HEROIC Narrative Assessment System: Helping Undergrads Navigate Transitions," by R. Feller, and M. Franklin, 2020, in P. Gardner & H. N. Maietta (Eds.). *Advancing Talent Development: Steps Towards a T-Model Infused Undergraduate Education,* p. 133.

their future story will undergo periods of stability and change.

Identifying one's question (left side of the top circle in Figure 4) starts the process as the client contemplates

- What should I do next?
- What possibilities are a better fit?
- How do I transition my past experiences into new opportunities?

The Career and Life Clarification circle (bottom left in Figure 4) challenges clients to reflect on past experiences to clarify three elements: *You, Other People, and Possibilities.* As clients identify possibilities, they create a *Clarification Statement* later used to gain feedback and resources, take inspired actions and identify a capability partner (e.g., mentor, peer support).

Intentional Exploration (bottom right circle, Figure 4) helps clients prioritize future possibilities by *welcoming opportunities*, *watching for clues*, and *taking inspired action* before making necessary decisions. This exploration avoids investing time and resources before ensuring a possibility is a good fit. Tasking clients to watch for clues effectively reframes accessing labor market information, so the client uses the knowledge of the world of work to identify matches or inconsistencies with the Clarification Statement (Feller & Franklin, 2020).

Clients who travel through the HNAS benefit from transparent, confident, well-informed decision-making because the framework bridges the latest career theory and thinking. Career coaches play a key role when clients engage in intentional storytelling by listening deeply to identify important story elements.

The Who You Are Matters! and Online Storyteller

Franklin and Feller (2014) used the HNAS to create Who You Are Matters! (WYAM) and the Online Storyteller. WYAM is a guided clarification exploration at the intersection of meaningful experience and work, personal lifestyle, and gaining a self-advocating voice. Through storytelling and meaningful conversations relevant to one's career and life, a Clarification Sketch is created as a takeaway that strengthens participants' self-advocacy voice and skills (Feller & Franklin, 2020). Clients who completed at least four sessions found significant increases in hope, efficacy (confidence), resilience, and optimism (abbreviated as HERO; Franklin et al., 2015).

Online Storyteller is a digital tool that guides clients through the HNAS framework to define and clarify the six key elements (Feller & Franklin, 2020). Online Storyteller is designed for collaborative use by helping professionals and their clients or for self-directed narrative assessment to generate meaningful future possibilities leading to well-informed choices.

WYAM and Online Storyteller help clients develop critical attributes and patterns sought after by all industries (Franklin & Feller, 2014). This constructive narrative method aligns with life design principles (Savickas, 2012) and exemplifies learning from a qualitative, post-modern career counseling lens (Franklin & Feller, 2017). In short, clients who explore using HNAS thrive when adapting to innovative environments and situations.

AIDA

AIDA is an acronym that stands for Awareness, Interest, Desire, Action. First devised in 1898 by E. St. Elmo Lewis as a customer service marketing funnel in the life insurance industry, AIDA explains the psychology of personal selling mechanisms (Mackey, 2005). Lewis's studies found that the most successful salespeople followed a hierarchical, structured approach to selling which used the four cognitive phases that buyers follow when accepting a new idea or buying a new product. Applying the AIDA concept to personal branding, the objective is to help the client see how they can live their dream in the present by developing effective strategies to communicate (as the sender) to better respond to the receiver's needs and desires.

Breaking down the AIDA acronym (see Figure

5), the A in AIDA increases the client's awareness towards the goal(s), such as a job search and tasks associated with goals (e.g., résumé creation, networking). One of the best approaches to attracting awareness is *creative disruption*, which breaks existing behavior patterns through highly creative messaging. The I in AIDA represents the ability to create and maintain interest related to the client's goals, which can be the most challenging aspect of the AIDA model. For example, a client's interest in the job search (prioritizing time commitments; effort level) directly impacts a client reaching their job search goals. Interest also relates to ease of understanding. Does the client understand the steps necessary to achieve the desired goal? If the goal is set too high, D for desire will decrease because the goal will feel less attainable. Therefore, the coach and the client need to focus on the client's desired outcome when applying the AIDA model to goal setting. Finally, A is for action or parsing the client's goals into measurable action items.

Figure 5
AIDA Model

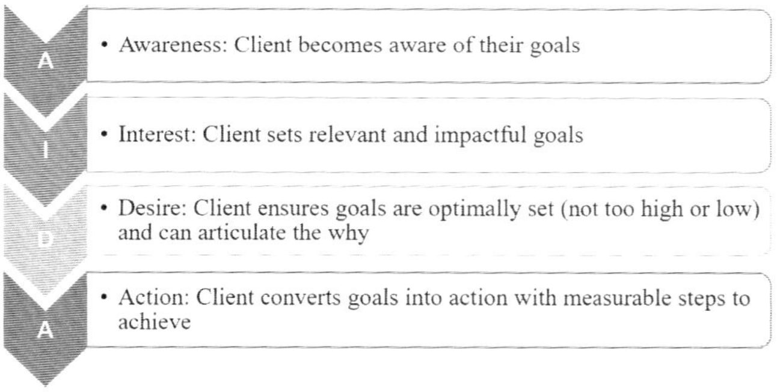

The AIDA model can be applied to many aspects of career exploration and is a valuable exercise for a single coaching session. Here are two examples of how AIDA can be used in career exploration.

Interviewing

A client can execute a job interview successfully using the AIDA model with the help of the coach.

A – Form awareness in the first few seconds. The interviewer forms an immediate opinion of the client, so instruct the client to smile, be polite, make eye contact (if culturally appropriate), and carry themselves with confidence.

I – Tailor responses directly to the advertisement or job description. Work with the client to craft answers that speak to the organization's needs and ensure they answer the question directly and concisely.

D – Exude passion in response. Practice connecting the client's competencies and skills to the position and their desire to work with the organization. Help the client research the company before the interview for value-driven job and organization connections and ensure the client knows specific examples of how to communicate these connections during the interview.

A – Post-interview action. Educate the client on how to follow up with all interviewers personally, reiterating their interest in the position. In addition, encourage the client to use this opportunity to highlight their skills to the organization (ones they might not have mentioned in the interview).

Résumé Development

A client and coach can craft a winning résumé using the AIDA model.

A – Write a targeted résumé or cover letter. Craft a message that communicates that the client is a direct match for the advertised position.

I – Grab the employer's interest in the potential employee. Show the employer that the client researched the position and the company by having the client reference the organization's accomplishments, goals, or philanthropic endeavors in the résumé and connect the client's experience and interests to these statements or activities.

D – Showcase the job seeker as irresistible by emphasizing skills and experience that will be an asset to their organization. Work with the client to offer something different by including examples that showcase the client's unique accomplishments and explain how, if hired, the client can bring these talents to the organization.

A – Any variety of actions, which may vary

depending on the situation and how far the job seeker travels through the application/attention-getting process. If the action is getting an interview lined up or, even better, an agreement made or, best of all, a contract signed, the coach will continue to walk with the client through these steps.

The AIDA model has stood the test of time in marketing and other areas where achievement and outcomes are paramount. Slightly altered versions of the model include AIDAS, which adds an S for *Satisfaction*. Applied to career coaching, the coach and client revisit outcomes related to action taken on set goals and determine satisfaction derived from those outcomes. Essentially, did the client achieve what they intended to achieve? Another version of AIDA includes *Commitment* (AIDCA), where commitment lives between desire and action. Proponents of this change argue that a desire to reach one's goal can be present without commitment to reach the goal. Therefore, to take action, the client must hold desire and commitment. Still, others use the acronym AIDCAS, combining awareness, interest, desire, commitment, action, and satisfaction. Whether a coach chooses the baseline model or the modern version of AIDA, the model is easy to remember and utilize for a client's multiple coaching needs.

G.R.O.W. Model

For centuries, the science of psychology has made great strides in understanding what goes wrong in individuals, families, groups, and institutions, but only within the past 20 years has attention turned to understanding what goes right (Gable & Haidt, 2005). Positive psychology is the science of life's most noteworthy moments–studying characteristics, conditions, and processes leading to positivity. Gable and Haidt (2005) stated that "positive psychology is the study of the conditions and processes that contribute to the flourishing or optimal functioning of people, groups, and institutions" (p. 104). This theoretical approach is concerned with strength, pays less attention to weakness, and is interested in building a positive approach to life while reframing negative situations. Positive emotions enhance cognitive, affective, and physical resilience (Fredrickson, 2003) and result in tangible outcomes such as higher earnings, creativity, work engagement, and health (Lyubomirsky et al., 2005).

Positive psychology coaching (PPC) suggests that the coach view the client as a whole, and the coaching process should focus on client strengths, positive behaviors, and purpose. When the client realizes their goals, the result is a sense of personal agency and the flow of happy emotions. PPC builds a client's thought to act, as the coach facilitates successful transitions through stages of change (Prochaska et al., 1994), providing challenges and supports appropriate for the client and the situation. The PPC process does not ignore unpleasant situations or barriers to change; it aims to reframe them into more tolerable, manageable circumstances that can–if possible–pivot the client to realize their situation with a higher measure of positivity.

The G.R.O.W. model is one of several coaching models that use a positive psychology approach. A coach can use the G.R.O.W. model to initiate change in a single session or as a multi-session coaching tool. The transtheoretical model (see Chapter 2) views change as a process that is not always linear and one in which individuals have varying degrees of readiness for change (Prochaska et al., 1994). Too often, coaching discussions begin during a deficit for clients: a job loss, a promotion that did not materialize, or perhaps a shattered professional dream. However, the discussion does not have to live in a deficit space. Negative emotions and experiences are more urgent and override positive ones because negative emotions often reflect immediate problems (Seligman & Csikszentmihalyi, 2000). Positive psychology coaching encourages the coach and client to acknowledge the problem, discuss appropriate adaptive responses, and elicit action. After that, the coaching focus should shift to experiences that promote happiness and well-being (Seligman & Csikszentmihalyi, 2000). As the client begins to conquer their limiting beliefs, change occurs. A client's perception of change transforms over time. In earlier stages, a client may see more cons than pros, but over time, in later stages, the balance shifts, and the client starts to see increased benefits to change (Prochaska et al., 1994). First used in corporate coaching in the late 1980s and 1990s, the G.R.O.W. model raises individuals' awareness and understanding of their aspirations, beliefs, resources, and reality.

G.R.O.W. is an acronym that stands for Goals, Reality, Options, and Way Forward. By working through these four steps, a client can envision their aspirations (goals) and apply these aspirations to their current situation (reality). Doing so offers the client a better sense of the possibilities and resources open to them (options) and helps them realize that they can achieve their goals (way forward). In addition, by setting goals that are inspiring and challenging, as well as S.M.A.R.T. (specific, measurable, achievable, relevant, and time-bound), using the G.R.O.W. model can promote confidence and self-motivation, leading to increased productivity and personal satisfaction.

Coaching with the G.R.O.W. Model

The advantage of working with the G.R.O.W. coaching model is that the coach does not need to be an expert in the client's specific situation. Instead, the G.R.O.W. coaching model offers a framework with general questions to elicit goals, obstacles, options, and more, without needing advice or forcing any particular direction. In a sense, the coach provides a dynamic vehicle for their client's development. The G.R.O.W. coaching model consists of a four-step journey taken by a client, facilitated by the coach.

Step 1: Goals. The first step in the G.R.O.W. coaching model is defining the goal of the coaching trajectory. In this step, the client needs to answer the question: "Where am I going?" That includes long-term (the central theme of the trajectory) and short-term (the goal for every session). Goals need to be S.M.A.R.T.: Specific, Measurable, Achievable, Relevant, and Time-bound.

Step 2: Reality. Step two of the G.R.O.W. coaching model is becoming aware of the client's actual situation. In this step, the client needs to answer the question: "Where am I coming from?" The coach's role is to stimulate self-evaluation with the client and identify the obstacles holding the client back. Summarizing and paraphrasing techniques (see Chapter 2) are also helpful. This step of the G.R.O.W. coaching model often reveals underlying fears and convictions that serve as future talking points or homework topics between coaching sessions.

Step 3: Options. Step three of the G.R.O.W. coaching model generates solution-focused ideas. In this step, the client needs to answer the question: "Where could I go?" The coach begins the creative brainstorming process without censure or conditionality. The client generates ideas then evaluates all ideas against desired outcomes. If needed, the coach can also offer some suggestions.

Step 4: Will. The fourth and last step of the G.R.O.W. coaching model is putting into action the choice of one option. In this step, the client needs to answer the question: "What do I need to get there?" First, the singular option is converted into a concrete plan to move forward and grow. Then the client's motivation to follow this plan is maximized. See Appendix L for coaching questions and a G.R.O.W. model worksheet.

The Impact

The G.R.O.W. model emphasizes the client's greater awareness and accountability to their circumstances and encourages proactive behavior and practical strategies to achieve goals and overcome obstacles through carefully framed questions. Continuous and progressive coaching support offers the framework that unleashes an individual's potential by developing confidence and motivation, resulting in both short- and long-term benefits. Table 4 is an example of the G.R.O.W. model applied to goal development.

Table 4
G.R.O.W. Model Applied to Goal Development

Goal Discuss and set goals for session or coaching program (single or multi-session)	**Clarify and focus** • What should the topic of today's session be? • What goal(s) do you want to achieve in this session related to that topic? • Why is this goal(s) important to you now? • How will you know you have achieved this goal(s)?
Reality Invite self-assessment of the topic and situation; Clarify any gray areas; Check assumptions	**Define current situation** • What impact or effect does this have? • How do you know that this is accurate? • How often does this occur? • Are there other relevant factors?
Obstacles Identify obstacle(s) (people, resources, environment)	**Explore and understand obstacles** • What prevents you from reaching your goal(s)? • What else gets in the way? • What personal changes will you have to make to achieve your goal?
Options Invite suggestions from the client. Here the coach is only the scribe.	**Brainstorm possibilities** • What options are possible? • What are the pros and cons of each option? • If you could choose, which option would you select?
Way Forward Get a commitment to act and devise a plan to move forward.	**Design an action plan and alternatives** • What are your next steps? • What is the timeframe? • What could get in the way? • What support and resources will you need? • How and when can you get the support and resources?

Appreciative Inquiry

Coaching through an appreciative inquiry (AI) lens is the belief that something works in every individual, and what an individual focuses on and the language an individual use creates their reality. It is "a collaborative and highly participative, system-wide approach to seeing, identifying, and enhancing the 'life-giving forces' that are present when a system is performing optimally in human, economic, and organizational terms" (Watkins & Mohr, 2001, p. 14). Cooperrider et al. (2005) offered a broader definition as a "cooperative, coevolutionary search for the best in people, their organizations, and the world around them. It gives 'life' to a living system" (p. 3). Proponents of AI believe in the model because it is strength-based, rooted in tenets of positive psychology, whereby people have more confidence in the future when they can carry forward positive parts of their past. The connection to positive psychology comes from its focus on a solution-based approach to problem-solving. During AI, the coach and client explore a coaching topic, clarify desired outcomes, brainstorm strategies, identify the next steps, create reality in the moment, and ask questions that influence and stimulate change. These generative moments or peak experiences help investigate the client's feelings, needs, and desires around their chosen topic (Moore et al., 2016). They are labeled generative because they inspire clients to generate new ideas or uncover capacities, leading to bold actions that can positively alter their future (Bushe, 2007). A career coach who takes a strengths-based approach to appreciative inquiry naturally creates generative moments because AI focuses on the individual, and coaching is rooted in information gathering and influencing behavior positively (Schutt, 2018). A strengths-based approach capitalizes on powerful, positive questioning to help clients move forward despite their obstacles, realize their potential, and develop clear visions for their future (Cooperrider & Whitney, 2005). It can be an advantageous model for career coaches as it is flexible and applicable to various settings.

There are five core principles of appreciative inquiry: the Constructionist Principle, the Simultaneity Principle, the Poetic Principle, the Anticipatory Principle, and the Positive Principle (Cooperrider & Whitney, 2000; Cooperrider et al., 2005).

The first is the Constructionist Principle, which postulates that knowledge is at the center of change, and how an individual gains knowledge is critical to our understanding of how to change and sustain the change that we make over time. In career coaching, knowing can manifest through storytelling (words, metaphors, narratives) to help clients create a sense of realness in bringing their vision to life and setting their dreams to reality (Cooperrider & Whitney, 2000). When clients understand who they are, they can envision (career, job) prospects and responses (goal setting, action planning) increases.

The second is the Simultaneity Principle, where asking questions prompts change and transformation; thus, questions are a key career coaching intervention (Cooperrider & Whitney, 2000). As a coach inquires, transformation immediately begins to take place. Like qualitative research, questioning promotes data gathering and directs the discussion's course. The third is the Poetic Principle, which suggests that individuals change their lives if they alter their perspectives (Cooperrider et al., 2005). A client's story is constantly being re-authored and open to interpretation. Thus people not only create but interpret their stories.

The fourth is the Anticipatory Principle, which suggests people can create their anticipated future. Creating one's future occurs by focusing on images that inspire action (Watkins & Mohr, 2001). People move toward positive images and avoid negative images because of the idea that "what is expected is often realized" (Cooperrider et al., 2005, p. 9). Change becomes less intimidating when one anticipates options, possibilities become part of mainstream conversation, and the client can envision a way forward. Finally, the premise of the Positive Principle is that one chooses to choose the most favorable interpretation of their story and, by doing so, focuses on strengths, affirming their forward movement and solidifying their choice for change (Cooperrider & Whitney, 2000).

Appreciative Approach Processes

There are five processes to follow when applying an appreciative inquiry model to career coaching. They are:

1. Begin with the positive focus
2. Use stories as the method of inquiry
3. Locate themes that appear in the stories and select talking points based on these themes
4. Co-create shared images with the client for a preferred future
5. Brainstorm innovative ways to create the future (Watkins & Mohr, 2001, p. 40).

Beginning with a positive focus from a coaching perspective simply means coaching with positivity – helping the client focus on times when things went well (the premise of positive psychology coaching). So often, inquiries elicit negative responses, as clients recall challenges. Coaches use powerful questioning (see Appendix A) to shift from deficit-based to strength-based approaches.

Patterns and themes emerge as the coach inquires into the client's story. From these themes, the coach and the client imagine a preferred future for the client based on the talking point derived from the themes that emerged from the client's stories. Naturally, future possibilities become clearer. The AI approach is solution-focused rather than problem-based, evidenced through the 4-D cycle: Discovery, Dream, Design, and Destiny (see Figure 6).

The 4-D Cycle

Cooperrider and colleagues (2005) described how the five principles of appreciative inquiry can be applied to career coaching using the appreciative approach process. The 4-D cycle demonstrates the phased process through which the appreciative intervention progresses when applying AI to career coaching. The steps of this cycle are as follows:

Pre-Cycle. The coach starts by determining why the client is seeking coaching and then positively reframes the issue.

Discover Phase. The Discover phase explores the client's background for strengths related to the issue, focusing on reframing solutions (see Chapter 2). During the Discover phase, the coach and client establish the purpose of the client's meeting. The coaching language moves from problem-focused to solution-focused. For example, instead of the client saying, "I can not find any jobs!" the coach suggests trying to say, "I want to identify three new job lists/resources that I have not yet explored." This phase is about helping the client realize they can change their future if they desire to and that the key is in making good choices. The coach identifies the client's strengths to build upon them as coaching moves forward.

Dream Phase. During the Dream phase, the coach helps the client examine hopes and dreams related to the future, focusing more on the dream itself, not the steps to get there. The coach encourages the client to begin thinking about steps to achieve those dreams and explores the client's strengths. The coach helps the client visualize a future where their dreams become a reality. This technique establishes motivation in the coaching process.

Design Phase. The coach provides the client with tools to create an action plan to achieve goals during the Design phase. The coach needs to help the client feel less overwhelmed as they design their future. As they create a plan of action, the coach ensures it is broken down into enough steps so that the client is comfortable and not overwhelmed. Once the client realizes they can tackle small steps toward their goal, they will feel confident to take on more at one time and be more proactive. This stage will likely last the longest, involving job searches, writing résumés, gaining work experience, compiling portfolios, and other career-related functions.

Destiny Phase. During the Destiny phase, the coach helps the client determine if they have made good career decisions. The focus should be on positive accomplishments and successes (e.g., job offers, internship placement). The coach should use this period to help the client reflect on their choices and encourage them to continue their personal growth in a like manner.

Figure 6
4-D Cycle

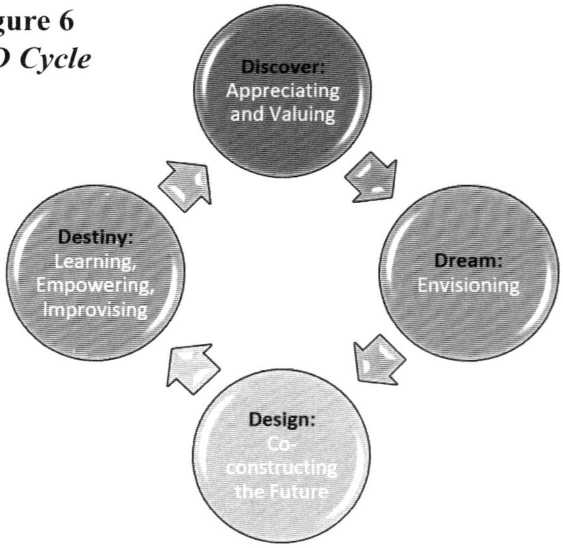

Adopted from "The Appreciative Inquiry Handbook: The First in a Series of AI Workbooks for Leaders of Change," by D. L. Cooperrider, D. Whitney, and J. M. Stravos, 2005, p. 30. Crown Custom Publishing, Inc. & Berrett-Koeler Publishers.

As a client enters a new step in the career development process, the cycle begins again. Clients may need to move through the cycle again until they achieve desired results, reevaluate these results, and repeat the cycle on a higher level. Re-cycling through the stages is part of the self-discovery process, and the AI model intentionally makes room for this exploration, so a client has maximum personal flexibility.

Bloom et al. (2008) adopted the appreciative advising model to advising, expanding the model to six phases: disarm, discover, dream, design, deliver, and do not settle (see Figure 7). In the Disarm phase or pre-cycle, the coach aims to create a welcoming environment that begins the rapport-building process. Once the coach establishes the groundwork for the helping relationship, the coach begins the Discovery phase by asking positive, open-ended questions that help them gather information about the client's goals. Next, the coach and client brainstorm and map possibilities, which is key in the Dream phase. Information from the Dream phase is necessary to co-create a plan to materialize the client's dreams into reality. Once the coach and client outline a plan of action in the Design phase, they can achieve their goal. The Deliver phase is the outcome generation of the hard work conceptualizing and planning a course of action. The coach continues to support the client as they execute their action plan, setting high expectations and check-points during the last phase of the AI advising model: Don't Settle. Appendix J contains a sample list of coach questions and prompts.

Figure 7
6D Cycle

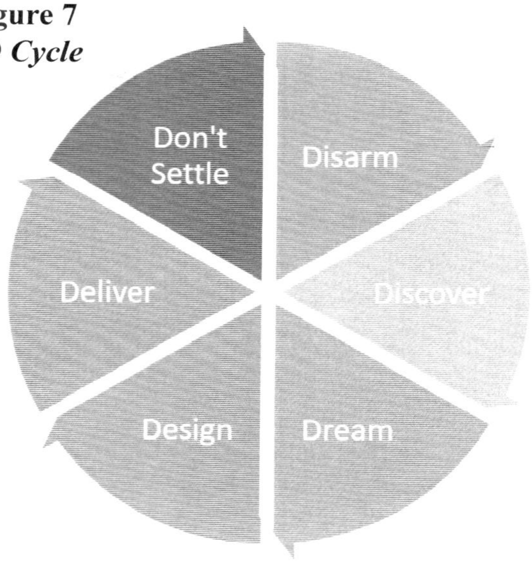

Behavioral Interviewing

Behavioral interviewing (BI) is a coaching technique that follows the premise that past performance predicts future performance in a similar setting (Society for Human Resource Management, 2016). BI uses open-ended, competency-based questions that assign a timeline to behavior, thoughts, analysis, values, and character - in story form. The coach asks questions about specific competencies or skills related to past situations, hoping to conclude how the client will perform in similar circumstances, unlike simply responding how they would perform hypothetically (Janz et al., 1986). A behavioral interview question might be, "Give me a specific example of a time when you resolved a conflict," whereas the standard interview question would be, "How would you handle a disagreement with a colleague?"

There are several reasons why it is helpful for clients to know how to demonstrate their competencies (knowledge, skills, and abilities) by giving specific examples from their past experiences. First, the coach can uncover the client's motivations, thinking patterns, likes, dislikes, preferences, temperament, style, and all else that traditional questions often overlook. This information is valuable to the goal-setting and decision-making process. Second, everyone likes a good story. Therefore, working with the client to craft and transmit valuable content efficiently and entertainingly is valuable interview preparation for the job search. Third, BI takes time because it asks the client to prepare in-depth, thorough, competency-based stories related to their desired goals. Finally, the preparation process is an exercise in self-reflection and self-understanding, and practicing behavioral interviewing can be eye-opening.

BI for the Job Search

Many organizations include behavioral interviewing in the hiring process, so practicing this technique in coaching prepares the client for the upcoming job search. The coach works with the client to prepare story-based responses to mock interview questions (see Appendix K). Responses should articulate the necessary competencies to perform the job using real examples with clear outcomes. The use of language is important in BI, as all questions will focus on what the client did, said, felt, or thought in the past. Therefore, the coach should prep the client to respond to questions with phrases such as "I accomplished…", "I said…", "I performed…." While working as part of a team is common and desirable, the interviewer wants to understand the individual's role in the probing example. Therefore, the client's responses should focus on individual contribution unless the question relates to team or group dynamics.

Every great story has a beginning, a middle, and an end. It also has a storyline that the listener can follow. It also has a moral, learning point, or outcome to describe the reason for telling the story. An effective way to execute the BI coaching technique is following the STAR method, which can be used for general coaching or to prepare a client for an upcoming interview in which the organization plans to use behavioral interviewing.

The STAR Method

STAR stands for a **s**pecific **s**ituation, **t**ask, **a**ction, **r**esult (Society for Human Resource Management, 2016). Dialog using the STAR method targets specific questions and answers to past situations. Responses should be past tense and preferably in the first person singular. Here is what the coach might encourage the client to prepare:

S = *specific situation.* Select one situation or project (that had a positive outcome) that illustrates your application of a particular skill. Describe the background and the issues involved.

T = *task or tasks.* What did you need to do? Describe the tasks involved in the situation. For example, did you rebuild a troubled department? Create a new program? Change the culture of an organization? Specify your objectives, using metrics where possible.

A = *action.* What specific action did you take or avoid to complete the tasks and achieve your results? Clarify your role and what you did as an individual, distinct from the team if it was a group effort.

R = *results.* What was the outcome? Be objective; use as many metrics as possible. If you consider the outcome a success, what defines it as such? You may also include what you learned from the project or task.

Many clients will encounter BI at some point in their job search. Helping the client prepare takes time, but the effort is worth it because they will understand their competencies related to the role if the coach helps them evaluate their education and experience against the position. Next, the coach helps map out 3-4 concrete examples using the STAR method based on sought-after workplace competencies (e.g., communication, problem-solving, leadership, initiative) and relevancy to the position. When crafting these stories, the client should be as specific as possible to showcase applicable skills, achievement, and effort. This strategy will prepare the client for an upcoming interview and increase their self-knowledge and ability to speak about how their competencies align with workplace needs.

Theory of Planned Happenstance

In 1996, career theorist John Krumboltz identified four workforce needs. First, for individuals to remain relevant in the workplace, continuous expansion of their knowledge, skills, and interests is necessary. Second, work stability is not guaranteed, nor should it be assumed. Therefore, individuals should plan for and be ready for change. Third, in order for individuals to be accepting of change, many need empowerment and reinforcement. Finally, when fully supported, clients will be most successful in all career difficulties, not just occupational/career choices (Krumboltz, 1996). Krumboltz went on to discuss working with clients as a chance to "facilitate the learning of skills, interests, beliefs, values, work habits, and personal qualities that enable each client to create a satisfying life within a constantly changing work environment" (Krumboltz, 1996, p. 61). This statement does not emphasize making a choice. Instead, the focus is on gathering information about how the self relates to the environment.

The theory of planned happenstance can be useful in career coaching because it maintains an exploratory attitude while encountering unexpected events, rapid shifts in the work environment, and workplace tensions (Krumboltz, 2009; Mitchell et al., 1999). Krumboltz (2009) posited, "human behavior is the product of countless numbers of learning experiences made available by both planned and unplanned situations in which individuals find themselves" (p. 135). Persistence, tenacity, and determination are essential in navigating career indecision and change. The attitudes to nurture are *curiosity, persistence, flexibility, optimism, and risk-taking* during these unexpected events (Krumboltz & Levin, 2004; Mitchell et al., 1999):

- Curiosity, or the ability to explore new learning opportunities or options resulting from an unplanned change
- Persistence, or the will to persevere despite setbacks
- Flexibility, or ability to pivot when unexpected events occur
- Optimism, or shifting the mindset to seek out new opportunities during a transition
- Risk-taking, or moving out of comfort zone despite uncertainty

Coaching clients using a planned happenstance approach replaces indecision with open-mindedness, using unplanned events to initiate the learning process and ignite curiosity. The four coaching steps are as follows (Mitchell et al., 1999):

Step 1: Use the client's history to normalize planned happenstance to build rapport with the client, as in a typical first coaching session (see Chapter 3), and make the client aware of how their actions can construct unexpected career opportunities. (i.e., "How have unplanned events influenced your career?")

Step 2: Materialize the client's curiosity into actual learning and exploration. Instead of meeting the client's request to match them to the perfect role or find them their ideal job, reframe the requests by helping the client identify opportunities to discover alternatives independently from the coach's guidance (e.g., "Describe an event that required you to change. How might you apply that experience to this situation?")

Step 3: Empower clients to create desirable change. Help raise the clients' awareness that unplanned events will inevitably occur but that they can initiate constructive action to generate more desirable chance events. (e.g., "What would happen if your life changed in X way?")

Step 4: Teach clients strategies to overcome anticipated and encountered barriers. Constructive action is necessary to overcome any challenges during the change process, and coaches must encourage and support their clients with strategies to overcome these barriers (e.g., "What steps can you take to overcome this barrier?")

The power of planned happenstance as a career theory is that unexpected events continue to happen in clients' lives. The coach and client should not misunderstand that happenstance is actually planned. The client (or coach) cannot (or should not) wait for change or wait to respond to change. Instead, the client becomes active in initiating that change, initiating connections that create change, or seeking out learning opportunities. Essentially, clients create unplanned events by acting (Feller et al., 2001). For this reason, promoting opportunities where the client can use their skills, interests, beliefs, values, work habits, and personal qualities to promote curiosity, persistence, flexibility, optimism, and risk-taking when unexpected events or change occurs is powerful.

Goal Setting Models

One of the fundamental principles of career coaching is to clearly understand where the client wants to get to before beginning the coaching journey. When clients seek the support of a coach, they are looking for a change. If clients could make a change on their own—they would have. Instead, they are looking for support, and one of the ways that coaches can make a difference is to help clients set effective goals. Below are various goal-setting models to assist this vital aspect of coaching.

S.M.A.R.T. Goals

S.M.A.R.T. goals are clear statements of outcomes with action steps. They indicate and give direction about what needs to be done and outline how much effort is required to obtain the goal. Clients who create S.M.A.R.T. goals find that their goals are:

- **Specific:** *What exactly do you want to accomplish?*
- **Measurable:** *How can you quantify this goal?*
- **Achievable:** *Is this goal within your capabilities to achieve? Do you need to depend on others to achieve?*
- **Relevant:** *What are you willing to let go of to get this goal completed?*
- **Time-bound:** *When will you start? What is your deadline? What are your measurables along the way?*

Writing goals sounds like a simple process – ask the client what they want and write it down. However, simply naming the goal and then materializing it can be difficult without specific measures, targets, and reasons why the goal is essential. Vague goals rarely become a reality.

Setting a goal that is specific means it needs to be as defined as possible. For example, a client might say they are interested in doing something different in their professional life. A coach may understand the client's direction, broadly speaking, but the specifics are arbitrary–they hold a different meaning for each individual. Therefore, more details are needed for the coach and client to set measures to achieve the goal. In this example, the client might specify their goal further by detailing that they would like to find a job using their culinary skills and artistic talents.

In addition to being specific, a goal must also be measurable. Asking the client a simple question like, "How will we know when you achieve your goal of using your culinary skills and artistic talents?" can help the client add a measure to their goal. In this example, the client might declare they are interested in being a Lead Chef or Sous Chef in a four or five-star restaurant.

A goal must also be achievable, which means it should be realistic to the individual setting the goal. For example, landing a job within two months could be an achievable timeline for a client moving within their current industry, but a client transitioning between industries or switching career paths may need additional time for their job search.

A goal must also be relevant to the client. For the coach and the client to establish relevancy, powerful questioning (see Appendix A) and a strong helping relationship (see Chapter 2) are key because the coach must gather information about the client's situation, including their values and interests to understand whether their goals are relevant to other aspects of the client's life. Continuing with the example above, the client set a goal to secure a job within two months, yet the client is conducting a job search during a pandemic. In addition, the economy is uncertain, and the industry where they seek employment is in massive flux. At this time, conducting a search within a two-month timeframe or transitioning into the restaurant industry may not be relevant to the economic climate.

Strength-based S.M.A.R.T. goals. Goals should inspire and motivate but can cause stress and anxiety when the client heavily invests in goal attainment and becomes aware that the possibility of failure exists. Using positive psychology and powerful questioning (see Appendix A), the coach can assist the client in mitigating these fears by focusing on progress made. For example, the coach can discuss the following with the client:

1. Let's explore what progress you have made so far.
2. When have you been successful in the past? Did you overcome setbacks in an attempt to reach that success?
3. What resources are needed to help achieve your goal? What have you tried so far?
4. What energy reserves do you have left related to meeting this goal?

S.O.A.R. Model

A well-known and widely used goal-setting model is the S.W.O.T. analysis: strengths, weaknesses, opportunities, threats. Conceptualized by Humphrey in the 1960s and 1970s to identify why corporations failed (Morrison, 2016), the S.W.O.T. and variations of the model are now used for developing and understanding individual decision-making. One such variation is S.O.A.R.: strengths, opportunities, aspirations, results (Stavros et al., 2003), which takes a more positive approach to goal setting and encouraging action. Many people find it easier to focus their attention and efforts on their strengths rather than improving their weaknesses. A coach may find S.O.A.R. beneficial when working with a client who is resistant to change or has difficulty developing an action plan. S.O.A.R. focuses on the positive while identifying adjustment needs. S.O.A.R. is a positive approach to strategic thinking and planning that allows clients to construct and achieve an action-oriented goal (Stavros & Hinrich, 2009). Using S.O.A.R. helps the client create value in their goal-setting process and aligns purpose as they relate to their career development in a meaningful way. S.O.A.R. questioning might sound something like this:

- What are your greatest strengths?
- What are your nearest opportunities for growth?
- What does the future you are working towards look like to you?
- What action can we take to achieve your goal?

Like S.W.O.T., S.O.A.R. planning should begin with the client defining the desired goal. Next, the coach works with the client to ensure the goal is a S.M.A.R.T. goal (see the previous section on S.M.A.R.T. goals). Next, the coach and client complete a S.O.A.R. analysis around the strengths of the goal ("where are we now?"), opportunities to help achieve the goal ("what resources do we have?"), aspirations for wanting to achieve the goal ("why do we want this?"), and results once the client reaches their goal ("where will we be once completed?"). Whether using S.W.O.T., S.O.A.R., or S.C.O.O. (strengths, challenges, opportunities, obstacles) model, the coach and client will benefit from structure and clarity in their goal-setting endeavors.

Decision-Making Models

As we learned in Chapter 2, career indecision is challenging for many clients. Resistance to change and the inability to make large or small decisions related to career growth can be crippling. After all, this is why a client seeks the support of a career coach: to help them make informed decisions related to their career. Several valuable tools can help clients make important decisions, especially when faced with several well-thought-out, viable options. One option is the decision-making matrix.

Decision-Making Matrix

A decision-making matrix is a valuable technique for a client making an important decision with several possible alternatives (e.g., job, volunteer, school, course of study) and several factors to consider. A decision-making matrix table can be hand-drawn, a simple Excel table, or Google sheets. Here are the steps the client would follow to create their matrix.

Step 1: *Create your spreadsheet.* List choices as rows and factors as columns. Add one additional row and column to be used after Step

2. For example, if you are trying to choose between three jobs options (loan officer, financial analyst, and business teacher), these options would be placed in rows. Next, place the factors impacting your choice (location, salary, and retirement contribution) in the columns on the spreadsheet (see Table 5).

Table 5
Decision Making Matrix Step 1

	Location	Salary	Retirement Contribution	
Loan Officer				
Financial Analyst				
Business Teacher				

Step 2: *Score each option.* Working your way down the columns, score each choice based on how well the factor is met in that option. Assign the scores from 0 (unsatisfactory) to 5 (excellent). Scores can be the same for different options (see Table 6).

Table 6
Decision Making Matrix Step 2

	Location	Salary	Retirement Contribution	
Loan Officer	2	1	3	
Financial Analyst	1	5	5	
Business Teacher	5	3	1	

Step 3: *Assign an importance score to each of your factors.* An importance score (from 1 to the total number of factors) will help you determine which of the factors is most important, with higher scores being more important to you. In this example, when choosing between three different jobs, which factor is more important in terms of your decision to accept a job offer? Is it location, salary, or retirement contribution? If it is the location, the importance score would be 3, if salary were the second most important factor in your choice, the importance score would be 2, and in this example, retirement contribution would receive an importance score of 1 (see Table 7). This is not to say that retirement contribution is unimportant, only that it is the least important of the three factors you are using to choose between the three job prospects currently available.

Table 7
Decision Making Matrix Step 3

	Location	Salary	Retirement Contribution	Total
Importance	3	2	1	
Loan Officer	2	1	3	
Financial Analyst	1	5	5	
Business Teacher	5	3	1	

Step 4: *Calculate your scores.* Simple math will give a weighted score for each option/factor combination. In step 4, multiply each of your scores from step 2 by the values assigned for importance and write the result in parentheses. For example, in Table 8, the client assigned an overall importance score of 3 to location and a score of 2 for loan officer position location; because 3x2=6, the 6 is written in parentheses; continuing in the next row, a score of 1 for financial analyst position location multiplied by the 3 for importance (3 x 1=3) equals (3); and a score of 5 for business teacher position location (3x5=15) for an overall importance score of 15.

Table 8
Decision Making Matrix Step 4

	Location	Salary	Retirement Contribution	Total
Importance	3	2	1	
Loan Officer	2 (6)	1 (2)	3 (3)	
Financial Analyst	1 (3)	5 (10)	5 (5)	
Business Teacher	5 (15)	3 (6)	3 (1)	

Step 5: *Add your weighted scores.* Finally, add the calculated scores in parentheses for each column for a total score for each row. Your highest score indicates the best decision, which, in this example, is the Business Teacher job option, considering the factors of location, salary, and retirement contribution (see Table 9).

Table 9
Decision Making Matrix Step 5

	Location	Salary	Retirement Contribution	Total
Importance	3	2	1	
Loan Officer	2 (6)	3 (2)	3 (3)	11
Financial Analyst	1 (3)	5 (10)	5 (5)	18
Business Teacher	5 (15)	1 (6)	3 (1)	22

Once the client completes the decision-making matrix, the coach can review the final scores together with the client and discuss the results. The coach should ensure the results sit well with the client's intuition. If the client feels the scores reveal a sound choice, proceed. If the results raise questions, reflect on the scores together and the weights that the client applied. For example, revisit the reasoning behind assigning greater weight to one category over the other. Further questioning may signify that certain factors are more important to the client than initially thought.

Mind Mapping

Mind mapping is a powerful technique to organize information visually. In general, mind maps begin with a central idea that leads to the branching out of sub-ideas (think of a tree with a trunk and branches). Individuals and groups trouble-shoot, visual think, decision-make, and problem-solve using mindmaps in virtually every industry globally. For example, mind mapping enables a client to view multiple perspectives and possibilities in a compact, visual format in career coaching. Coaches use mind mapping to help

Figure 8
Next Job Mind Map

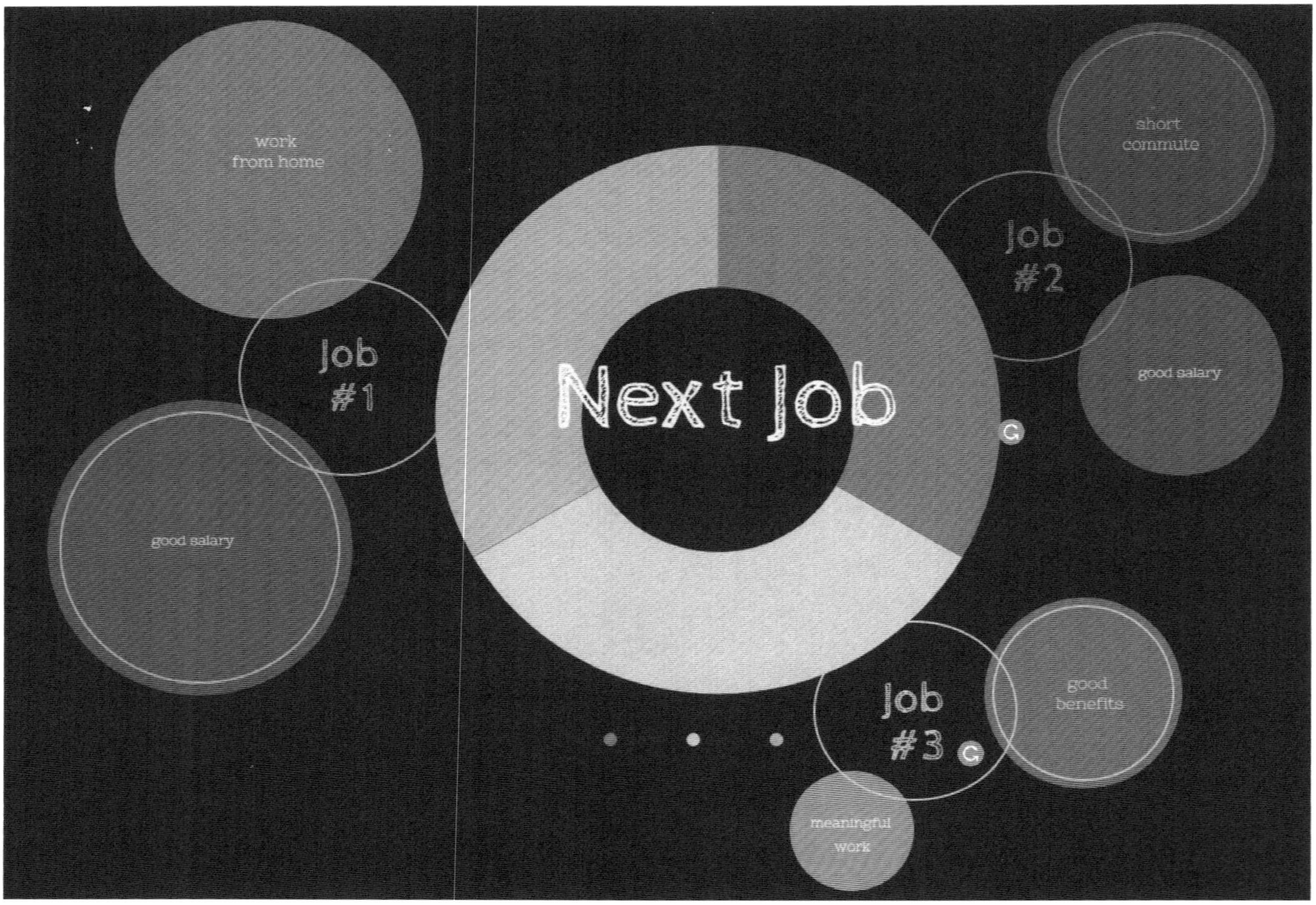

clients set and accomplish goals and brainstorm topics like interests, occupations, values, and more.

Usually, a single idea serves as the topic for a mind map. First, the creator draws an image in the center of a blank piece of paper (or mind mapping software). The creator then adds key ideas linked directly to the central subject (center image), and other ideas branch out from these (see Figure 8). Color and images create contrast, emphasize ideas, and encourage brainstorming. For example, if a client is drawing a mind map to decide between relocating to two different states that offer similar employment opportunities, the benefits of relocating to each state might be listed in one color, and the drawback of relocating to each state listed in another.

Typically, a client is grappling with their next career move, and various factors are at play, such as salary, location, work/life balance, job duties, promotional opportunities, benefits, and more. The client has three choices to consider: job 1, job 2, and job 3. Each choice offers a variety of pros and cons. A mind-mapping exercise can help the client identify the position that emerges as the most likely next professional step.

Here are 5 easy steps to mind mapping that can work in most career coaching scenarios:

Step 1: Provide the client with a blank sheet of paper and colored markers or pencils, or if you have access to mind mapping software (free or paid), offer this as an option. Let the client choose their preference: some clients prefer mind mapping software, while others prefer paper methods. Ask the client to begin in the center of the paper depicting their central idea in a word, short phrase, picture, or image. An example of a central idea might be *college to attend.*

Step 2: Next, ask the client to draw primary branches connected to the central image. There may be 3-5 primary branches stemming from the central idea. For example, from the central idea *college to attend,* your client might list 3-5 colleges they have received acceptances letters from, and the mind map exercise weighs the benefits and drawbacks of each college now that your client knows each choice is an attainable one.

Step 3: Ask your client to continue the brainstorming exercise by connecting second and third-level branches to the first and second levels. Encourage a combination of straight and curved lines, colors, images, and words.

Step 4: Brainstorm all the areas the client needs to consider for each of them – creating this wide array of ideas helps the client understand where they would like to go and how they will get there. In the *college to attend* example, what characteristics of each college make that college desirable? Undesirable? Depict the desirable characteristics as straight lines with circles for each desirable characteristic. The client may depict undesirable characteristics as curved lines with squares for each undesirable characteristic. The possibilities of depicting all the characteristics are limited only to the client's imagination.

Step 5: Once the client completes the mind map, use it to discuss the options available and then create a strategy to help them execute their career dreams.

A Mind Map is a creative outlet and should be approached with an open mind, without limitations, as the number of thoughts, ideas, and connections one makes is limitless.

Ideas for mind mapping topics could include job search, strengths, weaknesses or areas for improvement, values, interests, goals, education, barriers, occupations, volunteer options, companies of interest, and more!

Job Crafting

A job is a group of tasks and interpersonal relationships assigned to one person, typically by an organization (Ilgen & Hollenbeck, 1991). As technology advances and workers cope with new and different adversities, many employees seek meaningful work that provides a positive sense of self and increased human interaction (Barker Caza, 2007; Wrzesniewski & Dutton, 2001). Job Crafting is a career coaching technique that helps clients find satisfaction and meaning in their work, especially those unhappy and unable to make an immediate switch in their current roles. As Berg et al. (2008) posit, job crafting "captures what employees do to redesign their job in ways that can foster job satisfaction, as well as engagement, resilience and thriving at work" (p. 1). Job crafting is an employee's ability to change job characteristics in ways that can foster personal and professional fulfillment (Tims & Bakker, 2010). Whether a client is new to the search or currently working, job crafting can be a robust process for reenergizing and reimagining work life.

Many clients are in a situation where changing jobs or even roles within their organization is impossible. Career coaches can work with clients to help them think in more flexible terms regarding work situations or scenarios for change. Job crafting is possible if the employer is supportive, and the client has a flexible mindset and focuses on opportunities or boundary-spanning possibilities of their work (Wrzesniewski & Dutton, 2001). Job crafting begins with the coach and the client brainstorming gratifying elements of the client's current role. The coach and client then build on the good parts of the client's present work situation to create a more appropriate work plan. This process involves redefining the client's job or job search to incorporate their motives, strengths, and passions, prompting them to visualize the job, map its elements, and reorganize them to suit their needs and desires (Tims & Bakker, 2010). For instance, how might various aspects of their work tasks be altered to provide more day-to-day job satisfaction? How might they see their work environment from a different lens? Job crafting allows the client to add personal touches on how they see and do their job and, in the process, gain a greater sense of control at work.

Storytelling

As old as time, storytelling is a powerful right-brained activity that stimulates the neuropathways, enhancing the client's capacity to imagine movement towards the desired goal. Career construction theory (CCT) is a way to use storytelling to understand vocational behavior across the life cycle and provides career coaches with a model to help clients make vocational choices (Savickas, 2005). CCT looks at occupational choice and work adjustment, providing a way of thinking about how individuals choose and use work. The overall premise of CCT is to draw out the theme of work that connects to the client's overall life because it is the theme that matters in the client's life.

Being flexible and open to change is now seen as a necessary component of life-span, life-space theory (Savickas, 1997), and now more than ever, flexibility is needed when adjusting to new and changing work roles and work situations. To be life designers, individuals need to be autonomously and intrinsically motivated. Career coaches can help clients draw out life themes through stories (Savickas, 2012). Del Corso and Briddick (2015) described the coach's role as an audience for helping clients explore their career stories, reflect, and compose dominant narratives. Powerful questioning (see Appendix A) can help direct the client towards these self-defining stories as an active attempt at future decision-making. CCT's life themes address the client's work-life to date and focus on the why of vocational behavior: why has the client chosen the various occupations thus far (Savickas, 2005; Savickas et al., 2009)? The coach and client review the story to foster understanding and identify significant interests, values, strengths. Career objectives can spring from these stories, which helps the coach and client set appropriate action steps.

The Wheel of Life

A Wheel of Life is a powerful coaching tool useful in various situations, such as helping clients struggling to identify goals and ease clients into thinking about their personal lives, which benefit their careers. The Wheel of Life comprises eight domains, representing eight areas of an individual's life: career, money, health, friends/family, partnership, personal growth, fun/recreation, and physical environment.

How to Use. The wheel's center represents a rating of 0, moving outward to the edge of the wheel to a rating of 10. Thus, rating levels represent satisfaction within each of the eight areas. Present a client with a blank wheel (see Figure 9) to get started.

Using a dot or star, ask the client to mark their rating of the 8 domains in terms of satisfaction, with 0 being the least satisfied and 10 being the most satisfied. Next, connect each dot, creating a new outer edge of the wheel (see Figure 10). Low scores point to areas where a goal could raise their satisfaction in one or more areas of their lives.

The wheel also helps clients set priorities across the 8 domains. Take the basic rating exercise a step further by asking the client to identify their top three priorities of the lowest rated. For example, in Figure 10, the client rated romance, money, and career as the three areas of lowest life satisfaction. In this example, the coach could facilitate a brainstorming exercise with the client, having the client set a goal in each of those areas. Another exercise that works to identify priorities is to have the client set three priority areas on a blank wheel, then score their satisfaction on a scale of 0-10. What do they notice? How does the score for each of their top three priorities compare to the lower priorities? What actions could they take to set goals around these top three priorities?

Another more independent way to administer the Wheel of Life is to present the client with the wheel where the domain areas are blank. The coach then works with the client to create their Wheel of Life domain areas by identifying the primary areas of focus in their life. Once the client

Figure 9
Blank Wheel of Life

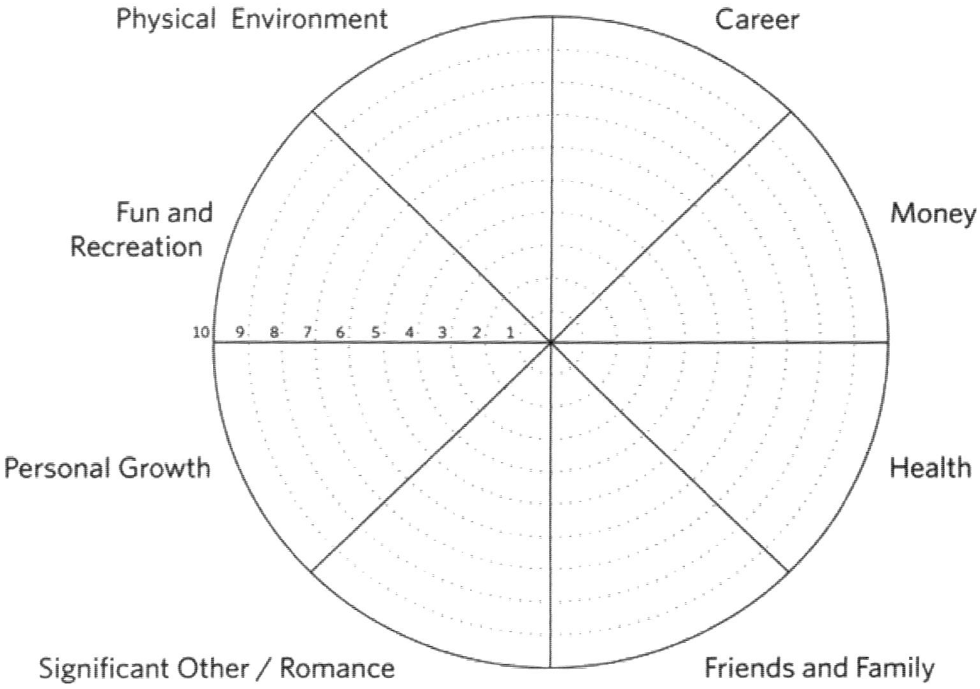

Figure 10
Completed Wheel of Life

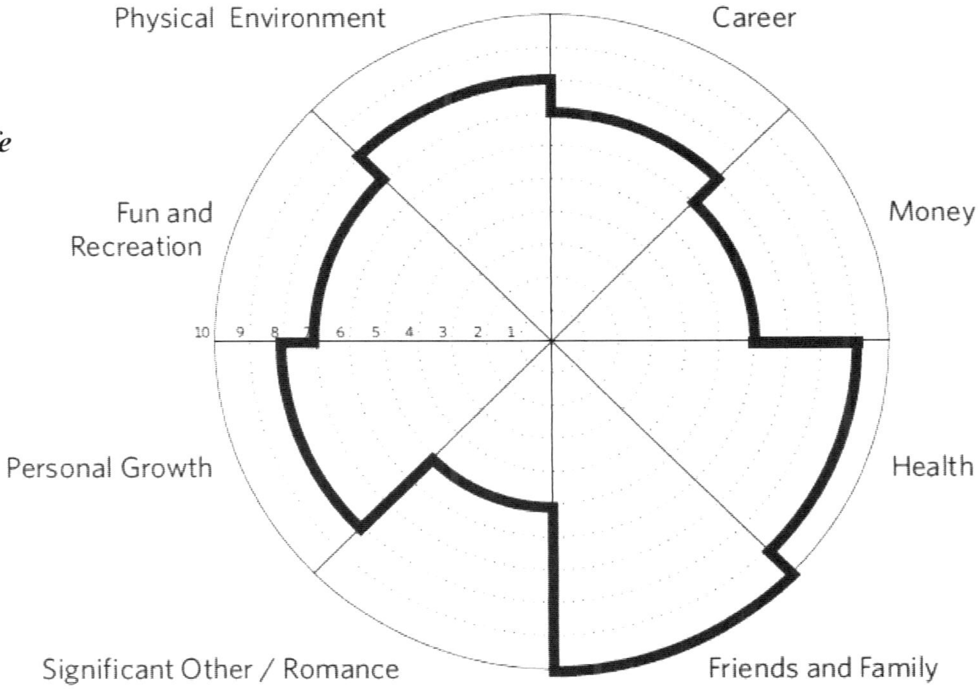

Adopted from "Physician Burnout: Coaching a Way Out," by G. Gazelle, J. Liebschutz, & H. Reiss, 2014, *Journal of General Internal Medicine (30)*4, p. 2.

establishes their areas, they then rank how they believe they are doing in each area from 0 to 10, where 10 is extremely satisfied, and 0 is highly dissatisfied (the coach and client can choose the measurement parameters, such as knowledgeable). Next, determine two or three actions the client can take to improve the least satisfying areas.

In short, the Wheel of Life activity has limitless possibilities in terms of career exploration. It can prompt a client to examine blind spots in areas of their life that directly or indirectly impact career growth. It is an excellent tool to initiate discussion around many aspects of the career development process, brainstorm growth and satisfaction areas, and set goals based on priorities.

Three Good Things Interventions

Three Good Things (TGT) or what-went-well journaling is an exercise helpful for career exploration. It is effective when clients have difficulty with change, motivation, or forward movement in the career development process (Seligman et al., 2005). The exercise takes approximately ten minutes to complete using a pen and a piece of paper (or computer/phone). To begin, the coach asks the client to write down three things that went well this week and explain why they went well. The coach must have the client write down the three items and their explanation, as the act of having a physical record is powerful; it is not enough for the client to do this exercise in their head. The things listed can be relatively small in importance (e.g., "my commute was better than normal") or relatively large in importance (e.g., "I had an article published in a professional journal").

As the client writes, the coach instructs them on the following:

1. Give your event a title (e.g., "received a promotion at work")
2. In the space below, write down precisely what happened in as much detail as possible, including what you did or said, and if other people were involved, what they did or said.
3. Include how this event made you feel (reflection) when it occurred and how it made you feel later (including now, as you remember it).
4. Use whatever writing style you please and in as much detail as desired.

The TGT exercise comes from positive psychology and is scientifically proven to increase happiness levels in positive affect and subjective well-being (Seligman et al., 2005). If the client is going through a difficult career transition or job loss, instruct the client to write down TGT as an end-of-the-day journaling exercise to help shed negative bias, foster hope, and increase job-search motivation. The exercise prompts the client to view things more positively and helps cultivate gratitude, increase optimism, and boost happiness.

Checklists

Using checklists is one way to increase accountability and connections from coaching sessions to sessions. It is also a way to keep the coach and client on track with progress. Simple checklists can be practical coaching resources, such as this sample Job Search Checklist.

- ❑ Work with a coach to gain clarity on job search direction
- ❑ Set goals for job search
- ❑ Create an elevator pitch or 30-second commercial introducing myself
- ❑ Revise or craft a résumé
- ❑ Revise or craft a base cover letter tailored to each job application
- ❑ Update/create appropriate social media (LinkedIn, ePortfolio) helpful for the job search
- ❑ Set a target list of companies/organizations of interest
- ❑ Scan my network to see if there are contacts at the above companies/organizations and reach out
- ❑ Find opportunities to network, in person or virtually

- ❑ Practice interviewing and do company research before an interview
- ❑ As interview invitations arrive, refine the search as needed
- ❑ Send a thank-you note post-interview and follow-up 1-2 weeks post-interview
- ❑ Maintain my network and continue to refine as needed
- ❑ Thank all who helped in the job search process

Checklists can be edited based on the client's needs and career-related goals. Each time the coach and the client meet, it is essential to go over checklist progress, discuss wins and challenge areas and refine the checklist as needed.

The Need for Theory and Connecting Theory to Practice

This chapter highlighted several theoretical options for use in career coaching, although it is not an exhaustive representation, and coaches should continuously advance their knowledge of career theory. Many authors have argued that a knowledge of theory is essential to help understand experiences. For example, Gothard (2001) reasoned, "theory has helped mold the way careers advisors have worked" (p. 35). Moreover, as the profession advances, new theories emerge, and current theories are revised to meet clients' complex needs and changing workplace demands.

Career coaches rarely use one theory, and it is improbable that one theory will meet all coaching needs for all clients. Additionally, many theories contain bias for racial-ethnic groups, gender, and the impact of workplace assimilation on diverse individuals and communities (see Chapter 6). Increasing exposure to theories allows for combination usage. Most coaches use theories in combination because they offer a more comprehensive strategy in meeting a client's holistic needs. Rather than assume that one theory applies to all clients, career coaches should familiarize themselves with multiple theories and become well-versed in several that are most applicable to their client population. It is essential to do homework when seeking the use of any theory: understand the client's needs, have a broad awareness of available theories and their application, choose the theory or theories best suited for the coaching situation, conduct further research, and, as always, proceed with care and caution. Sharf (2013) includes an excellent chapter in his text *Applying Career Development Theory to Counseling*, which discusses and offers relevant examples of using theories in combination.

One way to bridge theory to practice is through using career coaching models and assessments as a tool in the exploration process. Models and assessments operationalize theoretical constructs. For example, a coach can use interest inventories to efficiently expose job titles and offer clients a link to the world of work. Over the last century, models and assessments have been intricate in coaches' career support process to support their client's exploration and goal-setting needs. The effectiveness of coaching is that it is not inherently bound by one particular theory or model; rather, the idea is to be eclectic and borrow from various theories and models to engage the client in their coaching journey. Chapter 5 will discuss career assessments applied in a coaching context to complement the models just presented but first, it is important to take a deep dive into ethics in career coaching.

Knowledge Check

1. What are the two most prominent theories that guide your approach to career coaching?
2. How have you applied (or how do you intend to apply) some of the coaching models to your practice?
3. How will you know to combine models when needed?

K-W-L Model – What Have I Learned?

To conclude this chapter, revisit the K-W-L model to assess whether this chapter provided you with information to fill some of your knowledge gaps. Reflect on what you have ***learned*** from this chapter and how you will apply it to your coaching practice.

References

Adams, L. (2011). *Learning a new skill is easier said than done.* Gordon Training International. https://www.gordontraining.com/free-workplace-articles/learning-a-new-skill-is-easier-said-than-done/

Amir, T., & Gati, I. (2006, November). Facets of career decision-making difficulties. *British Journal of Guidance and Counselling, 34*(4). 483-503. http://doi.org/10.1080/03069880600942608

Baldwin, M., & Johnson, W. (1992). A test of the measures of non-discriminatory wages used to study wage discrimination. *Economic Letters, 39*(2), 223-227. https://doi.org/10.1016/0165-1765(92)90294-9

Barker Caza, B. (2007). *Experiences of adversity at work: Toward an identity-based theory of resilience* [Unpublished doctoral dissertation]. University of Michigan.

Berg, J. M., Dutton, J. E., & Wrzesniewski, A. (2008). *What is job crafting and why does it matter* [Theory-to-practice briefing]. Positive Organizational Scholarship University of Michigan. https://positiveorgs.bus.umich.edu/wp-content/uploads/What-is-Job-Crafting-and-Why-Does-it-Matter1.pdf

Biswas-Diener, R. (2010). *Practicing positive psychology coaching: Assessment, activities, and strategies for success.* Wiley.

Bloom, J. L., Hutson, B. L., & He, Y. (2008). *The appreciative advising revolution.* Stipes Publishing.

Bolles, R. (1978). *Three boxes of life.* Ten Speed Press.

Broadwell, M. M. (1969). Teaching for learning. *The Gospel Guardian.* http://www.wordsfitlyspoken.org/gospel_guardian/v20/v20n41p1-3a.html

Bushe, G. R. (2007). Appreciative inquiry is not (just) about the positive. *OD Practitioner, 39*(4). 30-35.

Cameron, K. S., Dutton, J. E., & Quinn, R. E. (2003). *Positive organizational scholarship: Foundations of a new discipline.* Berrett-Koeler.

Cooperrider, D. L., & Whitney, D. (2000). A positive revolution in change: Appreciative inquiry. In D. L. Cooperrider, P. F. Sorenson, Jr., D. Whitney, & T. F. Yaeger (Eds.). *Appreciative Inquiry: Rethinking Human Organization Toward a Positive Theory of Change.* Stipes Publishing.

Cooperrider, D., & Whitney, D. (2005). *Appreciative inquiry: A positive revolution in change.* Berrett-Koehler.

Cooperrider, D. L., Whitney, D., & Stavros, J. M. (2005). *Appreciative inquiry handbook: The first in a series of AI workbooks for leaders of change.* Crown Custom Publishing, Inc. & Berrett-Koeler Publishers, Inc.

Curtiss, P. R., & Warren, P. W. (1974). *The dynamics of life skills coaching. Life skills series.* Prince Albert, Saskatchewan: Training Research and Development Station, Dept. of Manpower and Immigration.

Del Corso, J. J., & Briddick, H. S. (2015). Using audience to foster self-narrative construction and career adaptability. In P. J. Hartung, M. L. Savickas, & W. B. Walsh (Eds.), *APA handbook of career intervention: Vol. 2. Applications* (pp. 255–268). American Psychological Association.

Eagan, M. K., Stolzenberg, E. B., Zimmerman, H. B., Aragon, M. C., Whang Sayson, H., & Rios-Aguilar, C. (2017). *The American freshman: National norms fall 2016.* Higher Education Research Institute, UCLA.

Fassinger, R. E. (2008). Workplace diversity and public policy: Challenges and opportunities for psychology. *American Psychologist, 63*(4), 252-268. https://doi.org/10.1037/0003-066X.63.4.252

Feller, R. (2017, May). *What is a HEROIC career mindset and how to have one*? MCDA Wellspring.

Feller, R., & Franklin, M. (2020). The HEROIC narrative assessment system: Helping undergrads navigate transitions. In P. Gardner & H. N. Maietta (Eds.), *Advancing Talent Development: Steps Towards a T-Model Infused Undergraduate Education.* (pp.125-140). Business Expert Press.

Feller, R., Honaker, S. L., & Zagzebski, L. M. (2001, March). Theoretical voices directing the career development journey: Holland, Harris-Bowlsbey, and Krumboltz. *The Career Development Quarterly, 49*(3), 212-224. http://doi.org/10.1002/j.2161-0045.2001.tb00563.x

Franklin, M. & Feller. R. (2014). *Who You Are Matters!* Onelifetools.

Franklin, M. & Feller, R. (2017). Using the one life tools framework: From clarification to Intentional exploration with an East Asian female. In L. Busacca & M. Rehfuss (Eds.), *Postmodern career counseling: A handbook of culture, context and cases* (pp. 273-284). American Counseling Association.

Franklin, M., Yanar, B., Feller, R. (2015). Narrative method of practice increases curiosity exploration, psychological capital, and personal growth leading to career clarity: A retrospective outcome-study. *Canadian Journal of Career Development, 14*(2), 14-23.

Fredrickson, B. L. (2003). The value of positive emotions: The emerging science of positive psychology is coming to understand why it's good to feel good. *American Scientist, 91*, 330.

Gable, S. L., & Haidt, J. (2005). What (and why) is positive psychology? *Review of General Psychology, 9*(2), 103-110. https://doi.org/10.1037%2F1089-2680.9.2.103

Gati, I. (1993). Career compromises. *Journal of Counseling Psychology, 40*(4), 416-424. https://psycnet.apa.org/doi/10.1037/0022-0167.40.4.416

Gati, I., Krausz, M., & Osipow, S. H. (1996). A taxonomy of difficulties in career decision making. *Journal of Counseling Psychology, 43*(4), 510-526. https://doi.org/10.1037/0022-0167.43.4.510

Goodman, J., Schlossberg, N. K., & Anderson, M. L. (2006). *Counseling adults in transition* (3rd ed.). Springer.

Gothard, B. (2001). Working with individuals. In B. Gothard, P. Mignot, M. Offer, & M. Ruff (Eds.), *Careers guidance in context* (pp. 10-37). Sage.

Gottfredson, L. S., & Richards, J. M. Jr. (1999). The meaning and measurement of environments in Holland's theory. *Journal of Vocational Behavior, 55*, 57-73. https://doi.org/10.1006/jvbe.1999.1697

Holland, J. L. (1985). *Manual for vocational preference inventory.* Psychological Assessment Resources.

Holland, J. L. (1997). *Making vocational choices: A theory of careers.* Prentice-Hall.

Holland, J. L., Powell, A. B., & Fritzsche, B. A. (1994) *Self directed search: Professional users guide.* Psychological Assessment Resources.

Ilgen, D. R., & Hollenbeck, J. R. (1991). The structure of work: Job design and roles. In M. Dunnette and L. Hough (Eds.), *Handbook of Industrial/Organizational Psychology* (pp. 165-207). Consulting Psychologists Press.

Janz, T., Hellervik L., & Gilmore D. (1986). *Behavior description interviewing*. Allyn & Bacon.

Koppi, S. (2018, May). Career coaching: A new paradigm for student-centered career services. *NACE Journal.* National Association of Colleges and Employers. https://ebiztest.naceweb.org/career-development/organizational-structure/career-coaching-a-new-paradigm-for-student-centered-career-services/

Krumboltz, J. D. (1996). The learning theory of career counseling. In M. L. Savickas & W. B. Walsh (Eds.), *Handbook of career counseling theory and practice* (pp. 50-80). Counseling Psychologists Press.

Krumboltz, J. D. (2009). The happenstance learning theory. *Journal of Career Assessment, 17*(2). 135-154. http://doi.org/10.1177/1069072708328861

Krumboltz, J. D., & Levin, A. S. (2004). *Luck is no accident.* Impact.

Lazarus, R. S. (1966). *Psychological stress and the coping process.* McGraw-Hill.

Lazarus, R. S., & Folkman, S. (1984). *Stress, appraisal, and coping.* Springer.

Lefkowitz, R., & Pate, D. (2018). *2018 Workplace learning report: The rise and responsibility of talent development in the new labor market* [LinkedinLearningContent; PDF]. https://learning.linkedin.com/resources/workplace-learning-report-2018

Lyubomirsky, S. L., King, L., & Diener, E. (2005). The benefits of frequent positive affect: Does happiness lead to success? *Psychological Bulletin, 131*(36), 803–855. https://doi.org/10.1037/0033-2909.131.6.803

Mackey, A. (2005). *The practice of advertising* (5th ed.). Elsevier Butterworth.

Maietta, H. N. (2022). The impact of forced transfer on students' college transition. In H. N. Maietta & P. Gardner (Eds.), *Ensuring success for students who transfer: The importance of career and professional development.* [Manuscript in Preparation], University of South Carolina, National Resource Center for The First-Year Experience and Students in Transition.

Mitchell, K. E., Levin, A. S., & Krumboltz, J. D. (1999, Spring). Planned happenstance: Constructing unexpected career opportunities. *Journal of Counseling and Development, 77*(2), 115-124. https://doi.org/10.1002/j.1556-6676.1999.tb02431.x

Moore, M., Jackson, E., & Tschannen-Moran, B. (2016). *Coaching psychology manual* (2nd ed.). Wellcoaches Corporation.

Morrison, M. (2016). *SWOT analysis (TOWS matrix) Made Simple.* RapidBI. https://rapidbi.com/swotanalysis/

Osipow, S. H. (1999). Assessing career indecision. *Journal of Vocational Behavior, 55*, 147-154. https://doi.org/10.1006/jvbe.1999.1704

Osipow, S. H., Carney, C. G. & Barak, A. (1976). A scale of educational-vocational undecidedness: A typological approach. *Journal of Vocational Behavior, 9*, 233-243. https://doi.org/10.1016/0001-8791(76)90081-6

Phelps, R. E., & Constantine, M. G. (2001). Hitting the roof: The impact of the glass ceiling effect on the career development of African Americans. In W. B. Walsh, R. P. Bingham, M. T. Brown, & C. M. Ward (Eds.). *Career counseling for African Americans* (pp. 161-176). Erlbaum.

Prochaska, J. O., Norcross, J. C., & DiClemente, C. C. (1994). *Changing for good: The revolutionary program that explains the six stages of change and teaches you how to free yourself from bad habits.* W. Morrow.

Rayman, J. R., & Gottfredson, G. D. (2020). *My life with a theory: John L. Holland's autobiography and theory of careers.* National Career Development Association.

Reilly, S. (2012). The 4 stages of competence. *National Underwriter Life & Health Breaking News*.https://www.thefreelibrary.com/The+4+stages+of+competence.-a0304411536

Savickas, M. L. (1997). Career adaptability: An integrative construct for life-span, life-space theory. *The Career Development Quarterly, 45,* 247–259. https://doi.org/10.1002/j.2161-0045.1997.tb00469.x

Savickas, M. L. (2005). The theory and practice of career construction. In S. D. Brown and R. W. Lent (Eds.), *Career development and counseling: Putting theory and research to work* (pp. 42-70). John Wiley & Sons.

Savickas, M. L. (2012, January). Life design: A paradigm for career intervention in the 21st century. *Journal of Counseling and Development, 90,* 13-18. https://doi.org/10.1111/j.1556-6676.2012.00002.x

Savickas, M. (2015). Life designing with adults: Developmental individualization using biographical bricolage. In L. Nota & J. Rossier (Eds.), *Handbook of life design: From practice to theory and from theory to practice* (pp. 135–149). Hogrefe Publishing.

Savickas, M. L., Nota, L., Rossier, J., Dauwalder, J-P., Duarte, M. E., Guichard, J., Soresi, S., Van Esbroeck, R., & Van Vianen, A. (2009). Life designing: A paradigm for career construction in the 21st century. *Journal of Vocational Behavior, 75*(3), 239–250. https://doi.org/10.1016/J.JVB.2009.04.004

Savickas, M. L., & Porfeli, E. J. (2012). Career Adapt-Abilities Scale: Construction, reliability and measurement equivalence across 13 countries. *Journal of Vocational Behaviour, 80,* 661-673. https://doi.org/10.1016/j.jvb.2012.01.011

Schlossberg, N. K. (1984). *Counseling adults in transition: Linking theory to practice*. Springer.

Schlossberg, N. K., Waters, E. B., & Goodman, J. (1995). *Counseling adults in transition: Linking practice with theory* (2nd ed.). Springer.

Schutt, D. A, .Jr. (2018). *A strength-based approach to career development using appreciative inquiry* (2nd ed.). National Career Development Association.

Seligman, M. E. P. (2011). *Flourish: A visionary new understanding of happiness and well-being.* Free Press.

Seligman, M. E. P., & Csikszentmihalyi, M. (2000). Positive psychology: An introduction. *American Psychologist, 55,* 5–14. https://doi.org/10.1037/0003-066X.55.1.5

Seligman, M. E. P., Steen, T. A., Park, N., & Peterson, C. (2005). Positive psychology progress: Empirical validation of interventions. *American Psychologist, 60*(5). 410-421. https://doi.org/10.1037/0003-066X.60.5.410

Sharf, R. S. (2013). *Applying career development theory to counseling* (6th ed.). Cengage.

Society for Human Resource Management. (2016). *A guide to conducting behavioral interviews with early career job candidates.* Author.

Solberg, V. S., Good, G. E., Nord, D., Holm, C., Hohner, R., Zima, N., Heffernan, M., & Malen, A. (1994). Assessing career search expectations: Development and validation of the career search efficacy scale. *Journal of Career Assessment, 2*(2), 111–123. https://doi.org/10.1177/106907279400200202

Stavros, J., Cooperrider, D., & Kelley, D. L. (2003). Strategic inquiry, Appreciative intent: Inspiration to SOAR. *AI Practitioner: International Journal of Appreciative Inquiry, 5,* 10-17.

Stavros, J., & Hinrichs, G. (2009). Thin book of SOAR: Building strengths-based strategy. Thin Book Publishers.

Swanson, J. L. & Gore, P. A. (2000). Advances in vocational psychology theory and research. In S. D. Brown & R. W. Lent (Eds.), *Handbook of Counseling Psychology* (3rd ed., pp. 233-269). Wiley.

Terrell, K. (2021). *Age bias in hiring hurts midcareer workers worldwide.* AARP. https://www.aarp.org/work/age-discrimination/midcareer-workers/

Tims, M., & Bakker, A. B. (2010). Job crafting: Towards a new model of individual job redesign. *South African Journal of Industrial Psychology, 36,* 1–9. http://doi.org/10.4102/sajip.v36i2.841

U.S. Equal Employment Opportunity Commission. (2020). *Discrimination by type.* EEOC. https://www.eeoc.gov/discrimination-type

Watkins, J. M., & Mohr, B. J. (2001). *Appreciative inquiry: Change at the speed of imagination.* Jossey-Bass.

Wrzesniewski, A., & Dutton, J. E. (2001). Crafting a job: Revisioning employees as active crafters of their work. *Academy of Management Review, 26*(2), 179–201.

CHAPTER 4
Ethics in Career Coaching

"We make a living by what we get. We make a life by what we give."

– Winston Churchill

Chapter Highlights

This chapter will discuss ethics in career coaching and the importance of adopting and applying sound ethical coaching practices in working with clients, including maintaining a professional code of ethics for career coaching. Implications for maintaining ethical coaching practices will be discussed, including legal implications of the profession.

Learning Objectives

This chapter highlights the following:

1. The importance of operating within a professional code of ethics in career coaching.
2. Roles and boundaries between coach and client, and the referral process.
3. How to apply ethical decision-making strategies to the career coaching practice.
4. Where ethics and legal issues in coaching overlap.

K – W – L

Now that you know what the chapter has to offer, take a few minutes to assess where you are in terms of your knowledge level and areas of learning using the K-W-L model. The first step in the K-W-L model is to self-assess what you already ***know*** about ethical issues related to career coaching. Next, think about what you ***want*** to know about ethical coaching practices. Where do you feel are the gaps in your knowledge of ethical codes or practicing ethical coaching? Finally, to conclude this chapter, you will be asked to revisit the K-W-L model to assess whether this chapter provided you with information to fill some of your knowledge gaps. You will reflect on what you ***learned*** from this chapter and how you can apply it to your coaching practice.

Ethical Foundations of Career Coaching

Career coaching exists to improve a client's situation and help them achieve their professional objectives. A positive coaching relationship promotes client growth and development while fully considering the client's welfare. Ethical and legal guidelines exist to protect clients and ensure coaches have a playbook for fair service delivery. They promote and ensure accountability by outlining service standards, educating career coaches on best practices, providing a framework for ethical decision-making when ethical dilemmas arise, and protecting coaches in the event conflict arises (Corey et al., 2014).

Trust is the foundation of the relationship between a coach and a client, and the coach must uphold that trust by adhering to acceptable boundaries. Because of the nature of the interaction between a coach and a client, ethical difficulties can arise. Consider a code of ethics as a moral compass: how decisions are made, how the coaching practice operates, and how connections occur with clients. These items are extremely important to the coach/client relationship. In addition, a coach wields authority over the client and has access to sensitive information about them. Therefore, legal and moral implications might accompany ethical problems. Ethically sensitive career coaches are more likely to detect unethical situations and respond appropriately.

There are many ways for a career coach to accomplish a positive coaching relationship within ethical and legal guidelines: maintaining confidential records, creating action plans, signing consent forms, and fostering a professional relationship are just a few examples. Clients want to know that their career coach will encourage them to discuss, plan, be vulnerable, take risks, and move forward in a confidential and safe environment. It takes respect, honesty, and trust to foster a coaching relationship. Practicing ethical coaching looks like this:

- *Avoid making hasty assumptions.* We all hold biases but understanding our biases and mitigating these biases is necessary for effective career coaching.
- *Be truthful.* Not everything you will say is feedback your client will want to hear; however, honesty is essential to help your client reach their goals and maintain rapport in the coaching relationship. Therefore, career coaches should consistently deliver sensitive feedback with care.
- *Know your limits.* The National Career Development Association *Code of Ethics* (2015) defines career professionals as "career counselors, career coaches, career consultants, career development facilitators, and anyone else who is a member of NCDA and provides career counseling, career advice/advising, career coaching, career planning, job search assistance, and/or related services" (p. 26). Within the scope of services that are the primary responsibility of a career professional are activities categorized as *career planning* (NCDA, 2015, p. 3). Career planning services include

  > active provision of information designed to help a client with a specific need, such as review of a résumé; assistance in networking strategies; identification of occupations based on values, interests, skills, prior work experience, and/or other characteristics; support in the job-seeking process; and assessment by means of paper-based and/or online inventories of interest, abilities, personality, work-related values, and/or other characteristics. (NCDA, 2015, p. 3-4)

The NCDA *Code of Ethics* distinguishes career planning services from career counseling services because counseling holds the potential for a professional counseling relationship beyond those included in career planning. The NCDA *Code of Ethics* calls for all career professionals, whether engaging in career planning or career counseling to provide only the services within the scope of their professional competence and qualifications. As we learned in the introduction, career coaching is a future-focused exercise of goal setting and action planning toward the desired state of career satisfaction. Ensuring a clear understanding of the client's needs and expectations and aligning qualifications with those needs and expectations is vital at the onset of the coaching conversation. If the coach cannot offer a service, an appropriate referral should be provided.

These and other coach/client relationship issues fall under ethical decision-making, which will be covered in greater depth later in this chapter. However, first, let us start with a definition of ethics and its application to career coaching.

What are Ethics?

The Oxford English Dictionary (OED, n.d.) presents the following definition of terms important to ethical decision-making. The OED defines ethics as *moral* principles that govern a person's behavior or activity. Morals are standards of behavior or beliefs concerning what is and is not acceptable. Our moral beliefs inform our thoughts and actions. An individual or group develops a code of *ethics* to provide rules for appropriate conduct in given situations. Ethics are contextual, based on *values*, which are principles or standards of one's behavior. Every career coach has their own unique set of values or blueprint for operating based on what they feel is good and desirable. In ethics, value denotes the importance of a thing or action. One's values heavily influence ethical decision-making. *Laws* are rules of behavior that stem from or are rooted in ethical principles. Ethics, values, morals, and laws are all considered when establishing a professional code of ethics.

Why Follow an Ethical Code?

Ethical codes or codes of conduct represent the ideal standards set by a professional organization or group of organizations and agreed upon by those who accept membership in those organizations (ACA, 2014). A code of ethics helps to define professional behavior and serves to protect the public, the profession, and those practicing in the profession (NCDA, 2015). Adopting and adhering to a code of ethics in career coaching is critical as it provides a road map of best practices or supports the construction of a course of action for the coach (de Jong, 2010; NCDA, 2015). It also aids in designing and implementing coaching strategies while dealing with individuals, groups, or diverse populations. Operating within a code of ethics also helps with assessment test administration and interpretation and processing of ethical inquiries and complaints (ACA, 2014). Finally, it provides coaches with a measure to be recognized as a legitimate, stand-alone profession (Brennan & Wildflower, 2018).

At the time of this publication, no single professional organization acts as the governing authority for the career coaching industry. Coaching professionals operate autonomously and with no obligation to comply with any regulatory body's code of ethics or conduct (Iordanou & Williams, 2016). However, there are codes of conduct available, such as the NCDA *Code of Ethics* (2015), which support career coaches. This regulatory absence has offered "fertile ground for the development of independent professional activity and, in consequence, idiosyncratic and self-imposed ethical standards in the coaching practice" (Iordanou & Williams, 2016, p. 2) -- precisely why following a code of ethics is essential. Career coaches currently rely on the ethical guidelines from the organization(s) that train, credential, and support them in their integral pursuit of professionalism.

The American Counseling Association (ACA, 2014), the National Career Development Association (NCDA, 2015), and the International Coaching Federation (ICF, 2021) recognize the value of adhering to an ethical code as a way to safeguard one's professional integrity through practicing in a competent, ethical, and transparent manner. ACA's mission is "to enhance the quality of life in society by promoting the development of professional counselors, advancing the counseling profession, and using the profession and practice of counseling to promote respect for human dignity and diversity" (ACA, 2014, p. 2). As mentioned in the introduction, many of the practices used by career coaches stem from the counseling industry. The National Career Development Association (NCDA) is one of the founding associations and a current division of ACA. NCDA's mission is to provide professional development, publications, standards, and advocacy to practitioners and educators who inspire and empower individuals to achieve their career and life goals (NCDA, 2021). NCDA's Ethics Committee acknowledged ACA's work in its code of ethics and endeavored to follow the structure of ACA's ethics code in its 2015 revision so that the two codes were compatible. ICF's mission is to lead the global advancement of the coaching profession and empower the world through coaching (ICF, 2021) and has a code of ethics for professional coaches working in various industries.

Career coaches practice in many settings and hold a variety of credentials. There are times when coaches desire ethical guidance targeted toward a specific work environment and task. Other times a code of ethics that speaks to a broad audience may be sufficient. "Due to the nature of their work, many people identify with more than one professional association or credentialing agency, making familiarization with multiple codes of ethics and standards of practice a professional necessity" (Makela & Perlus, 2017, p. 23). As a result, this chapter will draw from ACA (2014), NCDA (2015), and ICF's (2021) ethical codes, with primary reference to NCDA's (2015) *Code of Ethics*.

Key Questions to Consider

Coaches face numerous ethical decision-making challenges. For example:

- How do I coach ethically, and given the choices available, what ethical code do I adopt as practice?
- What ethical issues will I commonly encounter in career coaching?
- How and when do I identify and discuss ethical issues not recognized by my clients?
- How do I establish clear and dependable ground rules for confidentiality that protect my clients and our relationships?
- How do I determine when a client's needs require a referral beyond my training and credentials?
- Do I recognize and manage ethical dilemmas on my own?

Professional Values and Principles for Career Coaching

As mentioned earlier in this chapter, values are principles or standards of behavior (OED, n.d.). These principles guide ethical coaching and demonstrate ethical behavior and decision-making. NCDA (2015) highlights the following as essential values held by career professionals:

1. Enhancing career development throughout the life span;
2. Safeguarding the integrity of the professional working relationship;
3. Practicing competently and ethically;
4. Supporting the worth, dignity, potential, and uniqueness of everyone; and
5. Honoring diversity and promoting social justice. (p. 1)

These values provide a conceptual foundation for the fundamental principles of professional, ethical behavior. In surveying several professional bodies' ethical codes across various related professions, Brennan and Wildflower (2018) found a degree of consistency in the ethical principles that reinforce the professional practice. Common themes found across all codes were (a) Do no harm: Do not cause needless injury or harm to others; (b) Duty of care: Act in ways that promote the welfare of other people; (c) Know your limits: Practice within your scope of competence; (d) Respect the interests of the client; and (e) Respect the law (Brennan & Wildflower, 2018, p. 500). These common themes are revealed in NCDA's 2015 *Code of Ethics* fundamental principles of the profession:

- *Autonomy,* or fostering the right to control the direction of one's life. Respecting a client's autonomy refers to the coach allowing the client to exercise freedom of choice and action while also assisting the client in understanding how their decisions may be perceived within the context of the society in which they live and how they may infringe on the rights of others.
- *Nonmaleficence or do no harm* is avoiding actions that cause harm. When working with clients in any helping profession, the primary consideration is not to harm. The number one objective of career coaching is to practice in good faith.
- *Beneficence* or working for the good of the individual and society by promoting mental health and well-being. Beneficence is entering the coaching relationship with the client's best interests in mind and that all decisions made during the coaching process are for the client's benefit and well-being.
- *Objectivity* is coaching justly or treating individuals equitably. Objectivity ensures that clients are treated equally within the limits of the coach's abilities. Treating one individual fairly without violating the rights of another

is essential. For example, if a coach is holding virtual coaching sessions with a deaf or hard of hearing client, the coach may use closed captioning to ensure the client receives and fully comprehends all pertinent information.

- *Accountability* is honoring commitments and keeping promises. Being accountable refers to the trusting relationship between the coach and the client, including fulfilling one's responsibilities of trust in professional relationships. Confidentiality, for example, falls under accountability in that the coach has a responsibility to maintain a client's fidelity by keeping coaching conversations confidential.
- *Veracity* deals truthfully with individuals with whom career development professionals come into contact (NCDA, 2015).

In addition to these fundamental principles, it is important to look at NCDA's *Code of Ethics* and the necessary considerations to practice ethical career coaching.

Ethical Guidelines in Career Coaching

Ethical dilemmas are rarely black and white. Unlike laws governed by language easily understood and transparent to the public, ethics concern unique individuals and situations, which create gray areas. There is no such thing as a law of ethics, but rather a code or guidelines exist. Professional organizations that credential, certify, and train career coaches provide ethical guidelines for career coaching to ensure commitment and accountability to professional conduct. Many organizations have professional oversight processes where client concerns can be reported and investigated if needed. Although each organization's code of ethics offers a solid foundation in self-governance and every organization follows its own set of ethical guidelines, ethical codes across organizations are strikingly similar (Brennan & Wildflower, 2018). As you review the NCDA (see Appendix E), ACA (see Appendix F), and ICF (see Appendix G) codes, you may find the similarities and overlap unsurprising because the formation of ethical codes is not only based on earlier professional codes (psychologists, medical profession) but more general societal norms. For example, professionalism carries obligations of ethical conduct that have intended effects on one's behavior, and professional bodies carry regulatory power to oversee high standards of behavior (Brennan & Wildflower, 2018). Nonetheless, in the current unregulated coaching environment, where standards of behavior are self-imposed, ethical codes are critical to measuring standards and performance in this growing profession. Because the work of the career coach is most closely related to the National Career Development Association vision, it is helpful to study an overview of NCDA's 2015 *Code of Ethics*.

NCDA Section A: The Professional Relationship

Section A of the NCDA code outlines expected professional behaviors and responsibilities between coach and client. Career professionals form healthy relationships when they facilitate client growth and development to promote the client's interests and welfare. Trust, respect, confidentiality, and privacy are cornerstones of this partnership. In addition, career professionals treat clients with dignity to promote their welfare by offering supportive networks, respecting client boundaries, and maintaining a professional relationship at all times. The coach is also responsible for providing detailed and proper documentation, including informed consent, being clear about their services. Section A also states: "Career professionals actively attempt to understand the diverse cultural backgrounds of the individuals they serve. [They] also explore their own cultural identities and how these affect their values and beliefs about the working relationship" (NCDA, 2015, p. 5). Chapter 6 provides a deeper look at career coaching for diverse populations.

NCDA Section B: Confidentiality, Privileged Communication, and Privacy

Section B of the NCDA *Code of Ethics* outlines expected behaviors related to confidentiality, trust, and privacy. Section B states:

> Career professionals recognize that trust is a cornerstone of the professional relationship. Career professionals earn clients' trust by creating an ongoing partnership, establishing and upholding appropriate boundaries, and maintaining confidentiality. Career professionals communicate the parameters of confidentiality in a culturally competent manner. (NCDA, 2015, p. 8)

Confidentiality is key to the coach-client relationship when, for example, a client reveals a disability that might impede future hiring prospects. It is the coach's responsibility not to disclose this information to others. Respect and trust are also covered in Section B. Lack of transparency in communicating the parameters of confidentiality may impact the mutual trust between the coach and client, which may result in barriers to forward movement in achieving a client's goals.

NCDA Section C: Professional Responsibility

Section C discusses communication. In particular, coaches have a professional responsibility to provide accurate, honest, and open communication in their coaching practices and follow a code of ethics. Continued professional development also falls under professional responsibility. Career coaches must be educated on the codes governing the profession, be active in their professional organizations, and foster the growth of industry service delivery. Explicitly stated,

> Career professionals are encouraged to promote change at the individual, group, institutional, and societal levels in ways that improve the quality of life for individuals and groups and removes potential barriers to the provision or access of appropriate services being offered. Career professionals have a responsibility to the public to engage in ethical practice. (NCDA, 2015, p. 11)

NCDA Section D: Relationships with Other Professionals

Providing resources, consulting, and building and maintaining relationships with others in the profession are the cornerstones of Section D. "Career professionals recognize that the quality of their interactions with colleagues can influence the quality of services provided to clients" (NCDA, 2015, p.14). Section D explains that career professionals should develop positive working relationships and open communication lines with colleagues to enhance service delivery. In terms of advocacy, a population often silenced or quieted is the aging population or older workers (Jenkins, 2018). Professional advocacy can help reduce barriers when older workers experience ageism when seeking employment, promotion, or retirement compensation. Ageism is just one of the many career-related barriers that career professionals advocate against.

NCDA Section E: Evaluation, Assessment, and Interpretation

Coaches use formal and informal assessments as a tool in the career development process to help the client explore options for growth and discovery (see Chapter 5). "Career professionals promote the well-being of individual clients or groups of clients by developing and using appropriate career, educational, and psychological assessment instruments" (NCDA, 2015, p. 15). Coaches use assessments to help clients better understand themselves (skills, interests, values, personality, strengths) and how these attributes connect with various career options. The NCDA *Code of Ethics* Section E discusses the proper use of assessment evaluation and interpretation in career coaching and the selection and multicultural issues.

NCDA Section F: Providing Career Services Online, Technology, and Social Media

The use of technology and social media in career coaching is ever-evolving. Maintaining awareness of changes has been a constant struggle, particularly since the 2020 pandemic when most face-to-face coaching interactions moved virtually for an extended period. Applying a code of ethics in technology use, maintaining cultural sensitivity, and equity is a continued goal in the coaching profession. Section F of the NCDA code states:

> Career professionals strive to become knowledgeable about [technology and social media] resources, recognizing that periodic training is needed to develop necessary technical and professional competencies ... and make every attempt to protect the confidentiality and data security, ensure transparency and equitable treatment of clients, and meet any legal and ethical requirements for the use of such resources. (NCDA, 2015, p. 17)

Technology offers an excellent opportunity to serve clients in new and improved ways and requires coaches to practice ethically and inclusively.

NCDA Section G: Supervision, Training, and Teaching

Career coaches who work in the capacity of supervisors, trainers, and teachers should recognize the limitations of their knowledge and skills and seek guidance or counsel when needed. NCDA's Section G of the code states:

> Career professionals foster meaningful and respectful professional relationships and maintain appropriate boundaries with supervisees and students [and] ... have theoretical and pedagogical foundations for their work and aim to be fair, accurate, and honest in their assessments of other career professionals, students, and supervisees. (NCDA, 2015, p. 20)

Career coaches in a supervisory capacity should operate ethically by practicing culturally sensitive supervision and seek training and development in this area as needed.

NCDA Section H: Research and Publication

Many career coaches conduct research and publish research findings to advance the profession's scholarship. These contributions are necessary to progress as an industry, develop the profession, and learn from the literature. Therefore, scholars who research and publish in the field are asked to uphold NCDA's Section H ethical guidelines "by minimizing bias and respecting diversity in designing and implementing research" (NCDA, 2015, p. 24).

NCDA Section I: Resolving Ethical Issues

As career coaches practice and continue to grow within the profession, they are responsible for maintaining ethical coaching, which is emphasized in Section I. Simply put, it asks career professionals to incorporate ethical practices into their daily work. Not only do career professionals behave in a legal, ethical, and moral manner in the conduct of their professional work, they "engage in ongoing learning and development regarding current topics in ethical and legal issues in the profession" (NCDA, 2015, p. 24). Client protection and trust in the profession are dependent on a high degree of professional conduct. They hold other career professionals to the same standards as themselves and are prepared to take appropriate measures to meet these standards. Career professionals attempt to resolve ethical quandaries by a direct and open conversation among all persons concerned and, when required, seek counsel from colleagues and superiors.

Ethical Issues in Coaching

Avoiding ethical issues is not always possible, even though ethical codes define and set boundaries for coaching. It is essential to understand and practice ethical behavior, and part of doing so is developing ethical sensitivities. The term *ethical sensitivity* was coined to characterize the first step in professional decision-making: identifying and evaluating the ethical dimension. Scholars of professional disciplines have since conceptualized the term in various ways. While all have agreed that ethical sensitivity is essential in practice, there is no agreement on what it means, what it looks like, what conditions must exist for it to happen, or the consequences for professionals and society. For this publication, Bebeau et al. (1985) define ethical sensitivities as the "perception that something one might do or is doing can affect the welfare of someone else either directly or indirectly (by violating a general practice or commonly held social standard)" (p. 226). Career coaches must focus on building ethical sensitivities that support accountability and accessibility.

As mentioned earlier, governing bodies currently do not oversee or regulate the career coaching industry. Therefore, career coaches are encouraged but not required to hold and maintain certification and/or credentialing. However, just because career coaches are not subject to formal oversight does not preclude them from building ethical sensitivities and adhering to ethical guidelines set forth by their credentialing organization(s). A career coach, for example, may grapple with:

1. Whether or not to work with someone who holds personal affiliation (family member, friend)
2. Whether or not to meet with a client in a public setting where the risk of someone else seeing or overhearing the conversation is possible
3. Whether or not to share coaching conversations without the explicit written consent of the client

These questions contain gray areas depending on the particulars of the type of available service, environment, or consent given. This section highlights several common areas for self-monitoring.

Clarity of Qualifications

Some career coaches are also licensed to deliver counseling services. Depending on the type of licensure held, the career coach who is a licensed counselor has the professional capacity to diagnose and provide mental health counseling during the career coaching process if there is a client need. In this scenario, a referral model is not necessary. There are times in coaching engagements when it becomes clear that the coach is called to operate beyond their capability or the defined boundary of the coaching appointment. If a coach determines a client could benefit from a service the career coach is not licensed or trained to provide, the career coach is ethically responsible for referring the client elsewhere to receive those services. Career coaches who are not licensed to deliver counseling services must maintain a referral model for clients who need counseling services outside the coach's credentialing expertise. Career coaches without licensure should question referral when

- the client is depressed or having significant marriage/family problems
- the coach suspects or the client discloses a problem with addiction
- the coach questions his or her ability to address an issue unrelated to career
- the issues the client is facing go beyond workplace concerns
- the coach suspects other kinds of abuse
- the coach becomes aware of illegal conduct involving the client
- the coach sees incidents where behavior infringes on ethics policies

Communicating qualifications during the initial coaching session or intake (see Chapter 2) will be helpful to ensure transparency. However, waiting to disclose qualifications until the need arises or a situation warrants could put the client in a vulnerable position, stall support, disengage the client from the coaching process, or worse, cause harm to the client. Therefore, before rendering services, the coach should explain their credentials and qualifications to the client during the initial intake meeting and agree upon services in an informed consent form (see Appendix C).

Confidentiality

Confidentiality is a critical ethical consideration for maintaining rapport and trust between coach and client. ICF (2021) defines confidentiality as "protection of any information obtained around the coaching engagement unless consent to release is given" (p. 3). Coaches handle confidentiality issues in various ways, but all coaches have a professional responsibility (beyond the terms of the contract with the client) to apply high standards in their service. They frequently have access to highly sensitive information about clients and clients' life. Except as authorized by a client or required by the law, a coach's role is to respect the confidentiality of all client information (Brock, 2006). The coach needs to be open and frank about how confidentiality is met with the various methods and techniques used in the coaching process, maintain only appropriate records (e.g., coaching session notes), and respect the client's confidentiality (e.g., use pseudonyms and other means of hiding the client's true identity when contributing case studies).

Informed Consent

Section A.2.a. of NCDA's (2015) *Code of Ethics* details definitions and procedures related to informed consent. Fully considering and making decisions, without coercion, related to participating in a process that might impact the individual's well-being is the basis of informed consent. A client needs adequate information about the working relationship between coach and client to make an informed choice, and a coach has a professional obligation to review the rights and responsibilities of service before entering into coaching (NCDA, 2015). Services to be covered include:

1. Coaching goals, techniques, procedures
2. Limitations, potential risks, benefits of coaching
3. Coach qualifications, credentials, relevant experience
4. Use of tests/assessments and reports, fees, and billing arrangements
5. The role of technology, document storage, communication
6. Confidentiality, termination of services, and other pertinent information.

Section A.2.d. discusses the inability of the client to give consent when providing career services to minors or persons unable to give voluntary consent. If this situation arises, the career coach must seek the support of a guardian and include them in decision-making as appropriate (NCDA, 2015). A sample informed consent form can be found in Appendix C.

Documentation

Part of the informed consent process is recording and storing data. Informed consent must be received to document discussions throughout the coaching relationship. Records and conversations should be kept private, and for a coach to release, the client must give informed consent. Sessions should be documented accurately but collected and recorded only when necessary and shared if/when the client gives permission or the law requires (NCDA, 2015). The ICF (2021) ethics code suggests coaches "maintain, store and dispose of any records, including electronic files

COACH CORNER

Do you know the definition of Informed Consent?

"Informed consent is a process of information sharing associated with possible actions clients may choose to take, aimed at assisting clients in acquiring a full appreciation and understanding of the facts and implications of a given action or actions" (NCDA, 2015, p.26).

and communications … in a manner that promotes confidentiality, security, and privacy, and complies with any applicable laws and agreements" (p. 5).

Know Thyself

Several scholars (see Kitchener, 2000; Welfel, 2006 and others) discuss the need for coaches to understand their own ethical and moral beliefs in order to be able to grasp fully, understand, and apply ethical standards professionally, specifically when addressing conflict. Additionally, Makela and Perlus (2017) noted that it is important to tune into one's feelings when questionable situations arise to enhance ethical sensitivities. These feelings can serve as a prompt or indicator for more informed decision-making. The key to knowing thyself is practicing regular reflection on personal integrity, judgment, wisdom and the ethical principles discussed above: Autonomy, Nonmaleficence, Beneficence, Objectivity, Accountability, and Veracity (NCDA, 2015).

Keep it Professional

Section A of the NCDA (2015) *Code of Ethics* outlines the professional relationship between coach and client. Because a coach holds a professional role, this relationship encourages "client growth and development in ways that foster the interest and welfare of clients and promote the formation of healthy relationships" (p. 3). Therefore, coaches should have nothing but a working relationship with the clients they serve, avoiding personal relationships with clients while coaching.

Dual or multiple relationships can also challenge professional boundaries in coaching. A dual relationship is defined as a relationship having more than one role or interest (Buceta, 1993; Ellickson & Brown, 2000), for example, the client and co-worker or client and family member. If a dual coaching relationship presents itself, it is important to acknowledge and clarify conflict of interest, clearly defined roles, responsibilities and boundaries, and terms of coaching (Zur & Anderson, 2006). It is also essential for the coach to reflect on whether referral is necessary.

Respect for Diversity

Ethical coaching is necessary to understand and respect human differences and honor various cultures, races, and sexual orientations. The NCDA (2015) *Code of Ethics* outlines the expectation that career professionals minimize bias and respect diversity in all aspects of career coaching, including respecting clients, students, families, trainees, and research participants. Molinsky (2013) coined the term *global dexterity*, which implies adapting one's style of communication and behavior across cultures – regardless of one's culture of origin or destination. In addition, diversity should be considered when administering assessments (see Chapter 5), when acting in a supervisory capacity, or conducting and publishing research (NCDA, 2015).

Technology Considerations

The use of technology in career coaching practices continues to increase and is ever-changing, and with this ongoing advancement comes ethical fluctuations in the use and misuse of coaching practices. Technology benefits coaching because it provides greater access to clients and more efficient delivery of services. Yet, ethical considerations exist, including privacy, confidentiality, informed consent, data security, access rights, and responsibilities related to distance services. Although ethical codes cover many issues related to technology, ethical codes are not updated as rapidly as technology tends to change. Consult with the professional organization(s) for the latest updates related to ethics in technology use and misuse and consult and follow any ethical codes, such as NCDA's (2015) *Code of Ethics*.

Obtain a Mentor

Establishing a professional relationship with someone who can assist in assessing ethical dilemmas that may arise is helpful. No coach is an expert in all ethical (and legal) quandaries. When complex ethical issues arise, the coach will want support from a colleague or organization providing knowledgeable advice and acting as a sounding board. One example related to obtaining a mentor is the option for NCDA members to reach out to the Ethics Committee at any time with questions as part of their membership benefits.

Clarify Services Upfront

Coaches recognize the value in clarifying roles, agendas, expectations, and results at the onset of an engagement. Increasingly, coaches must intentionally do so in the context of ethics. Communicate with clients how to deal with perceived ethical dilemmas during the coaching engagement. Section A of the NCDA (2015) *Code of Ethics* is a valuable guide in establishing services rendered, means of communication, fees, gifts for service, non-payment, and termination of service. Highlights include:

- *Disclose costs:* If applicable, establish a consistent price and disclose the total price of services before the coaching starts. Have agreements for services in writing approved by both parties before beginning the work. If a client cannot afford the cost of service, help locate an appropriate alternative.
- *Set clear boundaries:* Have a conversation with the client on how feedback about the coaching engagement will be requested and delivered (number of sessions, in person, length of engagement).
- *Craft a specific exit strategy:* What will the client's growth and forward movement plan look like once the coaching contract ends? Ensure clear next steps follow coaching, and determine how the coach and client will manage the transition.

The ethical issues in coaching discussed in this section represent the most common challenges faced in career coaching. The message in this chapter and throughout this monograph is that resources and support are available! Nevertheless, career coaches should continue to develop their ethical sensitivities and adhere to a preferred ethical code at all times in the coaching process. The following section will present an ethical decision-making model for ethical dilemmas in coaching.

Ethical Decision-Making Models

This chapter has provided information related to ethics in career coaching, in addition to examining resources and strategies available to help career coaches address ethical dilemmas as they arise in working with clients. In researching ethics in the helping professions for this publication, several authors revealed standard components or models of ethical decision-making. While this

COACH CORNER

Ethical Dilemmas: What Would You Do?

- A parent of your client requests that you share assessment results with them without consent.
- You are not certified to administer an assessment a client has requested.
- Client discloses workplace misconduct by their supervisor, which is the main reason for seeking a new role.

monograph does not allow the inclusion of all theories and models, Makela and Perlus's (2017) meta-analysis offers nine components that apply to ethical decision-making in career coaching. These components are as follows:

Component 1: *Identify and define the problem.* Pause, reflect and gather all information as possible, consult peers, mentors, or appropriate sources if needed. A clear description of the ethical issue involving stakeholders and potentially affected relationships should result from the coach's problem identification.

Component 2: *Consider foundational ethical issues involved.* To enhance understanding of ethical problems at hand, a career coach should consider issues based on the ethical principles discussed earlier in the chapter: Autonomy, Nonmaleficence, Beneficence, Objectivity, Accountability, and Veracity (NCDA, 2015).

Component 3: *Tune in to feelings.* How the coach feels about the ethical dilemma at hand, the gut check, is essential to address in the ethical decision-making process. Attending to feelings helps create an internal compass and builds essential ethical sensitivities as the coach grows professionally.

Component 4: *Consult the code of ethics.* At this stage in the ethical decision-making process, consulting with a preferred code of ethics is the next step. Depending on the issue, it may also be necessary to review legal documents, organizational policies, ethics literature, and various policy statements. All resources may provide more straightforward guidelines on how to proceed next.

Component 5: *Seek appropriate consultation.* If needed, seek professional or supervisor consultation to gather outside expertise and perspective. This counsel can offer expertise and emotional support as the coach navigates the ethical dilemma.

Component 6: *Identify desired outcomes.* Rarely will the ethical dilemma produce one resolution; therefore, it is wise to identify all possible outcome scenarios and consider options based on components 1-5. Reflecting on potential outcomes informs consideration of possible actions.

Component 7: *Consider possible actions and their consequences.* Based on identified outcomes in component 6, what are possible actions and consequences? Next, consider each action based on components 1-6, including pros and cons related to social, time, economic, psychological, resources.

Component 8: *Select and implement an action.* Once the course of action has been identified, the next step is to implement the action. Finally, acknowledge and adjust for implementation challenges.

Component 9: *Document the process and reflect on the outcome.* Documentation should be an ongoing process beginning with component 1 through component 9; however, at this stage, finalize all documents for clarity and comprehensiveness. Take ample time to reflect on the process, including the outcomes of the decision.

COACH CORNER

Case Study: What Would You Do When Ethical and Legal Issues Collide?

You are a career coach in a community college career center who has worked for two years with a student now getting ready to transfer. This student has applied to a 4-year selective institution – the student's "dream school." In addition, the student has listed you as a reference on the admissions application. As a result, the admissions department requests that you provide access to the student's coaching records, specifically, any formal assessments on file as the admissions rep indicates fit is vital in the admissions decision process. What do you do?

Legal Issues in Career Coaching

When Law and Ethics Collide

Many ethical decisions are void of a legal obligation; however, occasionally, ethical dilemmas arise during the career coaching process with legal implications. Part of being a reflective career coach involves reviewing and considering all available solutions in the ethical decision-making process (see the previous section) and seeking the best course of action for both coach and client. It is impossible and unnecessary to know every law, but it is important to identify the core issue(s) and then determine possible options and available resources to resolve the ethical dilemma. For example, when does a law require a coach to break confidentiality? If a client's wellbeing is at risk, the law may obligate the coach to reveal a client's disclosures. NCDA's (2015) code states, "If the conflict cannot be resolved by acknowledging and discussing the applicable principles in the NCDA *Code of Ethics*, career professionals must adhere to the requirements of all applicable federal, state, local, and/or institutional statutes, laws, regulations, and procedures" (I.1.b). A coach should always consult their association's code of ethics and apply ethical principles to the situation to determine whether legal recourse is warranted.

As the coach moves through the ethical decision-making process (see the previous section), a seminal method of calculating a situation's ethical and legal implications is Engel and colleagues' (1990) 2 x 2 Ethical and Legal Quadrant (see Figure 11). This formula can help a coach analyze situations to decide on the most appropriate ethical and legal course of action. For example, consider the dilemma if the parent of a college student requests access to the student's coaching records. Does the career coach provide the parent with a copy of the requested records? This ethical and legal issue falls within the 2 x 2 formula, and the answer to the question depends more closely on the details of the situation. If the student consents,

Figure 11
2 x 2 Ethical and Legal Quadrant

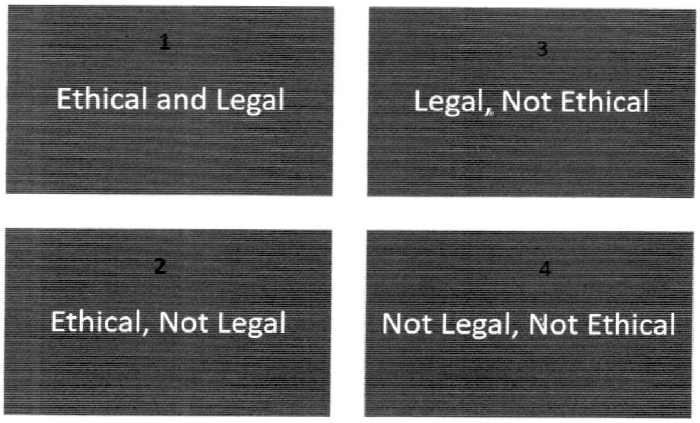

the career coach can ethically share coaching records (Quadrant 1 & 2). If the student does not provide the career coach consent to share records, sharing these records is unethical (Quadrant 3 & 4). Legally, the career coach must abide by the laws governing college students under the Family Educational Rights and Privacy Act (FERPA). FERPA is a statute that applies to federally funded institutions, which gives parents access to their children's educational records, the ability to have the records changed, and some control over the sharing of personally identifiable information from the education records. However, when a student turns 18 or enters a postsecondary institution at any age, the rights under FERPA transfer from the parents to the student (20 U.S.C. § 1232g; FERPA, 34 CFR Part 99). In this example, using the 2 x 2 formula, disclosing student records to the parent would violate Quadrant 2 and 4 regardless of whether the student provided the coach record sharing consent.

In addition to using the 2 x 2 Ethical and Legal Quadrant, it is important to consider the legal situation at hand based on the ethical principles of Autonomy, Nonmaleficence, Beneficence, Objectivity, Accountability, and Veracity (NCDA, 2015). Below are additional areas to be mindful of when legal questions arise.

Confidentiality

Most communication between a coach and client is confidential, yet there are exceptions. Fidelity describes the trusting relationship between the coach and the client, and confidentiality falls under fidelity in that coaches are responsible for maintaining a client's fidelity by ensuring that coaching conversations remain confidential (NCDA, 2015). An example of ethical and legal crossed lines is the case of a minor client disclosing sexual misconduct at her place of employment. Although there are confidentiality agreements between coach and client, it is within the coach's ethical and legal responsibility to report this disclosure to an authority.

Section B of the NCDA *Code of Ethics*, Confidentiality, Privileged, Communication, and Privacy (NCDA, 2015), discusses the parameters of confidentiality. As mentioned above, there may be times when the law requires coaches to break confidentiality if they believe the client intends to, for instance, inflict self-harm or harm others, elder or child abuse. Otherwise, outside of written release, coaches cannot share information regarding the client without client consent. The caveat to this confidentiality clause is that currently, career coaches are not regulated by a legal governing body, as are psychiatrists, psychologists, or other therapists. A career coach would operate under the do no harm clause; however, there is no legal recourse if the coach does not follow a code of ethics.

Risk Management Issues

In the 21st century, career coaches' work involves virtual connections and online tools and resources. Copyright and fair use laws can help career coaches make ethical and legal choices as remote work increases. There are many resources available to help navigate these areas. For example, the Library of Congress maintains a robust webpage and blog at https://blogs.loc.gov/copyright/2020/03/teaching-from-a-distance-and-copyright-considerations/ on distance teaching, online learning, and copyright considerations. Because this legal area is constantly evolving and changing, it is an essential professional development area for career coaches to remain versed in the betterment of their own ethical and legal practices. Professional associations provide ethical/legal resources, such as monthly columns on Legal Issues in Career Services in the National Association of Colleges and Employer's NACE Journal (https://www.naceweb.org/public-policy-and-legal/legal-issues/) and NCDA's *Career Developments* Magazine quarterly "Ethics in a Nutshell" column.

Coaching Agreements

Many coaches employ written agreements as communication protection or informed consent during the coaching process. Before the coaching relationship begins, written agreements allow a coach to clarify his or her ethical thought process, coaching procedures, and legal terms and conditions for the client. In addition, coaching agreements detail the coaching philosophy, terms and conditions of work performed, coaching approach and intended outcomes, confidentiality, fees and duration, and termination of service terms. Providing a client with a coaching agreement before work begins allows the client to clarify any nebulous areas, ask clarifying questions, and learn more about the coach before working together. The coaching agreement also outlines informed consent of the working relationship, ensures the coach and the client have the same understanding, and agrees to this understanding. See Appendix H for a sample coaching agreement.

Liability Insurance

Americans live in an ever-increasing litigious society. In 2019, combined filings in the United States district courts for civil cases and criminal defendants increased by over 18,000, up 5% from 2018 to 376,000 (U.S. Courts, 2019). Therefore, career coaches are strongly encouraged to secure liability insurance if practicing privately.

Professional liability insurance is an insurance policy to protect against a grievance from a regulatory board, claim, or lawsuit. Many career coaches and counselors carry liability insurance above and beyond their employer's offers. The American Counseling Association is one resource to help begin the liability insurance exploration process. Their website, Malpractice Insurance for Counselors (hpso.com), has many resources and references related to this topic. Career coaches who do not qualify for some types of malpractice insurance for counselors may choose to carry general liability insurance or errors and omission (EO) insurance. EO protects individuals and companies from claims of negligence or failure to perform duties. Clients sometimes file suits indicating there has been an act of negligence on the part of the coach or an unacceptable omission or error in their services, so having insurance is recommended.

A Summary of Ethics and Coaching

As the career coaching industry grows, the ethical and legal issues also increase. Ethical guidelines and principles put forth by the American Counseling Association (2014), the National Career Development Association (2015), and the International Coaching Federation (2021) strengthen the work performed by career coaches. These organizations exist for educational purposes and provide oversight to practicing coaches and their clients.

Although there is no way to prevent ethical dilemmas, the potential for their occurrence can be minimized. As discussed in this chapter, practicing ethical career coaching is one way. Another is regularly reflecting on ethical principles and their application to the coaching practice. Career coaches have various ethical codes to choose from, depending on their professional affiliations and credentialing. Following a code of ethics, such as the NCDA *Code of Ethics* (2015), is one way to ensure a trustworthy resource and a guiding compass are part of the coaching practice. When in doubt, seek assistance from a trusted professional or organization.

Knowledge Check

1. Define "ethics." Do ethics differ from values? If so, how?
2. Why is it important to operate within a professional code of ethics in career coaching?
3. When executing ethical decision-making, what are the six steps for addressing an ethical dilemma?
4. Why is informed consent necessary in career coaching?

K-W-L Model – What Have I Learned?

To conclude this chapter, revisit the K-W-L model to assess whether this chapter provided you with information to fill some of your knowledge gaps. Finally, reflect on what you ***learned*** from this chapter and how you can apply your new knowledge to your coaching practice.

References

American Counseling Association. (2014). *ACA code of ethics*. Author. https://www.counseling.org/resources/aca-code-of-ethics.pdf

Bebeau, M. J., Rest, J. R., & Yamoor, C. M. (1985). Measuring dental students' ethical sensitivity. *Journal of Dental Education, 49*(4), 225-235.

Brennan, D., & Wildflower, L. (2018). Ethics in coaching. In E. Cox, T. Bachkirova, & D. Clutterbuck (Eds.), *The Complete Handbook of Coaching* (3rd ed., pp. 500-517). Sage.

Brock, V. (2006). Where do we align our ethical code? Learning from other professions. *Choice, 4*(3), 42-45.

Buceta, J. M. (1993). The sport psychologist/athletic coach dual role: Advantages, difficulties, and ethical considerations. *Journal of Applied Sport Psychology, 5*(1), 64-77.

Corey, G., Corey, M. S., Corey, C., & Callahan, P. (2014). *Issues and ethics in the helping profession* (9th ed.). Thomas Brooks/Cole Cengage Learning.

de Jong, A. (2010). Coaching ethics: Integrity in the moment of choice. In J. Passmore (Ed.), *Excellence in Coaching* (2nd ed., pp. 204-214). Association for Coaching.

Ellickson, K. A., & Brown, D. R. (1990). Ethical considerations in dual relationships: The sport psychologist-coach. *Journal of Applied Sport Psychology, 2*(2), 186-190. https://doi.org/10.1080/10413209008406429

Engel, J. F., Blackwell, R. D., & Miniard., P. W. (1990). *Consumer behaviour.* Dryden Press.

International Coaching Federation. (2021). *ICF code of ethics.* https://coachingfederation.org/ethics/code-of-ethics

Iordanou, I., & Williams, P. (2016). Developing ethical capabilities of coaches. In S. D. Bachkirova (Ed.), *The Sage Handbook of Coaching* (p. 696-712). Sage.

Jenkins, J. A. (2018). *Let's keep legal protection for older employees strong.* AARP. https://www.aarp.org/politics-society/advocacy/info-2018/keep-fighting-age-discrimination.html

Kitchener, K. S. (2000). *Foundations of ethical practice, research, and teaching in psychology.* Lawrence Erlbaum Associates.

Makela, J. P. & Perlus, J. G. (2017). *A case study approach to ethics in career development* (2nd ed.). National Career Development Association.

Molinsky, A. (2013). *Global dexterity.* Harvard Business School Publishing.

National Career Development Association. (2015). *2015 NCDA code of ethics.* https://www.ncda.org/aws/NCDA/asset_manager/get_file/3395

National Career Development Association. (2021). Mission statement. https://ncda.org/aws/NCDA/pt/sp/about

Oxford English Dictionary. (n.d.). Ethics. *Oxford Lexicon.* Retrieved October 1, 2021, from https://www.lexico.com/en/definition/ethics

Oxford English Dictionary. (n.d.). Law. *Oxford Lexicon.* Retrieved September 10, 2021, from https://www.lexico.com/en/definition/law

Oxford English Dictionary. (n.d.). Morals. *Oxford Lexicon.* Retrieved October 1, 2021, from https://www.lexico.com/en/definition/morals

Oxford English Dictionary. (n.d.). Values. *Oxford Lexicon.* Retrieved September 10, 2021, from https://www.lexico.com/en/definition/values

U. S. Census Bureau. (2020). 2020 census state redistricting data (public law 94-171) summary file. Author. https://www2.census.gov/programs-surveys/decennial/2020/technical-documentation/complete-tech-docs/summary-file/2020Census_PL94_171Redistricting_StatesTechDoc_English.pdf

U.S. Courts. (2019). *Federal judicial caseload statistics 2019.* https://www.uscourts.gov/statistics-reports/federal-judicial-caseload-statistics-2019

Welfel, E. R. (2006). *Ethics in counseling and psychotherapy: Standards, research, and emerging issues.* Thomson.

Zur, O., & Anderson, S. K. (2006). Multiple-role relationships in coaching. In P. Williams & S. K. Anderson (Eds.), *Law and ethics in coaching: How to solve and avoid difficult problems in your practice* (pp. 126-199). Wiley & Sons.

CHAPTER 5
Assessments for Use in Career Coaching

"Your own self-realization is the greatest service you can render the world."

– Ramana Maharshi

Chapter Highlights

This chapter will discuss the use of assessments in career coaching. Assessments are one tool in a career coach's toolbox to help the coach and client better understand the client's sense of self and its impact on career choice and the world of work. In addition, assessments can help gather information to make informed career and workforce decisions.

Learning Objectives

This chapter highlights the following:

1. The theory behind assessment application
2. Evaluation and identification of assessments based on client preference and appropriateness to the coaching plan
3. Administration or triage of assessments as needed
4. Creating a coaching plan that incorporates the results of the client's assessment information in an ethical manner

K – W - L

Now that you know what the chapter has to offer, take a few minutes to assess your knowledge level and areas of learning using the K-W-L model. The first step in the K-W-L model is to self-assess what you already ***know*** about incorporating assessments in the career coaching cycle of exploration. What are things to consider when choosing to administer assessments? Are all assessments suitable for all clients? Next, think about what you ***want*** to know about assessments for use in career coaching. Where do you feel are the gaps in your knowledge or use of assessments for career coaching? Finally, to conclude this chapter, you will be asked to revisit the K-W-L model to assess whether this chapter provided you with information to fill some of your knowledge gaps. Reflect on what you ***learned*** from this chapter and how you can apply this learning to your coaching practice.

An Introduction to Assessments

Chapter 2, The Fundamentals of Career Coaching, covered how assessments are one of the many tools used in the coaching process. However, many people know very little about the career development process or the role of assessments to augment the process. Instead, they might imagine that taking an assessment is what career coaching is all about. Specifically, a client may think, "take a test, and this test will tell you what you want to do with your life." However, career coaches know this is not the case. No assessment exists to define one's career path. Instead, career exploration is a process, and assessments are an informative, reflective tool within that process. Using assessments as a coaching tool works because

- Clients reflect on information about themselves that they might have never thought to discover.
- The information produced from an assessment offers greater depth to coaching conversations.
- Assessments offer a common language to work with during the coaching process.
- Assessments offer a level of standardization within the career coaching industry.
- Formal assessments allow the coach to quantify and compare data accurately.

- Informal assessments offer creativity in the exploration process not offered by formal assessments.

Assessments help clients understand their own career needs and possibilities and aid career coaches in assisting their clients in realizing these possibilities. It is often difficult to cover all career coaching topics with clients in a single or even multiple coaching sessions. However, assessments can efficiently deliver valuable feedback, save time, and help clients gather information about themselves, career options, and other work-related opportunities. A deeper dive into assessments and their application can be beneficial to the practice of coaching.

What is an Assessment?

An **assessment** is "any systematic method of obtaining information, used to draw inferences about characteristics of people, objects, or programs; a systematic process to measure or evaluate the characteristics or performance of individuals, programs, or other entities, for purposes of drawing inference" (American Educational Research Association, American Psychological Association, National Council on Measurement in Education, 2014, p. 216).

A **test** is "an evaluative device or procedure in which a systematic sample of a test taker's behavior in a specified domain is obtained and scored using a standardized process" (American Educational Research Association, American Psychological Association, National Council on Measurement in Education, 2014, p. 224).

Although the words assessment, test, and instrument are distinct, they are often interchangeable. However, assessment is a broader term than test, and it usually refers to a process that combines test data with data from other sources, such as intake interviews, a client's work history, and other test results. In short, assessment is a verb and a noun. For example, a career coach might administer a values assessment (noun) to obtain detailed information about their client's value preferences. Upon receiving the assessment results, the coach conducts an assessment (verb) of the client's occupational interests.

Assessment Literacy

Career coaches should have a sufficient understanding of tests and assessments to make informed judgments about which tests to use and interpret results. This process is known as assessment literacy. The American Educational Research Association, American Psychological Association, and the National Council on Measurement in Education (2014) define assessment literacy as possessing "knowledge about testing that supports valid interpretations of test scores for their intended purposes, such as knowledge about test development practices, test score interpretations, threats to valid score interpretations, score reliability and precision, test administration, and use" (p. 216).

Assessment Measures

Assessment measures or constructs are the concept or characteristics that a test is designed to measure (The American Educational Research Association, American Psychological Association, and the National Council on Measurement in Education, 2014). Constructs include abilities, achievements, aptitudes, attitudes, career success, communication, intelligence, interests, job satisfaction, knowledge, managerial potential, motivation, personality traits, skills, strengths, vocation, work styles, work values, and more.

Measurement Techniques

Standardized and non-standardized tests, card sorts, checklists, memory boards, mind maps, questionnaires, inventories, observations, portfolios, performance assessments, rating scales, surveys, and interviews are some of the many quantitative and qualitative assessment measurement techniques.

Who Uses Assessments?

A wide variety of professionals in many industries use assessments. Some include career coaches/counselors, academic advisors, guidance counselors, workforce readiness professionals, military personnel, clergy, psychologists/psychiatrists, faculty, human resource professionals, management professionals, and more. These professionals administer assessments for decision-making, hiring, staff development, leadership, promotion, project management, learning, competencies identification, employee engagement, change, conflict management, strengths and needs, work style, personality, problem-solving, team synergy, values identification, and workplace philosophy development.

Career Assessments

Career or vocational assessments are instruments designed to help individuals understand how various personal and professional attributes or constructs impact their alignment and fulfillment with different career options and work environments. The American Educational Research Association, American Psychological Association, and the National Council on Measurement in Education (2014) define a vocational assessment as "a specialized type of psychological assessment designed to generate hypotheses and inferences about interests, work needs and values, career development, vocational maturity, and indecision" (p. 225).

Brief History of Career Assessments

Just as career counseling theory has evolved, so too have career assessments. Various assessments have met the changing needs of individuals and the workforce for over 100 years. This monograph aims not to offer an exhaustive account of the history of career assessments; however, in terms of career interventions using assessments, historians (Duarte, 2009; Pope, 2015; Pope, 2000) categorize these intervention periods into three models: vocational guidance, career education, and life design.

Period 1: Enhancing self-knowledge, increasing occupational information, and matching self to occupation via the *Vocational Guidance Model.* Vocational guidance encompasses intelligence, interests, and occupational assessments.

Period 2: Assessing development status, orienting the client to imminent developmental tasks, and developing competencies, beliefs, and attitudes for mastering tasks via *Career Education and Counseling Work Model.* Career education and counseling encompass career development (maturity, values, concerns) and career interest assessments.

Period 3: Constructing one's career through short stories, reconstructing those short stories into larger, identity narratives, and co-constructing the scenarios into one's life portrait via *Life Design Interventions Model.* Life design encompasses informal assessments, occupational information, and inventories related to social and cultural justice.

Today, career coaches are more imaginative and contextualized than ever before in incorporating career assessments into their work. As described in Chapter 3, bridging theory to practice has allowed the career industry to develop and utilize assessments in strategic and individualized ways to evolve the coaching process.

Assessments in Career Coaching

When deemed appropriate, assessments can be helpful in the career exploration, development, and planning process. However, the sheer volume of assessments available can be overwhelming. What criteria does a coach use to determine which assessment to employ to provide the type of feedback the client seeks? How does the coach measure the suitable construct to determine which assessment is the appropriate one to administer? Key constructs dictate the assessment; therefore, it is essential to clarify the client's goals. There are four areas where assessments are supportive to the career coaching process: career exploration, career decision-making, educational planning, and career adjustment.

Career Exploration

Using assessments for career exploration helps clients understand how their skills, interests, values, and personality preferences connect with possible career options. Drummond and colleagues (2016) posited that career interests are a set of beliefs or attitudes toward a given activity, and that interest is linked to motivation to engage in that activity. Work values are cognitive, emotional, and behavioral factors that manifest as beliefs (Osborn & Zunker, 2016), playing an important role in career decision-making. Work skills allow clients to organize, execute, and perform a specific job function based on certain skills (Stoltz & Barclay, 2019). Finally, personality assessments help clients determine current educational attainment and needs for developing and implementing a career plan based on preferences related to personality. For instance, clients might consider workplace culture or environment that positively aligns with their personality when making a career choice.

The career exploration process can be overwhelming and intimidating, quickly leading to frustration and burnout. Using assessments for career exploration helps clients better understand themselves and focus on the plethora of available resources. A few examples of career exploration assessments include O*NET Interest Profiler, Strong Interest Inventory, and others. In addition, many interest assessments use occupational matching based on the *Dictionary of Occupational Titles*, which has over 14,000 occupations categorized by career interest codes. A three-letter career interest code forms the results of a completed interest assessment, based on Holland's (1997) RIASEC model, which can then be cross-matched to the *Dictionary of Occupational Titles* to identify patterns in career interests with occupational options.

Career Decision-Making

Assessments can be useful in helping clients make effective career decisions by understanding their decision-making based on life stages or stages of the career planning process. Career indecision is the inability to express an educational or occupational choice and delays bringing closure to the career choice process (Slaney, 1988). Many clients will experience barriers to decision-making in various forms, such as:

- *Career decision-making self-efficacy.* Research suggests that individuals with higher levels of self-efficacy have little or no issue making career decisions. In contrast, those showing a lack of structure or confidence have difficulty making career decisions or avoid such decisions (Taylor & Betz, 1983).
- *Career beliefs.* Beliefs and assumptions block or prevent individuals from taking constructive action (Krumboltz, 1994).
- *Self-concept.* Self-concept is a person's assessment of themselves or what they think of themselves (positive or negative) and their ability to make career decisions based on this assessment (Super, 1990).

Assessments in this category also identify potential barriers to career exploration and decision-making. As a coach, it is important to empower clients to work through barriers to decision-making by recognizing first that the barriers exist, second, clients can overcome barriers, and lastly, there are strategies to help the client overcome the barriers. Career assessments can be a powerful tool in this process. A few examples of career decision-making assessments include Decisional Process Inventory, Career Decision Self-Efficacy Scale, the Career Beliefs Inventory, and Career Decision-Making Difficulties Questionnaire.

Educational Planning

Working with clients to identify education or training needs related to career advancement is a solid use of career assessments. For instance, a client might be interested in pursuing career paths that utilize a specific set of skills but unaware of how these skills might apply to the world of work. An inventory like SkillScan can offer occupations that match one's skillset. One could research these occupations to determine the education level needed to enter an occupation. Educational assessment systems geared toward early-career explorers (middle school to high school) combine multiple assessments (value, skills, interests) and match academic study with early career decision-making. One example is the COPSystem, which combines the Career Ability Placement Survey (CAPS), the Career Occupational Preference System Interest Inventory (COPS), and the Career Orientation Placement and Evaluation Survey (COPES).

Clients might also be interested in career assessments that measure achievement or aptitude. An aptitude is a skill, inclination, or talent inherited or developed due to upbringing and life experiences (Osborn & Zunker, 2016). An achievement test measures a client's mastery of a specific skill or knowledge in a subject area in which the person has received some instruction or training. In addition, aptitude tests estimate a client's future performance on a task and/or aptitude to develop new skills or knowledge if provided instruction or training. Essentially, achievement tests assess current performance after specific training; aptitude tests assess the potential for future performance. Examples include the Differential Aptitude Test, General Aptitude Test Battery, and the Adult Basic Learning Examination (ABLE).

Career Adjustment

Concerning career adjustment, a coach can be instrumental in helping clients determine appropriate next steps in their career transition. Career adjustment can reduce stress to address more serious career-related mental health issues. A coach can use assessments to help clients reposition their current working environment to be productive and satisfying when a career change is impossible. For example, the Career Adapt-Abilities Scale (CAAS) measures clients' perceived competence across four dimensions of career adaptability: concern, control, curiosity, and confidence (Savickas & Porfeli, 2012 as cited in Stoltz & Barclay, 2019). The Career Futures Inventory (CFI-R) provides insight into a client's optimism, career agency, support, work-life balance, and occupational awareness (Rottinghaus et al., 2012). Another assessment option related to career adjustment is job crafting (Berg et al., 2008). Clients who engage in job crafting alter the boundaries of their current job to create a more desired work environment. Altering boundaries might include taking on additional responsibilities in a partnering department to utilize an under-developed skill or learning a new aspect of a colleague's role so collaboration can take place. A client's imagination and support from their organization are two key ingredients to job crafting. The process could combine multiple formal and informal assessments to reveal needed information as the job crafting assessment is completed within the coaching setting.

Should an Assessment be Used?

It is not always necessary or fitting to use assessments in the coaching process. A career coach must set guidelines for evaluating when assessments (and what type of assessments) might enhance or contribute to the coaching conversation when working with clients. Here are general guidelines to follow in determining whether a coaching situation warrants the use of an assessment:

- **Client/instrument goals:** Be clear on the client's goals before deciding to administer an assessment and clearly define what information is intended to be learned from the instrument results.
- **Identify and research options:** Based on the information, coaches should think about how the information will contribute to the client's career goals and determine

the most appropriate assessments available. Determining the appropriate assessment may require research into the variety of assessments available. Next, create a list of available assessments that measure what needs to be measured.

- **Narrow the list:** From the list generated in step two, determine which assessments are accessible. The coach should ensure they are qualified to purchase, administer and interpret the selected assessments. For example, regarding accessibility, the cost is one point to consider: some assessments are free, while others have varying price points. Time is another factor to consider. Many assessments are open source or widely accessible for purchase, but others require author permission to administer. If author permission is required, it may take additional time to seek user approval.
- **Credentialing level** is also an important consideration. Ethically speaking, choosing assessments the coach is qualified to administer is essential. There are strict ethical guidelines associated with administering assessments in the helping professions. Career coaches should maintain the ethical standards set by the American Counseling Association (2014) *Code of Ethics* (see Appendix F) and the National Career Development Association (2015) *Code of Ethics* (see Appendix E).

If the assessment is unfamiliar, it may be worthwhile for the coach to complete pre-work before administering and interpreting. First, it is essential to review any assessment's validity, reliability, and credibility before administering. Next, the coach should test the assessment (on his or herself or a willing volunteer) to ensure familiarity in administering. Finally, review the test results to understand how to interpret them. To protect the welfare of clients, only share results with individuals who are qualified to interpret the results obtained from the instruments. These steps will ensure that the assessment under consideration will provide the information the client seeks.

Administering Assessments

Once a coach has determined that the use of an assessment is appropriate, the coach may want to answer additional questions:

- Why do I want to administer an assessment to this client?
- What do I want to know about this client (or what do they want to know about themselves)?
- What type of information can this assessment help us gather about the client to inform their goals?
- What type of assessment would be most appropriate in helping us gather the information we want to uncover?

Biswas-Diener (2010) uses a positive psychology approach to coaching, addressing the question, "What is going right for this individual?" This approach can also be applied when administering and interpreting assessments. Using assessments as a tool in a positive diagnostic (non-medical) coaching model works because assessments generally focus on depth and breadth of information not otherwise discussed in a typical coaching session. The assessment provides the coach and the client with valid, reliable data to guide or inform the discussion.

Once the coach has chosen a suitable assessment(s) to administer, ensure the following:

1. The coach is licensed and/or certified (see the Credentialing and Competencies section, to follow) and trained to administer the assessment
2. Schedule an assessment session; obtain access to assessment; prepare testing materials
3. Administer the assessment
   a. Discuss the instructions for taking the assessment with the client
   b. Reiterate the purpose and nature of the assessment and what will happen with the data once the assessment is completed
   c. Provide all materials (computer, pencil,

paper, assessment, room) needed to take the assessment comfortably

d. Ensure the client's space during the assessment is quiet and distraction-free

COACH CORNER

Things to Consider Before You Administer

Administering assessments must be done with care. There are many things to consider before a coach introduces an assessment into the career coaching conversation.

- Training, certification, or credentials needed to administer and interpret
- Administer with purpose (why) and specificity (how)
- Comfort-level with interpreting the test results
- Cost of assessment
- Ease of administering (in person, virtual, test-center)
- Flesch-Kincaid Readability Test Tool (i.e., suggested education level to easily understand the test)
- Accessibility (e.g., closed caption)
- Client's interest in taking an assessment
- Use as a tool in considering the whole-person approach to coaching

Interpreting Assessments

One of the most important aspects of the assessment process is interpretation, which helps the client understand the instrument results related to career decision-making. After administering an assessment, the coach should debrief the assessment results with the client as early as possible. When debriefing, there is a structure that the coach can employ, which aligns with the practice of positive psychology (see Chapter 3). This feedback is optimistic and motivating, keeping the conversation focused on what is possible (i.e., the future), less on past challenges or current setbacks. The assessment results become possibilities that correspond with the client's goals when the coach demonstrates what is conceivable and what opportunities exist. This purposeful, actionable, and specific feedback structure helps reduce anxiety in the debriefing session.

Before debriefing assessment results with the client, the coach must thoroughly analyze the results to understand the results, strengths, and limitations. The debrief session aims to inform clients of the results and actively encourage participation in test interpretation. Therefore having a strategy in place before the meeting is essential. The trust and rapport between coach and client are key to navigating a successful interpretation. A coach should formulate personal goals for the following questions:

- What do I want my client to take away from the debriefing session?
- What coaching methods will I employ to elicit client input during the debrief meeting?
- How will I know if the meeting was fruitful and achieved my client's objectives?

Begin the assessment debrief meeting by reviewing the client's previously disclosed professional goals or concerns and occupational interest areas highlighted during earlier coaching sessions. Next, remind the client why that particular

COACH CORNER

Assessment data
(i.e., standard scores, percentile ranks, etc.)
goes through three transformations:

1) Data must first be transformed into information (e.g., career options);
2) Options become actions (e.g., activities and experiences)
3) Activities and experiences become possible career plans.

assessment was chosen and the type of results the report generates (e.g., personality profile, interest inventory). Finally, give the client time to share their thoughts on taking the assessment (e.g., confusing, familiar, lengthy, enjoyable).

Provide the client with an electronic and hard copy of the assessment results (or elicit their preference before the meeting). Give the client time to think about their results and ask or jot down questions throughout each report section. Then, connect the results to the client's career plan as each section is detailed. Complete this step in phases: first, overview the assessment itself, and second, connect the client's results directly to their career goals. Taking the time to adequately explain the results, address client queries, and relate the results to career aspirations is critical, regardless of the debriefing strategy.

Actions After Assessing

Helping clients become self-aware is a critical skill that can contribute significantly to their success and well-being. Therefore, it is critical to co-create action items based on the client's career goals once they have a comprehensive and comfortable knowledge of the report contents. These action items should be believable, conceivable, and achievable. For example, a coach may ask a client, "Is it achievable to set a goal of investigating five of the occupations mentioned in the suggested occupational match section for us to discuss at our next appointment?" In this case, the coach may also ask the client which ones they would like to explore before the next meeting. If these are occupations that the coach is not familiar with, the coach may perform a preliminary occupational study in preparation for the next coaching session. Finally, revisit and weave report results into future career discussions, goal setting, and career wins as coaching sessions continue.

The Role of Technology in Career Assessments

Technology has and continues to evolve rapidly, making assessments more convenient and innovative in career planning. But, more importantly, technology has removed many barriers and limitations in connecting and delivering career assessments. Video, adaptive testing, administering to large numbers of people, rapid results generation, audio administration are examples of how technology has revolutionized what once was a paper and pencil, coach-to-client, face-to-face process.

With so many tools available and the growing incorporation of technology into assessments, career coaches must be careful in choosing and using these tools when assisting clients with their career decisions. Osborn et al. (2019) detail the use of computer-assisted career assessments (CACAs), discussing the current trends, benefits of use, limitations, ethical considerations, and future insights of these tools. In the COVID world, the use of CACAs will likely increase, as will virtual career coaching. However, be mindful of the ethical considerations surrounding using technology in administering assessments (see the section on Ethical Considerations in the Use of Assessments), storing data, and privacy. Online assessments may or may not have psychometric evidence to support their use. Individuals may purchase these online assessments without a coach yet cannot consider the assessment's results or limitations. A coach learning of a client's assessment purchase during a coaching session is one example of the many ethical challenges related to technology and assessment.

Credentialing and Competencies

Credentialing Level

Some assessments require specific qualifications to administer. Therefore, it is critical to understand the requirements for administering an assessment before using it. Psychological Assessment Resources (PAR; parinc.com), a publisher of psychological assessment materials, separates qualifications into the following levels:

Level A

Instruments require no special qualifications to administer. However, ethically, a coach should self-test the instrument before using it, observe the instrument being administered by a trained professional, and ask for a trained professional to supervise during the first solo instrument administration with a client. Examples of Level A instruments include Focus 2, Kuder Career Planning System, and the O*NET Interest Profiler.

Level B

In addition to meeting the requirements in Level A, to administer Level B instruments, a professional must hold a degree from an accredited four-year college or university in psychology or counseling-related field. Additionally, a professional must have completed coursework in test interpretation, psychometrics and measurement theory, educational statistics, or a closely related area; or hold a license or certification from an agency/organization with psychological testing standards that are ethical and require appropriate training and experience. Level B instruments include the Myers-Briggs Type Indicator (MBTI), Strong Interest Inventory, and the Campbell Interest and Skills Inventory.

Level C

In addition to Level A and B requirements, to administer Level C instruments, a professional must hold an advanced degree which encompasses appropriate training in the administration and interpretation of psychological tests; or a license or certification from an agency that requires appropriate training and experience in the ethical and competent use of psychological tests. The Minnesota Multiphasic Personality Inventory is an example of a Level C.

Level S

A professional must hold a degree, certificate, or license to practice in a physical or mental health care profession or occupation (e.g., nursing, social work), in addition to ethical training and experience with administration, scoring, and interpretation of clinical behavioral assessments.

Visit PAR's website at https://www.parinc.com/Support/Qualification-Levels to learn more about qualification levels and determine eligibility.

Competencies

In 2010, NCDA partnered with the Association for Assessment and Counseling in Education (AACE) to create coaching competencies to develop and evaluate training, workshops, and other continuing education opportunities and guide and evaluate the coach's professional development.

NCDA and AACE's goal was to set a standard by which all career coaches sought to exhibit the specific knowledge, understanding, and skills listed under each competency. Competencies related to knowledge, understanding, and skills of each are as follows:

Competency 1 - *choosing assessment strategies.*

Competency 2 - *identifying, accessing, and evaluating the most commonly used assessment instruments.*

Competency 3 - *administration and scoring assessment instruments.*

Competency 4 - *interpreting and reporting assessment results.*

Competency 5 - *using assessment results in decision making.*

Competency 6 - *producing, interpreting, and presenting statistical information about assessment results.*

Competency 7 - *engaging in professionally responsible assessment and evaluation practices.*

Competency 8 - *using assessment results and other data to evaluate career programs and interventions* (National Career Development Association, 2010).

Visit the NCDA.org website for a full explanation of the specific knowledge, understandings, and skills listed under each competency.

Ethical Considerations in the Use of Assessments

When administering and interpreting assessments, regardless of the code the coach chooses to follow (see Chapter 4), there are five ethical principles (Corey et al., 2014) essential to adhere to when using assessments in career coaching:

1. The primary consideration when administering and interpreting assessments is ***do no harm***.
2. As a career coach, make sure clients know and understand the services offered, qualifications related to those services, and how services will be offered. An ***informed consent form*** (see Appendix C) can help you communicate this information and ensure a common understanding.
3. Maintain ***Documentation*** to the best of your ability and recollection.
4. Assessment records and other documentation should be kept private, and to release these records, the client must give informed consent for release. Abiding by this ethical consideration ensures ***confidentiality***.

The NCDA website has several resources on ethical guidelines for administering and interpreting assessments, such as the "Career Counselor Assessment and Evaluation Competencies" (2010) and Stoltz & Barclay's (2019) *A Comprehensive Guide to Career Assessment* (7th ed.). In addition, see Chapter 4 for more on ethics related to using assessments in career coaching.

Assessment Quality and Appropriateness

A coach should understand that no assessment instrument will measure a trait or ability with perfect accuracy for every person and that no instrument will be completely accurate in predicting performance or job satisfaction. Selecting an instrument with confidence depends on several factors. Here are a few test qualities to consider:

Reliability

Reliability is the reproduction of assessment results when repeated under the same conditions. Reliability equals consistency (Capuzzi & Stauffer, 2018). It is important to note that a high-reliability score does not indicate accurate test results. The results might be reproducible, but they are not necessarily correct.

Validity

The degree to which the test measures what it intends to measure refers to its validity. A coach should read the manual or research to determine validity (Stoltz & Barclay, 2019). Validity provides integrity for assessments – the higher the validity, the more accurate the test measure (Capuzzi & Stauffer, 2018).

Standard Error of Measurement

As mentioned previously, no test can predict, with complete accuracy, performance, job satisfaction, or desired career path. Therefore, inherent variability also exists in scoring assessments. Listed below are factors that might cause variability (Capuzzi & Stauffer, 2018).

Psychological state. A person's psychological or physical state can influence assessment test performance. Anxiety, fatigue, or motivation levels may affect an individual's test results, as well as debriefing results post-assessment.

Environmental Factors. Testing environment fluctuations, like room temperature, lighting, noise, or site administrator, can influence a client's test performance.

Test version. Ongoing research continuously prompts language and measure updates, requiring new test versions. Items may differ on each version, but each version is still supposed to measure the same construct. Different test versions are parallel or alternate forms, designed with similar measurement characteristics but containing different items. A test taker might do better on one form than on another.

Multiple Raters. A rater's judgments of the test taker's performance or responses determine scoring in specific tests. Additionally, raters can have different experiences, training, and frames of reference, producing different test scores for the test taker. Multiple raters are also common in data collection for qualitative and mixed-methods research purposes.

Other Considerations. Limitation considerations are not always in the test itself. Free versions of the same or similar assessments may not meet the reliability or validity intended for more formal assessments. In addition, there may be limitations in the coach's or the department budgets, which prohibit specific assessment offerings. On the other hand, limited funding may lead to using free versions, which clients interpret themselves.

Assessment Bias

What is Bias?

Bias is an attitude or belief towards or against a person, group, or thing (Oxford English Dictionaries, n.d.). Coaches have biases that influence how they work with clients. Clients also bring biases into the coaching relationship. As a coach, (1) recognizing your biases, (2) understanding that your biases limit your effectiveness, and (3) knowing that biases impact your client's self-understanding in a variety of ways is essential.

There are two types of bias recognized in the literature: explicit or conscious bias and implicit or unconscious bias.

Explicit or Conscious Bias

Early learning and exposure to mainstream depictions of specific groups lead to conscious bias.

It is important to recognize bias in ourselves and others and manage them. Specific examples of conscious bias might be perceiving confident people as competent, women as natural nurturers, or men as mechanically inclined. Laws and policies combat prejudice based on color, age, gender, gender identity, physical ability, religion, sexual orientation, and other factors; however, bias still exists. Examples of how coaches could bring conscious bias into the coaching relationship may include:

- Feelings that younger clients are less-experienced
- Thoughts that international clients are harder to employ
- Opinions that coach is a better match with male clients

Examples of how clients could bring conscious bias into the coaching relationship may include:

- A male client wants to be a nurse but feels he cannot pursue this female-dominated occupation
- Female career coaches are more empathetic
- Thoughts about age, such as, "I cannot switch careers later in life; no one will hire me because of my age."

Unconscious or Implicit

Unconscious or implicit biases are social stereotypes about individuals or groups that form outside of conscious awareness. The Kirwan Institute for the Study of Race and Ethnicity defines implicit bias as

> the unconscious attitudes and stereotypes we hold about different groups of people that influence our actions. Operating outside of conscious awareness, the implicit associations we form through a lifetime of direct and indirect messages about groups of people can cause us to have unconscious attitudes about people based on characteristics like race, ethnicity, and gender. Whether we realize it or not, these associations, positive or negative, can influence our behavior and decisions. (Jackson, 2018, p. 2)

Unconscious bias operates outside of awareness and can directly contradict beliefs and values. People are hardwired to make unconscious decisions about others based on what feels safe, likable, and valuable. In the coach/client relationship, unconscious bias can impact assessment, decision-making, and clients' set career goals.

There are resources to evaluate implicit bias: The Implicit Association Test (IAT; https://implicit.harvard.edu/implicit) measures attitudes and beliefs that people may be unwilling or unable to report. The IAT may show that an individual has an unknown implicit bias. For example, you may believe that all genders should be equally associated with careers in engineering, but your automatic association may reveal that you associate males with careers in engineering.

Acknowledging Bias

Research by Dobbin et al. (2007) showed that simply acknowledging the existence of bias is not enough to prevent its adverse effects. To better understand and address implicit bias, Dr. David Rock, Director of the NeuroLeadership Institute (NLI), coined the term *neuroleadership*. The NeuroLeadership Institute creates brain-friendly talent strategies and educates learners about the brain at all levels, resulting in better decision-making, dialogues, and outcomes around bias. The NLI offers a three-step process for reducing the effects of bias:

1. ***Accept:*** Accept your own bias and the bias of others. Understand that bias is normal and that everyone holds bias.
2. ***Label:*** Label bias to create a shared language, calling out bias in a respectful and meaningful way. The SEEDS Model (described in the next section) is one example.
3. ***Mitigate:*** Implement strategies and commit to mitigating the adverse effects of bias.

How Does One Make Sense of Bias?

The NLI has condensed 150+ biases into five main categories that make up the SEEDS Model (Weller, 2019) to make them more accessible and easily retrievable:

- **Similarity: Preference (for people like oneself):** Similarity views people who look or think like me more favorably than people who do not look or think like me.
- **Expedience: Familiarity and ease:** Expedience tends to rush to judgment without considering all the facts (e.g., "she is too short to play professional basketball").
- **Experience: Belief that perception is accurate:** Experience tends to believe that seeing the world my way is inherently more

accurate than someone else's perspective (e.g., "my way of formatting a résumé will yield more interviews than your formatting method").

- **Distance: Proximity impacts perception:** Distance tends to assign greater value to things people perceive to be closer to themselves than further away (e.g., "in-person workers are more productive than remote workers").
- **Safety: Loss/gain:** Safety bias is about loss/gain and being "safe" in my decision-making (i.e., not taking healthy risks).

In summary, it takes time and energy to pay attention to and process information unique to each client. When coaches operate under a significant cognitive load, there is little energy available to attend to the uniqueness of any given client. Therefore, it is essential to recognize and accept biases and identify them early. Coaches should continue dissecting their biases and deciding which biases they will address first. Evans & Sejuit (2021) dedicate a chapter to exploring biases as a career professional in their recent publication *Gaining Cultural Competence in Career Counseling* (2nd ed.). Coaches can continue to educate and remind themselves that biases exist. Doing so is key to reducing individual biases so that coaches can open themselves up to the excellent work they do with their clients.

Formal and Informal Assessments

Formal Assessments

Formal assessments, often known as standardized tests, are content-specific tests produced by specialists with high scientific rigor, reliability, and validity. Formal assessments necessitate specialized procedures for preparing, conducting, and interpreting. As mentioned earlier, validity and reliability matter to establish confidence in the assessment results. Formal assessment validity and reliability scores are available in each assessment's technical manual (print or online) or in publications like NCDA's *A Comprehensive Guide to Career Assessment* (7th ed.; Stoltz & Barclay, 2019).

Formal Assessments Categories

Formal assessments measure abilities, interests, personality, skills, work values, and other constructs. Availability and use may largely depend on access (budget, subscription, membership) and qualification level (Level A, B, or C). Formal assessments typically produce scores or score profiles as part of their results as they are developed according to scientific principles of test construction. In print or digital format, a coach can administer in controlled conditions involving standard instructions, with suggested or specified time limits, and occasionally employ test monitors or testing materials. The following list of ways to measure abilities, beliefs, maturity, interest, personality, skills, work, and combined constructs are a few options available for career coaching.

Aptitudes/Abilities Tests. Abilities are developmental qualities of an individual. Aptitudes are natural strengths that precede abilities. Both provide clients with information on how well they match the demands of occupations under consideration. Examples include Tests of Adult Basic Education (TABE), Armed Services Vocational Aptitude Battery (ASVAB), WorkKeys, and YouScience.

Career Beliefs/Thoughts/Levels of Decidedness. These assessments help clients identify and understand internal barriers to career exploration and decision-making, for example, the Career Beliefs Inventory and Job Search Attitude Inventory.

Career Maturity. These assessments measure the degree to which individuals or groups have completed specific activities or tasks considered necessary for a given life stage or stage of the career planning process. Example: Adult Career Concerns Inventory (ACCI)

Interest Inventories: These provide clients with information on identifying and understanding clients' interest patterns or themes. Examples: Self-

Directed Search (SDS); Strong Interest Inventory; Career Decision-Making System (CDM); O*NET Interest Profiler; Career Key and the Kuder Career Planning System

Personality Inventories: These inventories help clients understand their preferences in school or work settings. Examples: The 16PF Questionnaire; Myers-Briggs Type Indicator (MBTI); Keirsey Temperament Sorter II

Skills Inventories: These assessments help clients identify specific skills or sets of skills they may not yet know about related to career choice. Example: SkillScan; Career Cluster Interest Survey; My Skills, My Future

Work Value Inventories: These help clients identify and describe the underlying values influencing their decision-making and career satisfaction. Examples: O*NET Work Importance Locator; True Colors; Super's Work Values Inventory

Combined Construct Platforms. These assessment platforms offer a combination of the above categories. Examples: ImaginePhD; Focus 2; O*NET; Who You Are Matters!

Informal Assessments

Many career coaches use informal or non-standardized assessments with their clients. Informal assessments are a fun, creative way to engage clients in exploration. A trained coach can help clients draw inferences from results to shed light on career choice or change. The benefit of informal assessments is that they gather information about clients through methods less structured than standardized tests. However, informal assessments are subject to misinterpretation and bias (cultural, personal) and are not scientifically measured. The validity and reliability of informal assessments are not scientifically measured, but these assessment methods can be effective in client self-exploration when used skillfully.

Informal assessments can be administered by a career coach, in person, or virtually. Informal assessment administration and interpretation often involve deep and ongoing reflection, where the coach helps the client understand themselves more thoroughly, thus supporting a clearer sense of direction and purpose for their career planning. This section offers a snapshot of several common informal assessments applicable to career coaching.

Career Portfolios. A career portfolio highlights a client's skills and experience related to a potential career path or responsibilities of an identified job through a series of artifacts collected by the client throughout their academic and professional career. Those in education, the arts, media, and other artistic domains are well-versed in using portfolios as a career and professional development tool; however, they can also be helpful in the career exploration process. To facilitate the exploration process, a coach uses powerful questioning to elicit open-ended responses from the client regarding how each artifact represents the client's skills, abilities, attributes, or knowledge and how these artifacts relate to their career goals. Clients can assemble a print or digital portfolio. Examples of digital portfolio platforms are LinkedIn, Parchment Credential, about.me, and Wix are just a few of the many options available.

Card Sorts. Various card sorts are available to assess a range of interpersonal qualities (interests, skills, values). Card sorts ask the user to rank or sort a set of options into categories. For example, an occupational card sort may have 50 cards with a different occupation listed on each card. A five-card ranking system asks the client to rank occupational options from most to least interesting. Once the ranking is complete, the coach and client discuss the reasoning behind the given answers. The coach may have the client research occupations that made it into the "most interesting" or "interesting" categories as a follow-up. O*NET Work Importance Locator is a card sort that is accessible in print for free. Additionally, Knowdell Card Sorts are a popular, cost-effective option.

Mind Mapping. Mind mapping is an informal assessment technique in which the client creates a visual representation of their ideas for career possibilities. Using a tree analogy, the client begins their exploration with a main idea (a strength, value, career interest) which serves as the trunk. From this main idea, related possibilities (branches and twigs) emerge as exploration takes place. These secondary connections are career or professional development opportunities. Mind mapping help clients visualize career possibilities and generate new ideas for growth based on relational links. Mindmup.com or Mindnode.com are two of many platforms that coaches and clients can use or simply pick up a pen and paper and begin to explore!

Guided Imagery (Visualization). Guided imagery or visualization takes the client from present career situations to imagining a more preferred state of career satisfaction. The coach facilitates this process through a structured set of questions that prompt clients to imagine their professional destiny and envision achieving that destiny. Guided imagery techniques may be helpful in career coaching because they promote divergent thinking, which enhances problem-solving ability. Appendix D highlights a simple career-related guided imagery exercise.

Career Genogram. A genogram is a three-dimensional family tree showing the linear relationships between clients and their family members and the family dynamics associated with those relationships. A career genogram is a tool that helps the client gain a clearer picture of work exposure, preferences, and attitudes based on family work history (see Figure 12). The

Figure 12
Career Genogram Example

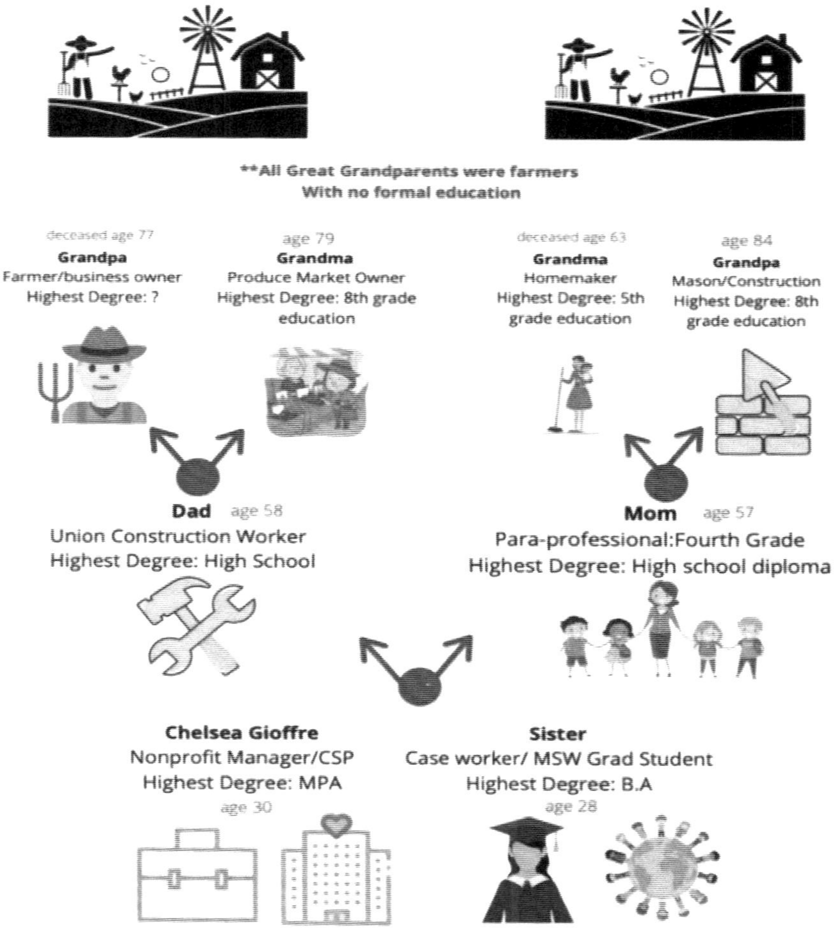

Career genogram created by Chelsea Gioffre. Used with permission.

COACH CORNER

"Informal assessments give me a chance to get to know my clients better and to connect with them where they are in the exploration process."
— Heather

family tree may include educational background, occupations, avocations, and other interests. A genogram typically spans three generations, including the client, siblings, parents, and grandparents. Also included are family members' ages of employment and retirement. Assessment debriefing occurs when a coach and client review the career genogram for patterns in skills, values, or interests. This knowledge might help the client expand their decision-making capabilities based on past family preferences.

Other Examples of Informal Assessment. Journal writing, forced-choice activities; structured or unstructured interviewing; checklists of interests, values, abilities; group discussion; job shadowing; games; and simple questionnaires are other informal assessment options for coaches to employ.

Final Thoughts on Assessments for Career Coaching

First and foremost, a career coach must realize that assessments are one piece of the comprehensive coaching process. Career coaches use assessments in working with various populations in various situations; however, they should be selective when using them, as sometimes clients think assessments will give them a quick answer to solve their career dilemmas. Often assessments confirm what the client already knows, while other times, they give the client new ideas to investigate, but self-validation is needed regardless. If a client lacks any direction, the assessments can be a good starting point. Regardless of which assessment career coaches administer, the coach needs to work closely with the client to choose an appropriate assessment based on the client's specific needs. *A Comprehensive Guide to Career Assessment* (Stoltz & Barclay, 2019) offers a deep dive into instruments and applications of a wide variety of assessments and contexts.

Checklist for Selecting and Utilizing Assessments in Coaching

- ❑ Do use assessment tools **purposefully**. Assessments are one tool in a more extensive exploration process.
- ❑ Do use the **whole-person** approach. Assessments are available to help guide the client toward making sound career decisions.
- ❑ Do **compare** career assessments to see which ones might meet the client's needs.
- ❑ Do consider **free** online assessments, but do homework on the assessment's reliability, validity, and credibility.
- ❑ Do not discount **career ideas** and **directions** the client never thought of – all possibilities are worth further exploration.
- ❑ Do critically evaluate assessments for potential bias, unfairness, or adverse impact and seek assessments **appropriate** for the client.
- ❑ Do ensure **reliability** and **validity** when using formal assessment instruments and procedures.
- ❑ Do consider having the client take **several different assessments** to help them learn more and determine which tests provide the most valid results.
- ❑ Do have the client print out and retain the results of the assessments. Then, **compare** results and look for **patterns.**
- ❑ Do **check for bias**. Assessments that create labels can potentially impact coaching.
- ❑ Do not **overthink** or rely too heavily on assessment results.
- ❑ Do ensure **proper** training and that test conditions are **suitable** for all test takers.
- ❑ Do maintain the **confidentiality** of assessment results and store results **securely.**

Knowledge Check

1. Am I able to link theory to assessment through application?
2. Am I able to identify assessments based on client preference and appropriateness to the coaching plan, including formal and informal assessment use?
3. Do I understand the importance of exploring biases and the impact of bias in the assessment process?
4. Do I feel more confident in incorporating assessment into the coaching process?
5. Do I have a stronger awareness of the assessment resources available?

K-W-L Model – What Have I Learned?

To conclude this chapter, revisit the K-W-L model to assess whether this chapter provided you with information to fill some of your knowledge gaps. Finally, reflect on what you ***learned*** from this chapter and how you can apply it to your coaching practice.

References

American Counseling Association. (2014). *ACA code of ethics*. Author. https://www.counseling.org/resources/aca-code-of-ethics.pdf

American Educational Research Association, American Psychological Association, National Council on Measurement in Education. (2014). *Standards for educational and psychological testing*. American Educational Research Association.

Berg, J. M., Dutton, J. E., & Wrzesniewski, A. (2008). *What is job crafting and why does it matter* [Theory-to-practice briefing]. Positive Organizational Scholarship University of Michigan. https://positiveorgs.bus.umich.edu/wp-content/uploads/What-is-Job-Crafting-and-Why-Does-it-Matter1.pdf

Biswas-Diener, R. (2010). *Practicing positive psychology coaching*. Wiley & Sons.

Capuzzi, D., & Stauffer, M. D. (2018). *Career counseling: Foundations, perspectives, and applications* (3rd ed.). Routledge. https://doi.org/10.4324/9781315166797

Corey, G., Corey, M. S., Corey, C., & Callahan, P. (2014). *Issues and ethics in the helping profession* (9th ed.). Thomas Brooks/Cole Cengage Learning.

CPP, Inc. (2014). *Strong Interest Inventory.* Consulting Psychologists Press.

Dobbin, F., Kalev, A., Kelly, B. (2007). Diversity management in corporate America. *Contexts 6*(4). 21–28.

Drummond, R. J., Sheperis, C. J., & Jones, K. D. (2016). *Appraisal procedures for counselors and helping professionals* (8th ed.). Merrill.

Duarte, M. E. (2009). The psychology of life construction. *Journal of Vocational Behavior, 75,* 259-266. https://doi.org/10.1016/j.jvb.2009.06.009

Evans, K. M., & Sejuit, A. L. (2021). *Gaining cultural competence in career counseling* (2nd ed.). National Career Development Association.

Holland, J. L. (1997). *Making vocational choices: A theory of careers.* Prentice-Hall.

Jackson, V. W. (2018). *Institutional interventions to prevent implicit bias from undermining organizational diversity.* The Kirwan Institute for the Study of Race and Ethnicity. http://kirwaninstitute.osu.edu/wp-content/uploads/2018/04/Combating-Implicit-Bias-in-the-workplace.pdf

Krumboltz, J. D. (1994). The Career Beliefs Inventory. *Journal of Counseling and Development, 72,* 424-428. https://doi.org/10.1002/j.1556-6676.1994.tb00962.x

Lewis, P., & Rivkin, D. (1999). *Development of the O*NET Interest Profiler.* National Center for O*NET Development Employment Security Commission. https://www.onetcenter.org/dl_files/IP.pdf

National Career Development Association. (2015). *2015 NCDA code of ethics.* https://www.ncda.org/aws/NCDA/asset_manager/get_file/3395

National Career Development Association & Association for Assessment in Counseling and Education. (2010). *Career counselor assessment and evaluation competencies.* NCDA. https://associationdatabase.com/aws/NCDA/asset_manager/get_file/18143/aace-ncda_assmt_eval_competencies?ver=47302

Osborn, D. S., Carr, D. L., Riner, M. M., Sides, R. D., Lumsden, J. A., & Sampson, J. P. (2019). Computer-assisted career assessment. In K. B. Stoltz & S. R. Barclay (Eds.), *A comprehensive guide to career assessment* (7th ed., pp. 43-58). National Career Development Association.

Osborn, D. S., & Zunker, V. G. (2016). *Using assessment results for career development* (9th ed.). Cengage Learning.

Oxford English Dictionary. (n.d.). Bias. Oxford Lexicon. Retrieved October 16, 2021, from https://www.lexico.com/en/definition/bias

Pope, M. (2000). A brief history of career counseling in the United States. *The Career Development Quarterly, 48,* 194-211.

Pope, M. (2015). Career intervention: From the industrial to the digital age. In P. J. Hartung, M. L. Savickas, & W. B. Walsh (Eds.), *APA handbook of career intervention* (pp. 3-19). American Psychological Association.

Rottinghaus, P. J., Buelow, K. L., Matyja, A., & Schneider, M. R. (2012). The career futures inventory-revised: Measuring dimensions of career adaptability. *Journal of Career Assessment, 20*(2), 123-129. https://doi.org/10.1177/1069072711420849

Savickas, M. L., & Porfeli, E. J. (2012). Career Adapt-Abilities Scale: Construction, reliability and measurement equivalence across 13 countries. *Journal of Vocational Behavior, 80,* 661-673. https://dx.doi.org/10.1016/j.jvb.2012.01.011

Slaney, R. B. (1988). The assessment of career decision-making. In W. B. Walsh and S. H. Osipow, (Eds.), *Career decision-making* (pp. 33-76). Lawrence Erlbaum Associates.

Stoltz, K. B., & Barclay, S. R. (Eds.). (2019). *A comprehensive guide to career assessment* (7th ed.). National Career Development Association.

Super, D. E. (1990). A lifespan, life-space approach to career development. In D. Brown & L. Brooks (Eds.), *Career choice and development* (2nd ed., pp. 197–261). Jossey-Bass.

Taylor, K., & Betz, T. (1983). Applications of self-efficacy theory to the understanding and treatment of career indecision. *Journal of Vocational Behavior, 22,* 63-81.

Weller, C. (2019, April 9). *The 5 biggest biases that affect decision-making.* NeuroLeadership Institute. https://neuroleadership.com/your-brain-at-work/seeds-model-biases-affect-decision-making/

CHAPTER 6
Career Coaching for Diverse Populations

"Diversity doesn't look like anyone. It looks like everyone."

– Karen Draper

Chapter Highlights

This chapter will discuss career coaching for diverse populations, including how cultural diversity plays a vital role in workforce development. It will overview key terminology and offer language that provides a mutual understanding of multicultural career services. The chapter will discuss the challenges that clients and coaches face related to diversity and career development and identify several strategies coaches can use to work with diverse populations on their career decision-making journey.

Learning Objectives

This chapter highlights the following:

1. Common language related to career coaching for diverse populations
2. Knowledge of cultural competence applied to career coaching and an understanding of its importance in practice
3. Applying career coaching models in working with diverse clients/groups
4. Specific and unique challenges that certain populations face and ways to support these populations

K – W - L

Now that you know what the chapter has to offer, take a few minutes to assess your knowledge level and areas of learning using the K-W-L model. The first step in the K-W-L model is to self-assess what you already ***know*** about working with diverse populations? Have you challenged yourself to learn about and experience cultures other than your own? What is your comfort level in working with clients who do not share similar racial, ethnic, cultural, or religious identities as your own? Are you familiar with communication customs related to other cultures? These questions are ones to ponder as you read through this chapter. Next, think about what you ***want*** to know about culturally diverse coaching. Where do you feel are the gaps in your coaching knowledge and performance? To conclude this chapter, you will revisit the K-W-L model to assess whether this chapter provided you with information to fill some of your knowledge gaps. Finally, you will reflect on what you ***learned*** from this chapter and how you can apply it to your coaching practice.

Serving Diverse Populations

The demographic of the typical United States citizen has changed significantly since the 1970s, due in part to higher birth numbers, aging trends, and immigration rates. The U.S. Census Bureau (2020) projects that the non-Hispanic White population will shrink from 199 million in 2020 to 179 million people in 2060. Furthermore, the population's racial composition will change in the coming decades, with one in every three Americans—32 percent of the population—being a race other than White by 2060 (U.S. Census Bureau, 2020). Vespa et al. (2020) reported that in 2030

> immigration is projected to overtake natural increase (the excess of births over deaths) as the primary driver of population growth for the country. Beyond 2030, the U.S. population will grow slowly, age considerably, and become more racially and ethnically diverse. (p. 1)

Specifically, the "population of people who are Two or More Races is projected to be the fastest-growing racial or ethnic group over the next several decades, followed by Asians and Hispanics" (Vespa et al., 2020, p. 2). Clients may turn to coaches to help them navigate cultural matters given the rise in globalization, immigration, and the diverse workforce. As discussed in Chapter 1, techniques developed for White, middle-to-upper-class clients no longer supported all clients (Hays & Mcleod, 2018). Changing demographics require those in a coaching role to be aware of and continuously explore their own cultural identity and how it shapes their ethical decision-making. With the rise of multiculturalism and social advocacy, more equitable interventions exist. Now more than ever, there is space for coaches to focus on cultural diversity, privilege, oppression, and resilient strategies related to career development.

Who Do We Serve?

The National Career Development Association (NCDA) *Code of Ethics* (2015) defines multicultural/diversity competence as "cultural and diversity awareness and knowledge about self and others, and how this awareness and knowledge is applied effectively in practice with clients and client groups" (p. 26). Multicultural counseling is the practice of counseling between or among people from various backgrounds based on race, ethnicity, ability, sexual orientation, religion, national origin, and culture (Sue, 2001). Career coaching for multicultural populations serves clients who are racially and ethnically diverse. Section A of the NCDA *Code of Ethics* (2015) states: "Career professionals actively attempt to understand the diverse cultural backgrounds of the individuals they serve. [They] also explore their own cultural identities and how these affect their values and beliefs about the working relationship" (NCDA, 2015, p. 5). Needs across different populations include multigenerational, justice-involved, mental/emotional needs, K-12, inclusive populations, veterans, gap workers, gig economy, LGBTQ+, international, geographically challenged, socioeconomic, undocumented individuals, race, ethnicity, religion, national origin, and physical/emotional/developmental abilities.

Important Terms

A universal understanding of key concepts in multicultural career counseling is important. Below are a few terms to be aware of when career coaching with multicultural populations and when bringing the information together to conceptualize client issues in a culturally relevant manner (Hays & Mcleod, 2018).

- *Cultural Identity* – degree to which individuals identify themselves as belonging to subgroups of various cultural groups or categories (i.e., race, ethnicity, gender). Cultural identity shapes interactions, experiences, worldviews, and beliefs and can contribute to psychological well-being and resilience (Moore-Thomas, 2018).
- *Disability* – a mental or physical impairment that affects at least one of an individual's daily activities. Ableism is discrimination faced by people with disabilities. Non-apparent disabilities are hidden or invisible disabilities because they may not appear to others (i.e., dyslexia, learning challenges, chronic health issues; Rowe & Murphy, 2021).
- *Ethnicity* – shared characteristics of culture, religion, and language with which a group may identify.
- *Gig Economy* – a labor market characterized by the prevalence of short-term contracts or freelance work as opposed to permanent jobs (Oxford English Dictionary, n.d.).
- *Gender* – masculinity and femininity are normative expressions of maleness and femaleness in a given society or social context. Androgyny is a blending of masculinity and femininity. Intersex and transgender demonstrate a complexity of gender and gender norms.

- *Generational Status* – cluster of particular age groups within a particular social and historical context generally within a 15-20 year timeframe. A group's particular historical or life-changing experiences (i.e., financial collapse, war, pandemic) categorize the generations.
- *Race* – socially constructed classification of individuals based on physical distinctions such as skin color, hair texture, facula forms, and eye shape; used as a classification system to divide and exploit individuals throughout history, resulting in racism.
- *Sexual Identity* – identification with a particular sexual orientation (i.e., heterosexual, gay, lesbian, bisexual, questioning).
- *Sexual Orientation* – sexual or affectional attraction to the same or opposite gender, or both.
- *Socioeconomic Status (SES)* – indicated by household income, education level, occupational status, access to health care and public assistance use; lower SES is associated with poor physical and mental health and plays an important factor in multicultural coaching.
- *Spirituality/Religion* – spirituality refers to the connection individuals have with themselves and the universe. Religion refers to organized affiliation with an individual's practice of their faith.

Why is a Multicultural Worldview Important?

Many scholars and practitioners have and continue to call for career coaching practices that consider and serve multicultural clients. "The need to develop competencies in multicultural counseling is an issue of a pluralistic philosophy of life. It is also a matter of professional ethics" (Sodowsky, 1996, p. 284). Further, Leong and Brown (as cited in Hartung 2002) concluded that "the central problem with most, if not all the majority career theories is their lack of cultural validity for racial and ethnic minorities in this country" (p. 13). Osipow and Fitzgerald (1996) opined that

> Possibly the most profound challenge to the generalizability of career development theories is posed by the assertion that many racial/ethnic minority individuals do not share the value systems on which the traditional theoretical explanations are based...and to the degree that such an assertion is correct, it constitutes a profound limitation on the validity of vocational development theories, suggesting that they may not be applicable to many minority individuals. (p. 275)

Although progress has been made in coaching theory, research, and techniques over the past few decades, much work remains. As the United States continues to diversify, coaching practices must respond to the needs of its changing clientele. To be considered multicultural-minded, career coaches must be sensitive to the intricacies of cross-cultural differences and the context in which these differences impact four areas: the career coach, the coaching relationship, the client's worldview, and coaching interventions (Hays & Mcleod, 2018).

Social Justice and Cultural Competence

In the early 20th century, Frank Parsons (1909) emphasized situating vocational guidance at the heart of the call for awareness, advocacy, attention to social problems, and concern for marginalized groups. He saw vocational guidance as a means to improving the lives of others, especially recent immigrants, and was an advocate for social change as part of the Progressive Movement (Blustein & Ellis, 2006; Hooley & Sultana, 2016; Stebleton & Eggerth, 2012). Vocational guidance helped individuals find work as they migrated from the country to the cities, serving a social and political function (Hooley & Sultana, 2016). This gallant effort was spearheaded by White scholars and dominated by Western European and masculine ideals, mainly that employment be accessible and attainable to all (Cook et al., 2002; Gysbers et al., 2014). Although 21st century workplace challenges are vastly different from Parsons's day in 1909, inequalities stemming from the vocational guidance era continue to plague growth and upward mobility for millions of Americans. As Hooley and Sultana (2016) posited:

> Poverty, inequality, shifts in the nature and location of work, a lack of social mobility, and the growth of geographical mobility all remain as social, political and economic themes that 21st century career guidance has to deal with just as much as the progressives who originated the area. … Ethnicity, gender, religion, age, sexual orientation, and nationality all offer other poles around which unfairness congregates, often in ways where multiple, intersectional and overlapping burdens are carried by the same individual and group. (p. 3)

with the end goal of eradicating oppression (Lee, 2014). Young (1990) identified five faces of oppression: exploitation, marginalization, powerlessness, cultural imperialism, and violence. Used interchangeably, one can argue that the goal of social advocacy leads to social justice (Gnilka et al., 2018). For example, career coaches can work with individual clients and contribute to that work and beyond it by advocating for fair and equal pay across gender. This advocacy contributes to social justice in gender equality. Career coaches can help in a professional capacity through increasing their knowledge, applying their coaching skills, and furthering the research in the areas of social justice and career development, together with political action in whichever way this is conceived around these faces of oppression to further a social justice agenda.

COACH CORNER

The list of social issues (e.g., food insecurities, economic downturns, workplace injustices, systematic racism) in the U.S. and around the globe is ever-changing and impacts all aspects of career coaching. How can you remain educated and current on these important conversations? How does this affect the welfare of your clients and the practice of career coaching?

Social Justice

Young (1990) stated that a socially just system does not oppress, and Gnilka et al. (2018) defined social justice as equitable treatment, including equity among groups, distribution of advantages and disadvantages, and nondiscrimination. In employment counseling, social justice interventions "challenge systems, institutions, and cultural norms that result in oppression and marginalization of certain groups in society" (Arthur, 2014, p. 51). Coaching with a social justice mindset is based on the belief that all people have the right to equitable resources and fair treatment,

Culture

Culture is a dynamic relational process in which common meanings develop through human interactions (Carpenter-Song et al., 2007), creating a set of boundaries, identifying what is acceptable, and establishing processes, guidelines, and norms of behavior. Betancourt (2004) described culture as a pattern of teaching ideas, values, and behavior shared within a community, including language, communication techniques, traditions, conventions, and attitudes influencing roles and relationships. It is our mental patterns of thinking, feeling, and acting or our "the software of the mind," according to Hofstede et al. (2010, p. 5). Ethnic groups, nations, organizations, occupations, genders, generations, and social classes are all considered cultures, although individuals learn and experience culture differently (Lennard, 2010). Schein (2010) posited:

> if we understand culture better we will understand ourselves better and recognize some of the forces acting within us that define who we are. We will then understand that our personality and character reflect the groups that socialized us and the groups with which we identify and to which we want to belong. (p. 9)

Examining cultural values and behaviors, such as Hofstede's cultural dimensions, can help career coaches better understand how clients live, interact, and negotiate within a culture.

Hofstede's Cultural Dimensions

The premise of Hofstede's cultural dimensions is that cultural variations exist between country and region, rooted in history, and differ in identity, values, and institutions. Entrenched in the question of "what group do I belong to?" identities are explicit, can be expressed in words, and tend to shift over a lifetime. Examples of identities are women (individual) and American citizens (collective) (Hofstede et al., 2010; Hofstede, 2011). Values are the invisible software of the mind, implicit, and sometimes difficult to express because they imply questioning our motives, emotions, and taboos. The gender values Americans place on masculinity and femininity are examples of values imposed by a culture (Hofstede et al., 2010; Hofstede, 2011) and are often found within the workplace. Our world now interacts more closely with broader and varied cultures, increasing our learning and life perspectives. Expanded interactions cause uncertainty and questions such as, "How do I relate to individuals from another culture? Am I acknowledging and respecting customs and traditions? Are communication patterns the same or similar?"

Dimensions of Culture

Benedict and Mead developed the view that all societies, modern or traditional, face the same cultural differences (Hofstede et al., 2010). Inkeles and Levinson (1969) and Hofstede and colleagues (2010) furthered this research to confirm that dimensions exist from culture to culture, and as society evolves, dimensions evolve simultaneously. Five dimensions currently exist, four of which apply to this monograph:

1. **power distance** (from small to large): social inequality, including the relationship with authority. The degree to which less powerful members accept and anticipate power distribution is power distance (Hofstede, 2011).
2. **collectivism versus individualism:** the relationship between the individual and the group. Individualism is one side vs. its opposite. The degree to which people integrate into groups is collectivism (Hofstede, 2011).
3. **femininity versus masculinity:** the concepts of two roles, the social and emotional implications of being born as a boy or a girl; distribution of values between the two genders (Hofstede et al., 2010).
4. **uncertainty avoidance** (from weak to strong): ways of dealing with uncertainty and ambiguity, related to controlling aggression and expressing emotions (Hofstede et al., 2010).

In application, Hofstede's cultural dimensions have many benefits to the career development process. Cultural dimensions affect all levels of communication: verbal (words and language), non-verbal (body language, gestures, symbols), etiquette (dress, dining, protocol, customs), and written communication (Adair et al., 2016; Gabelica & Popov, 2020; Wardrobe, 2005 as cited in Makambe & Pellissier, 2014), Increasing one's awareness of different cultures can also improve aspects of the job search and success in the workplace. Examples of this include greater success with negotiating (LeBaron, 2003).

Makambe and Pellissier (2014) stated (as cited in LeBaron, 2003)

> When negotiating in western countries where time is looked at as a commodity, the aim is to work out a mutual understanding and reach an agreement quickly (sign a contract) and then shake hands to signal the conclusion of the agreement and the starting of working together ... whereas Chinese and Japanese negotiators spend time on preliminaries (non-business activities) such as small talk, hospitality and drinking coffee and so on with preferences to protocol and form in order to establish a solid relationship first. (p. 94)

As cultures change, so too do the individuals living within a culture, impacting existing cultural dimensions. Failure to consider cultural differences in terms of cultural dimensions leads to miscommunication between coach and client and an inability for the coach to provide the proper support for the client's needs. Possessing cultural proficiency and responding accordingly to create a harmonious working relationship is where cultural competence comes into play.

Cultural Competence

Cultural competence is a person's capacity to understand, connect, work, and form meaningful relationships with others from varied cultural backgrounds (de Guzman et al., 2016). Williams (2001) defined cultural competence as "the ability of individuals and systems to work or respond effectively across cultures in a way that acknowledges and respects the culture of the person or organization being served" (p. 1). Sue et al. (1982) argued that it is critical to recognize that for one to be different does not mean to be "deficient," "deprived," or "disadvantaged" (p. 46). Developing cultural competence is a lifetime process that involves improving self-awareness, developing social skills and behaviors related to diversity, and learning to advocate for others. It goes beyond tolerance, which indicates a willingness to overlook differences. Instead, it entails recognizing and valuing variety through words and actions in all circumstances.

Developing Cultural Competence

Developing cultural competence offers those who hold diverse customs, traditions, and communications the freedom and space to express themselves, increasing communication channels. Deardorff (2006) offered seven cross-cultural attitude strategies to develop and enhance one's ability to practice effective communication in intercultural situations:

- Demonstrate acceptance of difference by practicing openness
- Demonstrate acceptance of ambiguity by exercising flexibility
- Show humility by suspending judgment and demonstrating the ability to learn
- Appreciate cultural differences through sensitivity to others
- Show curiosity and see opportunities in different situations through an adventurous spirit.
- Use humor to laugh at ourselves
- Demonstrate a successful interaction with the identified culture by practicing positive change or action

Culturally Competent Coaching

Like the lifelong pursuit of developing one's coaching skills, cultural competence development is ongoing and requires diligent educational and applicable pursuits. Burchum (2002) described cultural competence as "a non-linear dynamic process that is never-ending and ever-expanding. It is built on increases in knowledge and skill development related to its attributes" (p. 5). The influence of a culture can both promote and inhibit change, and coaches who are aware of this can be instrumental change agents by bringing cultural influences to the surface. Change can occur when culture is understood and respected.

Based on the Universal Integrated Framework (UIF), four areas can increase cultural competence and skills development: personal, social, cultural, and professional competence (Passmore & Law, 2009). Personal competence is having self-awareness or self-management of one's cultural understanding and identification. Sue et al. (1982, 1992) posited that attitudes and beliefs speak to a [coach's] ability to examine personal biases and stereotypes, and preconceptions may negatively impair effective service delivery; therefore, a level of awareness is important. As Peterson (2007) noted

> The broader a coach's understanding of culture, the better they are able to identify important dimensions of human behavior and explore their meaning. The deeper a coach's insights into how culture has shaped their own beliefs and values, the more sensitive they can be to how their assumptions shape their reactions and advice to the people they coach. (p. 262)

A career coach should begin by examining their cultural history as a gateway for developing multicultural career counseling competencies (Evans & Sejuit, 2021; Rush, 2010). For a coach to fully support a client's growth and forward career development, a deep understanding of their own cultural biases and assumptions is essential.

Additionally, a coach should strive to increase cultural competence related to empathy and social skills. A career coach must inventory their skills in observing, assessing, and communicating non-judgmentally about a culture by asking internally-focused questions such as "Do I realize that others may have needs and expectations that are unexpressed or expressed indirectly?" A coach's understanding of their worldview, historical and sociopolitical influences impacting their clients can impart judgment and understanding (Sue et al., 1982, 1992). For example, a typical Western approach like direct eye contact is not always productive in the coaching relationship, as there are certain cultural situations where direct eye contact can be off-putting. A coach can develop a more indirect means of gathering information from the client or group (Peterson, 2007) if empathy and social skills development is a coaching priority.

The UIF also noted the need for ongoing cultural development, broad stroke awareness, and championing of other cultures to increase and practice culturally competent coaching. Coaching across cultures includes looking for hidden layers, adapting the coaching approach to the person, and implementing the change to best suit the individual or group (Hicks & Peterson, 1999). Peterson (2007) noted

> As the coach gains insight into the individual's makeup, they can ask questions to identify the most effective methods and approaches for this particular person independent of their culture: What's the best way to foster the coaching relationship with this person? What's the best way for this person to learn? What skills, approaches, and style will be most useful for this person in their context? (p. 264)

Developing culturally appropriate skills help a coach employ culturally relevant and effective intervention strategies, which are helpful and often necessary in working with specific individuals and groups (Sue et al., 1982, 1992).

Finally, striving for cultural competence and skills development from a professional lens is necessary for more impactful, multiculturally based coaching. Sodowsky et al. (1994) studied the counselor's interaction with minority clients, including comfort level, worldview, and counselor's trustworthiness. The authors found that racial identity development is essential in developing multicultural competencies and that we realize cultural change when we understand it. Career coaches can develop cultural competence in various ways, both formally and informally. As coaches develop their cultural competencies, practicing is critical to adopting a more culturally-minded skillset. Hicks and Peterson (1999) recommended adapting the coaching approach to the person – every client is unique, and needs vary from situation to situation. For example, clients may be hesitant to share parts of their culture or heritage, so coaching techniques (see Chapter 2) can help draw out critical details. Looking for hidden layers in meaning as the coaching relationship progresses and gaining as much knowledge as possible for increased understanding can help a coach become more proficient in coaching through a multicultural lens.

Career coaches need to recognize that the questions they ask, and their ideas about the process and direction of the coaching, will contain their own cultural biases. Therefore, it is essential to regularly take an inventory of one's skills in observing, assessing, and communicating non-judgmentally about culture (Peterson, 2007). Additionally, learning to "perceive and decipher the cultural forces that operate in groups, organizations and occupations" (Schein, 2010, p. 12-13) is necessary for coaching success and gains towards adapting to the client's communication style and cultural behavior.

Global Dexterity

Molinsky (2013) described global dexterity as the ability to adapt one's style of communication and behavior across cultures – regardless of one's culture of origin or destination. He described six dimensions of behavior, representing key aspects of communication that differ across cultures: degree of directness, enthusiasm, formality, assertiveness, and self-promotion that is considered appropriate, and the extent to which personal information can acceptably be shared or requested. In addition, the ability to function with humility and honor differences in culture, race, and sexual orientation are aspects of a coach's ethical behavior. In contrast, responding with sensitivity to the client's tone and tempering one's style to set the client at ease are essential coaching skills.

Johari Window: A Tool for Coaching Across Cultures

As mentioned in the previous section, understanding clients' perspective is the first step in coaching across cultures. However, understanding requires ongoing development, and it also requires both coach and client to be on the same page--meaning, clients must also be self-aware. Once a client is self-aware, they can improve their communication with others. The Johari Window can help clients better understand their relationship with themselves (Luft, 1970) to improve cross-cultural communications.

Johari Window

As mentioned previously, cultural orientations, preferences, and personalities that inform one's view of the world can also block, inhibit, or disallow other views. The Johari Window is useful for looking at the impacts and influences of cultural orientation as it depicts areas where things are known and hidden from an individual and others. The Johari Window was developed in 1955 by Luft and Ingham to help clients recognize how they perceive themselves and how they are perceived (Luft, 1970). The Johari Window represents a person or group's attitudes, beliefs, skills, and experiences concerning others from four perspectives, depicted as quadrants or windows (see Figure 13). It can provide valuable insight for improving interpersonal communication through self-awareness and understanding in two key ideas (1) building trust with others through disclosing information about yourself; and (2) getting feedback from others, which increases self-awareness.

Bennett and Bush (2013) provided details on each quadrant: open area, hidden area, blind area, and the unknown area. Each quadrant represents feelings and motivation regarding whether the information is known or unknown to the person and others.

Open Area. The open area, also known as the arena, is the open or conscious self, including behaviors, attitudes, motivation, beliefs, and ways of life that others are aware of (Saxena, 2015). A free and open exchange of information occurs within the arena; the arena increases as confidence and trust between coach and client grow and more information, particularly personally relevant information, is communicated (Bennett & Bush, 2013).

The Goal. Coaching in the arena aims to explore

with the client what they know to be true about themselves and brainstorm ways to apply the knowledge revealed during exploration. Positive attributes might sound like the client sharing, "I am organized. I enjoy helping people make sense of their space. I really like helping people feel free of an unnecessary burden so they can be more creative and productive." Negative attributes by the client might sound like, "I'm a perfectionist. It is impacting my work performance productivity, and I don't know this for sure, but I suspect my coworkers don't want to work with me on team projects because I delay completion."

While coaching in the arena, both the coach and the client are aware of the deficits that exist, and the client shares more personally relevant information. It is essential to help the client understand that awareness is the first step in creating positive change.

Hidden Area. In the hidden area or façade, information is unknown to others unless the client discloses it. When operating in the hidden area of coaching, only the client is aware of their deficit or area of need. There is an inhibition or fear factor (rejection) that stops the client from being open if the coach does not appear supportive by the client (Saxena, 2015). If the client starts revealing thoughts, feelings, and reactions, the coach (or others) might judge or react negatively. These feelings might sound like, "If an employer finds out I was fired from my last job, I will not get hired." Or: "I'm afraid to mention it took me eight years to complete my degree when everyone else seems to finish in four years."

The Goal. Before taking the risk of telling others something, the client must know the coach and others will provide a support system (Bennett & Bush, 2013). The client may want others (including the coach) to positively judge their feelings, thoughts, and reactions. The goal of coaching in the hidden area is to work with the client to uncover insecurities, explore limiting beliefs, and discuss worst-case scenarios. Fear is a normal response when approaching something new, so the client will need a plan that allows smaller steps to achieve their broader goals.

Blind Area. This area contains information that the client does not know about, but others, including the coach, may recognize with clarity. Bennett and Bush (2013) posited that the coach learns information about the client from verbal cues, mannerisms, how things are said, or how the client relates to others. The client may not be aware of action or mannerism, yet the coach perceives it differently. For example, a client may be unaware of their tendency to look away from a person when speaking or touching their hair when nervous. Coaching in these moments might sound like

> Coach: "You are very articulate and are good at public speaking."
>
> Client: *[surprised]* "Ooh am I?! I didn't know that about me."

Or:

> Coach: "I notice that each time you talk about an uncomfortable topic, you bite your bottom lip."
>
> Client: *[surprised]* "Really?! I thought that was just a habit of mine. I've been doing that since I was a child."

During this blind area of coaching, the coach is aware of the client's strengths and growth areas; however, the client is unaware that they have attributes that may be attractive to employers and areas for potential growth.

The Goal. Helping the client raise their self-awareness, based on a fuller picture of themselves, is the goal when coaching in the hidden area. The coach needs to ensure the client does not overlook their strengths because they come naturally.

Unknown Area. Whether through ignorance or pre-existing motives, neither the client nor the coach knows or understands the deficit areas, barriers, or potential within the client. Early childhood memories, latent potentialities, intrapersonal dynamics, and unrecognized resources come into play (Bennett & Bush, 2013). Coaches, in these moments, might say, "There can be circumstances or occasions that hold us back from achieving our goals, but often, we are unsure what those circumstances are. Coaching could help uncover and set aside or manage those obstacles."

It is improbable for the client to know all about themselves, and the unknown area of the model represents the unconscious, which is the part of the client that will remain unknown (Saxena, 2015).

The Goal. Unknown areas of potential or deficit are often a result of subconscious feelings, fears, limiting beliefs, conditioned behaviors. Coaching in the unknown area is to engage in deep and lengthy dialog because internal boundaries of this area change depending on the amount of feedback sought and received.

The Johari Exercise

In a Johari exercise, the client picks several adjectives from a list (see Table 10), choosing ones they feel describe their personality. The client then inserts all chosen adjectives into cells of a Johari Window (see Figure 13) - depending on the client's awareness level, the words will go in either the Open or Hidden area. The coach also instructs the client to share the same list with several peers (co-workers, friends, colleagues), asking each to pick adjectives that describe the client. The client positions words their peers chose in the Blind Area if the word is not in the Open area. The client moves words out of the Hidden cell if peers chose the word. Finally, all words from the original list not chosen by the client or peers are placed in the Unknown Area.

The Johari window helps career coaches and clients identify biases in communication blind spots and growth areas (Kegan & Lahey, 2001). From a career coaching perspective, feedback should be direct and specific as the coach minimizes the Unknown area and maximizes the Open area throughout coaching (Mehay, 2012). Promoting discussion and awareness of what is known and hidden gradually develops a larger arena (open area) of shared information. This model can be constructive for a career coach in facilitating a discussion with an individual or group on navigating culture in an organizational or workplace setting, such as revisiting policies and procedural manuals for inclusive language and workplace practices.

Figure 13
The Johari Window Model

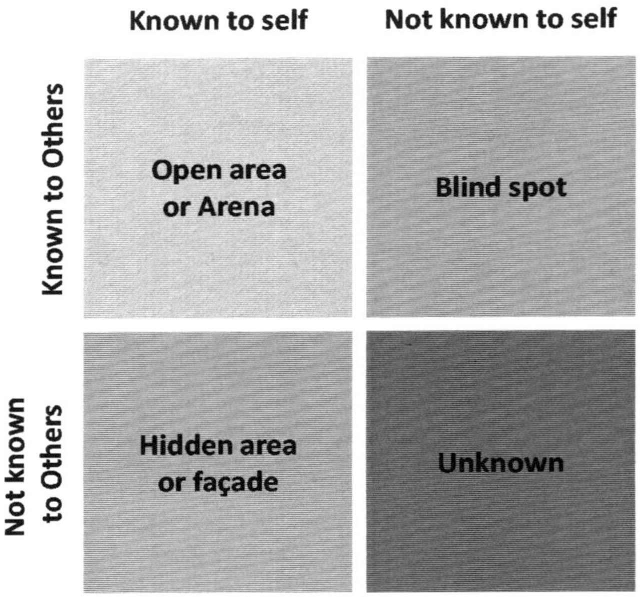

Adopted from "Coaching for Change," by J. L. Bennett & M. W. Bush, 2013, p. 104. Routledge.

Table 10
Johari Exercise List of Adjectives

able	accepting	adaptable	bold	brave	calm	caring	cheerful
clever	complex	confident	dependable	dignified	empathetic	energetic	extroverted
friendly	giving	happy	helpful	idealistic	independent	ingenious	introverted
kind	knowledgeable	logical	loving	mature	modest	nervous	observant
organized	patient	powerful	proud	quiet	reflective	relaxed	religious
responsive	searching	self-assertive	self-conscious	sensible	sentimental	shy	silly
smart	spontaneous	sympathetic	tense	trust	warm	wise	witty

Integrating the cultural dimension into coaching is necessary to increase coaching's validity and allow coaches to learn from the client in communication, reasoning, identity, and purpose. Instead of minimizing the importance of cultural differences, embracing and leveraging differences can support the coaching process. For example, one way to ask a new client whether there are cultural considerations that the coach should be aware of is through an intake (see Chapter 2). This prompt might open up a dialog that positively impacts the coaching discussion and lines of communication between coach and client.

Multicultural Considerations in Career Coaching

Ethics

NCDA's *Code of Ethics* (2015) discusses various ways career professionals can deliver culturally sound career-related services.

Informed Consent

Section A.2. discusses the importance of using clear and understandable language when addressing issues related to informed consent or providing accommodations should language be challenging to understand (e.g., interpreter, computer voice translation). A career coach examines the cultural implications of their informed consent procedures and adjusts practices accordingly (NCDA, 2015). If the client cannot provide consent (minors or persons unable to give voluntary consent), it is recommended that assistance be sought from a guardian or translator.

Respecting Clients Rights

Although career professionals have differing views, they are aware and sensitive to cultural meanings of confidentiality, privacy, and disclosure of information. The sensitivity afforded clients also extends to families and parents/guardians over the welfare of their children/charges according to the law (NCDA, 2015).

Professional Responsibility

Being a culturally competent career professional is the responsibility of all career professionals. Career professionals should actively gain knowledge, personal awareness, sensitivity, dispositions, and skills pertinent to cultural and diversity training. Furthermore, career professionals should never practice outside of their competence, education, training, credentials, and professional experience (NCDA, 2015).

Nondiscrimination

> Career professionals do not
> condone or engage in discrimination against any individual based on age, culture, mental/physical disability, ethnicity, race, religion/spirituality, creed, gender, gender identity, sexual orientation, marital/partnership status, language preference, socioeconomic status, any other characteristics not specifically relevant to job performance, or any basis prohibited by law. (NCDA, 2015, C.5)

Administering Assessments

Clients benefit from career assessments because they gain a better understanding of themselves. Administering career assessments through a multicultural lens requires the counselor to be aware of their own biases, understand their own culture (including racial identity development), and recognize areas where unearned privilege exists. Successful multicultural assessment administering also requires knowledge of the historical context of marginalized groups and making efforts to understand their worldviews. Finally, administering career assessments through a multicultural lens requires applying coaching skills effectively (Sue et al., 1992).

Common Pitfalls

Wilkins-Yel and colleagues (2019) identified three concerns in administering career assessments in a multicultural context: White ethnocentric biases, historical overemphasis on personal variables, and the role of language. White ethnocentric biases cloud the judgment of cultural and minority identities, which can cause misinterpretations in assessment results (Marsella & Leong, 1995). There has also been a strong and ongoing overemphasis on personal over environmental variables in assessment interpretation (Leong, 1997). The idea that an individual might pursue a career, for example, in veterinary medicine because their assessment results align with this occupational choice is only part of the career discussion. Many environmental variables influence the path to and through veterinary medicine, such as how competitive the application process is or the comfort with student loans. The role of language is also a pitfall in assessment interpretation, specifically around translation and multilingual issues (Marsella & Leong, 1995). Instrument translation can result in misinterpretation of both language and cultural context. Receiving regular diversity training, examining one's cultural identity and judgment, and consulting and adhering to a code of ethics can minimize pitfalls to assessment administration.

Ethics in Multicultural Career Assessment Administration

The NCDA *Code of Ethics* (2015) section E.1. highlights the primary purpose of qualitative and quantitative educational, psychological, and career assessments, which is to provide valid and reliable measurements in either comparative or absolute terms. As discussed in Chapter 5, it is a client's right to know and understand their assessment results and a coach's ethical duty to interpret the results to the best of their professional knowledge and offer conclusions and recommendations based on these interpretations. Coaches must utilize only those testing and assessment services they have been trained in and are competent in administering and interpreting to meet this duty. Before administering any assessment, the coach must explain the nature and purpose of the assessment(s) in the client's language. Assessment choice must include consideration of the client's personal or cultural context, how the client understands the results, and how the results impact the client.

The NCDA *Code of Ethics* recognizes that cultural sensitivity is needed when administering and interpreting assessments because, as was explained earlier in the chapter, culture affects how clients' issues are defined. For example, cultural identities and experiences influence a coach's selection, judgment, and interpretation of assessment tools and results (Wilkins-Yel et al., 2019). In addition, historical and societal prejudices influence diagnosis in specific persons and groups, and career professionals have an ethical responsibility to reduce the maintenance of these prejudices by correct diagnosis, recommendations, and service provision (Fitzgerald & Betz, 1994; Pope, 2009). Section E.8. of the NCDA code (2015) outlines the possible "effects of age, color, culture, disability, ethnic group, gender, race, language preference, religion, spirituality, sexual orientation, and socioeconomic status on test administration and interpretation" (p. 14). To effectively address multicultural issues in administering assessments, career professionals must use caution when selecting assessments for culturally diverse populations to avoid using instruments that lack appropriate needs or considerations for the client population.

Career coaches can educate clients on the benefits and limitations of assessments in career choice and offer the client assessment options. After all, there are many topical assessments available for the choosing. In addition, the use of more exploratory, open-ended, qualitative assessments, such as mind mapping, journaling, or vision board exercises (see Chapter 3), can augment formal, quantitative assessments (Wilkins-Yel et al., 2019) because the less rigid exercises spark idea generation and personalized response.

Blustein and Ellis (2006) posited that "ethical and moral use of tests within a culturally diverse context offers perhaps the greatest challenge for career practitioners of the 21st century" (p. 380). Failure to pay attention to a client's cultural context might heighten the use of mismatched or inappropriate career assessments (Fouad, 1995). Whether career assessments meet the needs of the rapidly changing cultural landscape is ongoing.

Coaching and Assessment Use for Diverse Populations

A variety of population-specific assessment instruments exist to meet the needs of diverse groups. This chapter cannot address assessment needs for all populations; however, highlighted here are a few populations for which the use of assessments warrants additional consideration. The populations covered here face higher unemployment and underemployment, more significant challenges in hiring and workplace stigmas, discrimination, discomfort, and even danger while employed (Bailinson et al., 2020; Baboolall et al., 2021).

LGBTQ+ Population. A 2020 Gallup poll found that 5.6% of the U.S. general population identifies as LGBTQ+ (Jones, 2021). Although legislative efforts to address discrimination in the workplace have progressed, such as Executive Order No. 13,672 (2014), expanding the definition of anti-discrimination in employment and the 2020 Supreme Court ruling making it illegal for an employer to fire someone because of their sexual orientation or gender identity (Williams, 2020), the workplace is far from equal and unbiased. There are multi-faceted issues the LGBTQ+ client navigates relating to career advancement and job-related decision-making. The lines are often blurred between sexual orientation and gender (Cenizal, 2014), and often employers focus more on supporting sexual orientation in the workplace than on gender identity or expression (Thoroughgood et al., 2020). For example, the LGBTQ+ community is underrepresented in the workplace, even at the entry-level, and across all companies, LGBTQ+ women are underrepresented by more than half (Elisworth et al., 2021). Furthermore, transgender adults are twice as likely as cisgender adults to be unemployed, and those employed make 32 percent less money in a year (Baboolall et al., 2021).

Acceptance of identity and orientation is one of the critical components to building rapport with the client, and with a client who may identify as LGBTQ+ it is essential to ascertain the level of openness to their identity. In addition, clients need a safe and confidential environment to discuss personal issues, fair and equal employment, and any concerns about career exploration options. Unfortunately, many LGBTQ+ clients do not understand the full range of career options or safe and appropriate assessments available and seek out coaching because they feel limited opportunities exist. In addition, because some LGBTQ+ clients may not be aware of the laws that protect them from discrimination and mistreatment in the workplace and hiring process, a coach must remain abreast of the most recent laws pertaining to LGBTQ+ clients.

When choosing and administering assessments, a coach must be mindful of test language and client population. Some questions a coach might ask are:

- Has the assessment been updated to reflect 21st century gender equality?
- Do the assessment results allow for gender adaptability?
- Am I (the coach) qualified, and do I feel comfortable administering this assessment?
- Are there coaches more proficient in administering assessments for the LGBTQ+ population in my network that I can call upon for support?
- Have I done my research and have support, referrals, and resources readily available should the client need?

A career coach cannot control the legal and regulatory environment of the workplace, but they can support their clients in the exploration and search process. A coach influences the coaching experience and a client's progress. LGBTQ+ clients will have a greater chance of healthy workplace success if they are educated on their workplace rights, understand their strengths and positive contribution to an organization, confidently share those attributes with employers, and feel supported and included.

Veteran Clients. Per the 2020 census, approximately 10% of the total population in the United States are veterans (Vespa, 2020). A report released in March 2021 by the U.S. Bureau of Labor Statistics reported that the veteran unemployment rate was 6.5% for males and 6.7% for females. Among the 581,000 unemployed veterans in 2020, 54% were aged 25 to 54, 41% were aged 55 and over, and 5% were aged 18 to 24. Interestingly, although the veteran unemployment rate tends to be higher than for non-veterans, unemployment rates for White, Black, Asian and Hispanic veterans were lower than for their non-veteran counterparts (U.S. Bureau of Labor Statistics, 2021).

Understanding veteran clients' family obligations and transitional needs are crucial when coaching, especially in administering and interpreting assessments. It is also important to respect and consider military tradition and unique language use while remembering that clients may not be familiar with the coaching industry's assessment language. Because of veteran clients' previous military experience, specifically a regimented work style and highly structured environment, it is essential to explain assessment purposes and benefits/drawbacks. In some circumstances, clients may have a long history of being over-assessed or assessed in error, so they could be hesitant about the process. Once results are available, thoroughly discussing pathway options and instructions for the next steps can increase communication and decrease resistance.

Cultural competence and skills translation are two common barriers to veteran transition from the military to the civilian workforce (McFarland & Ford, 2017). Career coaching can help clients unpackage and overcome these barriers in myriad ways, including assessment administration and interpretation. For example, veterans have many strengths (leadership, initiative, agility, collaboration, resiliency, resourcefulness) that they bring to the workplace. A strengths assessment can identify these assets. Likewise, a skills assessment can reveal many hard and soft skills desirable to employers. Veterans can learn a great deal about themselves and articulate their strengths and skills from military to civilian life as the coach decodes the results of these assessments and discusses scenarios in which the client's strengths and skills apply to non-military work situations. In short, veterans enhance productivity and performance, diversify the workforce, improve a company's market strength and bottom line, and are an excellent source of talent (McFarland & Ford, 2017).

Clients with Disabilities. Many policies are in place to support clients with disabilities, such as the 1990 Americans with Disabilities Act (ADA) and the Rehabilitation Act (42 U.S.C. § § 12111-12117), which prohibits discrimination against qualified individuals with disabilities in application procedures, hiring, compensation, training, advancement, and other terms, conditions and privileges of employment. For example, ADA requires employers to provide reasonable accommodations for disabled employees. However, clients with disabilities often need assistance in understanding and navigating the laws and available resources. For a coach to successfully discern and administer the appropriate assessment and navigate appropriate support resources, being aware of and understanding the client's disability is essential.

Clients often hesitate to reveal their disability for fear of recourse. Disabilities can cause stress for the individual and their support group, especially if a client's disability is hidden (e.g., mental health challenges). A recent report from the Center for Disease Control and Prevention (CDC) indicated that stress and other mental health issues play a significant factor in the lives of adults within the United States, with nearly 40% of the adult population in 2020 reporting they were struggling with mental health and substance abuse issues (Czeisler et al., 2020). There are many ways to discriminate against people based on disabilities, including psychological ones, but any person known to have a history of mental disorders can be considered disabled. Clients with disabilities often search for adaptable programming and services, but they often do so alone or in isolated groups because of the challenges inherent in sharing information about a disability with others.

Clients may seek out assessments to determine their skill levels, aptitudes, and interests and explore how these meet the requirements of the current labor market. Clients may require assessment waivers and adaptability accommodations to complete the assessment, therefore, considering the client's needs and available resources before administering an assessment is necessary. Upon receiving the results, clients with disabilities sometimes have difficulties seeing themselves in the possibilities identified on an assessment and may see the results as overwhelming. However, ethically and professionally administered assessments can help clarify vocational goals, whether the person with a disability has never worked, has a long work history, or needs to consider a new career. It is essential to align the debriefing conversation with the client's physical and intellectual abilities.

Overall, career assessments can be an impactful part of any coaching journey, uncovering new and exciting employment possibilities. However, for some populations, such as those highlighted in this section, assessments are less accurate in identifying special abilities or talents ideal for outside mainstream employment. Therefore, career coaches should continue professional development related to laws and regulations and best practices in assessments administration for diverse populations.

Multicultural Career Models

There have been recent improvements in career assessment with culturally diverse populations, given the rise of multicultural career coaching. As a result, several models and frameworks have been established to help the career evaluation process and comprehend culturally diverse individuals' professional demands. Included here are two of the many available models for consideration.

Intercultural Sensitivity Development Model

Bennett's (1986) Developmental Model of Intercultural Sensitivity is a communication, engagement, and equity model. The model is often called the Bennett Scale, representing how people experience, interpret and interact across cultural differences. As a result, a developmental continuum exists where people move toward greater knowledge and respect of cultural diversity and more social competence when navigating cross-cultural dissimilarity.

The model comprises six intercultural sensitivity and communication stages, progressing from *ethnocentric* (denial, defensiveness, and minimization) to *ethnorelative* worldviews (acceptance, adaptation, and integration). Included next is a summary of each stage.

***denial*:** the perception that an individual's cultural perspective is the only accurate or valid interpretation of reality (e.g., believing employment discrimination does not exist based on race or gender).

defense: when others view cultures as polarized or competitive; when one culture imposes their culture over another; or when an individual feels victimized or attacked in discussions about bias or racism (e.g., blaming the victim in a sexual harassment case).

minimalization: the idea that one's cultural worldviews apply to everyone and everyone is similar or the same (e.g., one career coaching assessment applies to all populations).

acceptance: recognizing and embracing cultural differences; increased curiosity and interest around different cultures and cross-cultural relationships (e.g., learning about assessments geared towards diverse populations for future application).

adaptation: authentically, emotionally, and intellectually interacting with individuals from other cultures (e.g., researching cultures different from your own).

integration: internalizing multicultural awareness and interacting productively across cultural differences (e.g., volunteering your expertise at a job seekers networking group hosted by cultural groups different than your own).

In short, the development of intercultural sensitivity describes how an individual can create an alternative experience that compliments or mirrors that of those in another culture. People who can create an alternative experience can communicate cross-culturally and have an intercultural worldview. The intercultural sensitivity development model is not predominately a description of cognition, affect, or behavior but how one's worldview moves from an ethnocentric to a more ethnorelative state (Bennett, 2004). When this happens, a coach generates greater intercultural sensitivity, increasing the potential for more intercultural competence.

Cultural Intelligence or CQ

Cross-cultural confidence is the capacity to adapt effectively across cultures and is essential for successfully coaching in a multicultural world with diverse clients. Earley and Mosakowski (2004) defined cross-cultural confidence or cultural intelligence (CI) as the ability to "tease out of a person's or group's behavior those features that would be true of all people and all groups, those peculiar to this person or this group, and those that are neither universal nor idiosyncratic" (p. 140). A coach that possesses cultural intelligence creates new frameworks for understanding what a client sees and experiences and reshapes their thinking to be more sympathetic to culture and behaviors so that coaching interactions are more skilled and appropriate (Early et al., 2006; Thomas & Inkson, 2003).

Similar to working with clients who are stuck, when a coach experiences a new situation or tries a new coaching technique, the coach may retreat from this new experience. The first response is to situate oneself in a familiar environment. Yet, this is not always possible or realistic, nor does it allow one to develop new skills or expand thought processes beyond what is known. In intercultural interactions, the equipment—our skill sets and our knowledge—may not be enough to navigate successfully in a new cultural environment. A coach's ability to recognize and express cultural diversity, solve problems caused by cultural differences, and work in harmony with clients with various cultural backgrounds while minimizing cultural conflicts, demonstrates possession of deep cultural intelligence (Brislin et al., 2006).

Cultural intelligence is a framework to help a coach learn to turn off the automatic response to familiar situations to reset mental programming in three areas: metacognition and cognition, motivation, and behavior.

Metacognitive intelligence deals with an individual's level of awareness when engaged in cross-cultural interactions and the strategies employed that allow the individual to interact in new cultural environments. A career coach who understands when to refrain from making eye contact with clients of certain cultures out of respect is practicing metacognitive intelligence. It challenges coaches to question preconceived norms, think differently about clients and cultural settings, be introspective in their cultural views, and revise conventional strategies when necessary (Ang et al., 2011). *Cognitive intelligence* is cultural knowledge or knowledge about the cultural environment that a career coach possesses, obtained from education or personal experience. Individuals with high cognitive intelligence have strong inductive reasoning skills and quickly adapt to unfamiliar cultures (Ang et al., 2011).

Motivational intelligence is one's interest in learning and responding to cultural situations, adapting to different cultures, appropriately behaving when acculturating, and generally assimilating to a new culture with greater ease (Ang et al., 2011). Individuals with higher motivational intelligence enjoy and actively engage with different cultural situations and others from different cultural groups. Finally, *behavioral intelligence* is one's ability to communicate on high levels with individuals from other cultures verbally and non-verbally (Ang & Van Dyne, 2008). Individuals with high behavioral CQ first recognize what to do and how to act appropriately in a given situation and then strive to adapt to that situation (Earley & Peterson, 2004).

CQ offers coaches a framework to communicate across cultures. The important thing to note about CQ is that it can be learned and developed over time. Career coaches help clients uncover limiting beliefs and constraints placed by their cultural setting, experiment with new habits, and form new assumptions and beliefs. However, career coaches must develop their CQ before they can help their clients do the same. Engaging in continued professional development and experiential learning to address cultural blind spots and improve cross-cultural competence can help clients make sense of their internal cultural struggles.

Future Directions in Multicultural Models

Many current career models point to the importance of understanding personal variables that influence career development. Multicultural career models look beyond personal variables and consider the context and environmental variables that affect career decisions and career development. As with many coaching techniques, multicultural models suggest that one theory or technique may not be suitable or culturally valid to all clients. Important environmental and contextual factors include an individual's family influence, cultural background, racial, ethnicity, acculturation, socioeconomic status, gender, worldview, environment, and perceived personal strengths. These factors support the career assessment process by helping the client identify factors that may contribute to or influence thoughts, feelings, or actions in the career development process. Coaches aware of their perceptions and beliefs about environmental factors that influence their own lives can mitigate these biases from impacting their clients' career support.

Multicultural Considerations in Delivery Modality

Technology has expanded opportunities for career support in ways most could not have ever imagined. Yet, it has also raised concerns about equity, inclusion, and reasonable accommodations for all populations. For example, technology can make cultural and language barriers more pronounced, yet specific applications offer translation tools. In addition, the delivery mode for job applications instructions might be via computer video, making it impossible for visually impaired clients, but adding audio services might provide reasonable accommodations.

Section F.4. of the NCDA *Code of Ethics* (2015) outlines the benefits and limitations of using technology applications in providing career services. "When providing technology-assisted services, career professionals make reasonable efforts to determine that clients are fully capable of using the application and that the application is appropriate for the needs of the client" (p. 16), which includes maintaining websites and other technology resources that are accessible to persons with disabilities.

Multicultural Considerations in Research

Career counselors, vocational and educational psychologists, and career coaches are some of the many groups researching and studying multicultural career issues. All those engaged in helping professions should continuously educate themselves with empirical research and literature regarding the career development of culturally diverse clients and apply their knowledge and skills to clinical practice (Flores et al., 2005). Strides have been made in policy and practice to try and address the challenges marginalized populations encounter in career development, but more work is needed. For example, investigating the validity of current measures for research and practice has been one of the central tenants of multicultural career investigation. The career coaching profession must continue to develop culturally valid and targeted career assessments that meet the needs of the growing multicultural population. Understanding the research landscape of multicultural career services is essential because research informs practice and supports the growing needs of our ever-changing, diverse client base.

Multicultural Career Coaching Concluding Thoughts

Multicultural coaching strategies are essential in supporting the diverse workforce of the 21st century. Career coaches can use helping skills to promote a strong coaching alliance while understanding their own biases in the coaching process. Numerous resources are available that encourage individuals to recognize and understand their biases. Coaches who work with diverse clients should establish a comprehensive working plan with exploration strategies and client support systems and identify existing factors that pose barriers to the career exploration process. Then, together, the coach and client can discuss these barriers and brainstorm potential solutions.

Knowledge Check

1. What is the common language related to career coaching for diverse populations?
2. Can you describe the importance of cultural competence in career coaching and its importance in practice?
3. Can you apply one or more models learned from this chapter to your client population? If newer to the field, are you interested in learning more about the models presented in this chapter?
4. Do you understand the specific and unique challenges that certain populations face in the workplace/job search, and did you come away from this chapter with ways to support these populations?

K-W-L Model – What Have I Learned?

To conclude this chapter, revisit the K-W-L model to assess whether this chapter provided you with information to fill some of your knowledge gaps. Finally, reflect on what you ***learned*** from this chapter and how it can apply to your coaching practice.

References

Adair, W. L., Buchan, N. R., Chen, X.-P., & Liu, D. (2016). A model of communication context and measure of context dependence. *Academy of Management Discoveries, 2,* 198–217.

Ang, S., & Van Dyne, L. (2008). Conceptualization of cultural intelligence: Definition, distinctiveness, and nomological network. In D. L. Sam & J. W. Berry (Eds.), *The Cambridge Handbook of Acculturation Psychology* (pp. 3–15). Cambridge University Press.

Ang, S., Van Dyne, L., & Tan, M. L. (2011). Cultural intelligence. In R. J., Sternberg & S. B. Kuffman (Eds.), *The cambridge handbook of intelligence* (pp. 582–602). Cambridge University Press. https://doi.org/10.1017/CBO9780511977244.030

Arthur, N. (2014). Social justice and career guidance in the age of talent. *International Journal for Educational and Vocational Guidance, 14,* 47–60. https://doi.org/10.1007/s10775-013-9255-x

Baboolall, D., Greenberg, S., Obeid, M., & Zucker, J. (2021). *Being transgender at work.* McKinsey & Company. https://www.mckinsey.com/featured-insights/diversity-and-inclusion/being-transgender-at-work

Bailinson, P., Decherd, W., Ellsworth, D., & Guttman, M. (2020, June). *LGBTQ+ voices: Learning from lived experiences.* https://www.mckinsey.com/business-functions/organization/our-insights/lgbtq-plus-voices-learning-from-lived-experiences

Bennett, M. J. (1986). A developmental approach to training for intercultural sensitivity. *International Journal of Intercultural Relations, 10*(2), 179–196.

Bennett, M. J. (2004). Becoming interculturally competent. In J. S. Wurzel (Ed.), *Toward multiculturalism: A reader in multicultural education.* Intercultural Resource Corporation.

Bennett, J. L., & Bush, M. W. (2013). *Coaching for change.* Routledge.

Betancourt, J. R. (2004). Cultural competence—marginal or mainstream movement? *New England Journal of Medicine*, *351*(10), 953-955.

Blustein, D. L. & Ellis, M. V. (2006). The cultural context of career assessments. *Journal of Career Assessments, 8,* 379-390.

Bolles, R. (1970). *What color is your parachute?* Ten Speed Press.

Brislin, R., Worthley, R. & Macnab, B. (2006). Cultural intelligence: Understanding behaviors that serve people's goals. *Group and Organizational Management, 31,* 40–55.

Burchum J. L. (2002). Cultural competence: An evolutionary perspective. *Nursing Forum*, *37*(4), 5–15. https://doi.org/10.1111/j.1744-6198.2002.tb01287.x

Carpenter-Song, E. A., Schwallie, M. N., & Longhofer, J. (2007). Cultural competence reexamined: Critique and directions for the future. *Psychiatric Services*, *58*(10), 1362-1365.

Cenizal, P. M. A. C. (2014). Pride and progress: Gender expression as a factor in career progression. *The Reflective Practitioner, 2,* 43-63.

Cook, E. P., Heppner, M. J., & O'Brien, K. M. (2002). Career development of women of color and White women: Assumptions, conceptualization, and interventions from an ecological perspective. *Career Development Quarterly, 50,* 291-305. https://doi.org/10.1002/j.2161-0045.2002.tb00574.x

Czeisler, M. É., Lane, R. I., Petrosky, E., Wiley, J. F., Christensen, A., Njai, R., Weaver, M. D., Robbins, R., Facer-Childs, E. R., Barger, L. K., Czeisler, C. A., Howard, M. E., & Rajaratnam, S. M. W. (2020). Mental health, substance use, and suicidal ideation during the covid-19 pandemic—United States, June 24-30, 2020. *Morbidity and Mortality Weekly Report, 69*(32), 1049–1057. https://doi.org/10.15585/mmwr.mm6932a1

de Guzman, M. R. T., Durden, T. R., Taylor, S. A., Guzman, J. M., & Potthoff, K. L. (2016). *Cultural competence: An important skills set for the 21st century.* Nebraska Extension NebGuide.

Deardorff, D. K. (2006). Identification and assessment of intercultural competence as a student outcome of internationalization. *Journal of Studies in International Education, 10*(3), 241-266. https://doi.org/10.1177/1028315306287002

Earley, P., Ang, S., & Tan, J-S. (2006). *CQ: Developing cultural intelligence at work.* Stanford University Press.

Earley, P. C., & Mosakowski, E. (2004). Cultural intelligence. *Harvard Business Review, 82*(10), 139–146.

Earley, P. C., & Peterson, R. S. (2004). The elusive cultural chameleon: Cultural intelligence as a new approach to intercultural training for the global manager. *Academy of Management Learning & Education, 3,* 100–115.

Elisworth, D., Hancock, B., & Schaninger, B. (2021). LGBTQ+ inclusion in the workplace [Podcast]. McKinsey & Co. https://www.mckinsey.com/business-functions/people-and-organizational-performance/our-insights/lgbtq-plus-inclusion-in-the-workplace

Evans, K. M., & Sejuit, A. L. (2021). *Gaining cultural competence in career counseling* (2nd ed.). National Career Development Association.

Exec. Order No. 13,672, 3 C.F.R. 42,971 (2014). https://www.govinfo.gov/content/pkg/FR-2014-07-23/pdf/2014-17522.pdf

Fitzgerald, L. F., & Betz, N. E. (1994). Career development in cultural context: The role of gender, race, class, and sexual orientation. In M. L. Savickas & R. W. Lent (Eds.), *Convergence in career development theories: Implications for science and practice* (pp. 103-117). CPP Books.

Flores, L., Lin, Y., & Huang, Y. (2005). Applying the multicultural guidelines to career counseling with people of color. In M. Constantine & D. Sue (Eds.), *Strategies for building multicultural competence in mental health and educational settings* (pp. 73-90). John Wiley & Sons, Inc.

Fouad, N. A. (1995). Balancing client and cultural sensitivity. *Counseling Psychologist, 23*, 63-67.

Gabelica, C., & Popov, V. (2020). "One size does not fit all": Revisiting team from a cultural dimensions perspective. *Group and Organization Management, 45*(2), 252-309. https://doi.org/10.1177/1059601120910859

Gnilka, P. B., O'Hara, C., & Chang, C. Y. (2018). Social justice counseling. In D. G. Hays & B. T. Erford (Eds.). *Developing multicultural counseling competencies: A systems approach* (3rd ed., pp. 66-91). Pearson.

Gysbers, N. C., Heppner, M. J., & Johnston, J. A. (2014). *Career counseling: Holism, diversity, and strength* (4th ed.). American Counseling Association.

Hartung, P. (2002). Cultural context in career theory and practice: Role salience and values. *The Career Development Quarterly, 51,* 12-25.

Hays, D. G., & Mcleod, A. L. (2018). The culturally competent counselor. In D. G. Hays & B. T. Erford (Eds.). *Developing multicultural counseling competencies: A systems approach* (3rd ed., pp. 1-36). Pearson.

Hicks, M. D., & Peterson, D. B. (1999). Leaders coaching across borders. In W. H. Mobley, M. J. Gessner & V. J. Arnold (Eds.), *Advances in global leadership* (Vol. 1, pp. 295–314). JAI Press.

Hofstede, G. (2011). Dimensionalizing cultures: The Hofstede model in context. *Online Readings in Psychology and Culture, 2*(1). https://doi.org/10.9707/2307-0919.1014

Hofstede, G., Hofstede, G. J., & Minkov, M. (2010). *Cultures and organizations: Software of the mind*. McGraw Hill.

Hooley, T., & Sultana, R. G. (2016). Career guidance for social justice. *Journal of the National Institute for Career Education and Counselling, 36*(1), 2-11. https://doi.org/10.20856/jnicec.3601

Inkeles, A., & Levinson, D. J. (1969). National character: The study of modal personality and sociocultural systems. In G. Lindzey & E. Aronson (Eds.), *The Handbook of Social Psychology IV* (pp. 418-506). McGraw-Hill.

Jones, J. (2021). *LGBT identification rises to 5.6% in latest U.S. estimate.* Gallup 2020. https://news.gallup.com/poll/329708/lgbt-identification-rises-latest-estimate.aspx

Kegan, R. & Lahey, L. (2001). *How the way we talk can change the way we learn.* Jossey-Bass.

LeBaron, M. (2003). *Culture-based negotiation styles.* Beyond Intractability. https://www.beyondintractability.org/essay/culture_negotiation

Lee, J. (2014). Asian international students' barriers to joining group counseling. *International Journal of Group Psychotherapy, 64,* 445-464. https://doi.org/10.1521/ijgp.2014.64.4.444

Lennard, D. (2010). *Coaching models: A cultural perspective: A guide to model development for practitioners and students of coaching*. Routledge.

Leong, F. T. L. (1997). Cross-cultural career psychology: Comments on Fouad, Harmon, and Borgen (1997) and Tracy, Watanabe, and Schneider (1997). *Journal of Counseling Psychology, 44*, 355-359. https://doi.org/10.1037/0022-0167.44.4.355

Luft, J. (1970). *Group processes: An introduction to group dynamics* (2nd ed.). Mayfield Publishing Company.

Makambe, U., & Pellissier, R. (2014). The application of Hofstede's cultural dimensions at Botho University: A model for workplace harmony in a multi-cultural business environment. *Information and Knowledge Management, 3*(4), 92-99.

Marsella, A. J., & Leong, F. T. (1995). Cross-cultural issues in personality and career assessment. *Journal of Career Assessment, 3,* 202-218.

McFarland, B. M., & Ford, C. (2017). *Integrating and engaging veterans in the workforce.* https://www.shrm.org/foundation/ourwork/initiatives/engaging-and-integrating-military-veterans/documents/4-17%20vet%20summit%20report%20final.pdf

Mehay, R. (2012). *The essential handbook for gp training and education.* Radcliffe Publishing Ltd.

Molinsky, A. (2013). *Global dexterity.* Harvard Business School Publishing.

Moore-Thomas, C. (2018). Cultural identity development. In D. G. Hays & B. T. Erford (Eds.), *Developing multicultural counseling competencies: A systems approach* (3rd ed.). Pearson.

National Career Development Association. (2015). *2015 NCDA code of ethics.* https://www.ncda.org/aws/NCDA/asset_manager/get_file/3395

Osipow, S. H., & Fitzgerald, L. F. (1996). *Theories of career development* (4th ed.). Allyn & Bacon.

Oxford English Dictionary. (n.d.). Gig economy. *Oxford Lexicon*. Retrieved December 14, 2021 from https://www.lexico.com/en/definition/gig_economy

Parsons, F. (1909). *Choosing a vocation*. Houghton-Mifflin.

Passmore, J., & Law, H. (2009). Cross-cultural and diversity coaching. In J. Passmore (Ed.), *Diversity in coaching: Working with gender, culture, race and age* (pp. 4-16). Kogan.

Peterson, D. (2007). Executive coaching in a cross-cultural context. *Consulting Psychology Journal: Practice and Research*, 59(4), 261–271.

Pope, M. (2009). Jesse Buttrick Davis (1871-1955): Pioneer of vocational guidance in the schools. *Career Development Quarterly, 57,* 248-258. https://doi.org/10.1002/j.2161-0045.2009.tb00110.x

Rowe, J. M., & Murphy, M. (2021). Inclusive career services programming for students with non-apparent disabilities. In H. Maietta (Ed.), *Cases in career services: A working guide for practitioners.* National Association of Colleges and Employers.

Rush, L. C. (2010). The needed development of multicultural career counseling skills: If not now when? If not us who? *Vista Online.* https://www.counseling.org/docs/default-source/vistas/the-needed-development-of-multicultural-career-counseling-skills-if-not-now-when-if-not-us-who.pdf

Saxena, P. (2015). Johari window: An effective model for improving interpersonal communication and managerial effectiveness. *SIT Journal of Management, 5*(2), 134-146.

Schein, E. H. (2010). *Organizational culture and leadership* (Vol. 2). John Wiley & Sons.

Sodowsky, G. R. (1996). The multicultural counseling inventory: Validity and applications in multicultural training. In R. Sadowsky & J. C. Impara (Eds.), *Multicultural Assessment in Counseling and Clinical Psychology.* Buros Institute of Mental Measurements, University of Nebraska–Lincoln. https://digitalcommons.unl.edu/burosbookmulticultural/13

Sodowsky, G. R., Taffe, R. C., Gutkin, T. B., & Wise, S. L. (1994). Development of the Multicultural Counseling Inventory: A self-report measure of multicultural competencies. *Journal of Counseling Psychology, 41,* 137–148.

Stebleton, M. J., & Eggerth, D. E. (2012). Returning to our roots: Immigrant populations at work. *Journal of Career Development, 39,* 3–12. https://doi.org/10.1177/0894845311417131

Sue, D. W. (2001). The superordinate nature of cultural competence. *The Counseling Psychologist, 29,* 850–857.

Sue, D. W., Arredondo, P., & McDavis, R. J. (1992). Multicultural counseling competencies and standards: A call to the profession. *Journal of Counseling and Development, 70,* 477-486. https://doi.org/10.1002/j.1556-6676.1992.tb01642.x

Sue, D. W., Bernier, J. E., Durran, A., Feinberg, L., Pedersen, P. B., Smith, E. J., Vasquez-Nuttal, E. (1982). Position paper: Cross-cultural counseling competencies. *Counseling Psychologist, 10,* 45-52.

Thomas, D. C., & Inkson, K. (2003). *Cultural intelligence: People skills for global business.* Berrett-Koehler Publishers.

Thoroughgood, C. N., Sawyer, K. B., & Webster, J. R. (2020). Creating a trans-inclusive workplace: How to make transgender employees feel valued at work. *Harvard Business Review.* https://hbr.org/2020/03/creating-a-trans-inclusive-workplace

U.S. Bureau of Labor Statistics. (2021, March 18). Employment situation of veterans summary. Author. https://www.bls.gov/news.release/vet.nr0.htm

Vespa, J. (2020). *Those who served: America's veterans from World War II to the war on terror: American community service report.* U.S. Census Bureau. https://www.census.gov/content/dam/Census/library/publications/2020/demo/acs-43.pdf

Vespa, J., Medina, L., & Armstrong, D. M. (2020). *Demographic turning points for the United States: Population projections for 2020 to 2060.* U.S. Census Bureau. https://www.census.gov/content/dam/Census/library/publications/2020/demo/p25-1144.pdf

Wilkins-Yel, K. G., Chung, Y. B., Cheng, J., & Li, Y. (2019). Multicultural considerations in career assessment. In K. B. Stoltz & S. R. Barclay (Eds.), *A comprehensive guide to career assessment* (7th ed., pp. 59-69). National Career Development Association.

Williams, B. (2001). Accomplishing cross-cultural competence in youth development programs. *Journal of Extension, 39*(6), 1-6.

Williams, P. (2020). In landmark case, Supreme Court rules LGBTQ workers are protected from job discrimination. *NBC News.* https://www.nbcnews.com/politics/supreme-court/supreme-court-rules-existing-civil-rights-law-protects-gay-lesbian-n1231018

Young, I. M. (1990). Five faces of oppression. In E. Hackett & S. Haslanger (Eds.), *Theorizing Feminisms* (pp. 3-16). Princeton University Press.

CHAPTER 7
Group Career Coaching

"Individually, we are one drop. Together we are an ocean."

– Ryunosuke Satoro

Chapter Highlights

This chapter will discuss the growing interest in group career coaching, a less labor-intensive, more cost-effective, social justice-focused delivery model compared to individual career coaching. Various ways career coaches work with groups, including identifying characteristics of effective group facilitation, creating an ideal learning environment, and outlining a plan to deliver effective group coaching, will be discussed. The chapter will also overview how to create lesson plans considering varied learning styles and group dynamics. Lastly, the chapter will introduce several specialized emerging group career coaching interventions.

Learning Objectives

This chapter highlights the following:

1. Various ways career coaches can work effectively with groups
2. How learning styles affect group facilitation strategies
3. Stages and how to navigate group dynamics
4. Ways to improve your skills for delivering career services to groups
5. Knowledge of emerging career coaching interventions related to social justice

K – W - L

Now that you know what the chapter has to offer, take a few minutes to assess your knowledge level and areas of learning using the K-W-L model. The first step in the K-W-L model is to self-assess what you already ***know*** about working with groups and group facilitation. What coaching techniques have you applied to your practice that have helped you become more proficient in group work? Next, think about what you ***want*** to know about coaching in a group setting. Where do you feel are the gaps in your coaching knowledge and performance? Finally, to conclude this chapter, you will be asked to revisit the K-W-L model to assess whether this chapter provided you with information to fill some of your knowledge gaps. Reflect on what you ***learned*** from this chapter and how you can apply it to your coaching practice.

Group Facilitation

The majority of career coaching has and continues to be performed individually, despite attempts to expand and legitimize the practice of group coaching. Meldrum (2021) posited, "Career guidance, counseling and coaching practice over the years has predominantly been delivered on a one-to-one basis and focused on the development of the practitioner-client relationship to facilitate growth at an individual level" (p. 214). Thomsen (2012) posited that approaches that focus on collaborative problem-solving need to be brought to the forefront, deemphasizing a focus on one-on-one coaching. In the busyness of everyone's lives, it is often more convenient to arrange one-on-one coaching appointments with clients than small or even large group coaching sessions or seminars. The one-on-one relationship between coach and client may provide clients the direct attention they seek and other clients may prefer one-on-one due to feeling intimidated by the group (Pyle & Hayden, 2015). That said, group coaching is emerging as an approach with many benefits, including collective empowerment and social justice potential (Hooley & Sultana, 2016). This chapter will examine the impact of group coaching on career-related decision-making in this larger context.

There are several definitions of group coaching in the literature depending on the applicable discipline. This publication will use Cockerham's (2011) group coaching definition, which is "a facilitated group process that is led by a professional coach and formed to maximize the combined energy, experience and wisdom of individuals who chose to join in order to achieve organizational objectives and/or individual goals" (p. 1). Working in groups or *group work* is an opportunity to bring together disparate individuals who share a common purpose to meet the desired objective. Benson (2019) posited, "Groupwork is a productive, healthy, and creative experience, carried out based on explicit agreements, openly pursued and clearly arrived at, about the purpose and task of the group, rights, and responsibilities of members" (p. 8). Participants of group work engage in two-way, emotional interaction with other members. Benson highlighted that when the group work is synergistic, the following principles are present:

- The group experience is fundamental
- The group provides consistency and predictability
- The group is organic and natural
- The group is an energetic experience
- The 'here and now' is important
- The 'hidden' must be made visible
- Experience in the group is multidimensional
- There is an organizing principle in the group. (Benson, 2019, p. 2)

Individual, community and organizational settings can all benefit from group coaching. This chapter will overview the benefits and challenges of group coaching, career coaching techniques for working in groups, and nuances associated with group career coaching when working with varied clientele.

Team vs. Group Coaching

While a number of people may be brought together under one coach, there are variations between team and group coaching, and the two serve different purposes. In a team coaching setting, individuals work in synergy towards a common goal or objective. Team coaching improves effectiveness within members of a group, typically within an organization, to better the whole. The team may work on communication, productivity, accountability among team members, conflict resolution, and leadership dynamics. A career coach working with a team might help members reconfigure roles and responsibilities based on strengths – a form of job crafting (Berg et al., 2008; see Chapter 4) – to showcase and apply more directly the talents of each member within the organization. Since individuals work closely towards a defined and mutually accountable goal (Bloisi et al., 2003), career coaching within a team environment works for the individual and the team.

Group coaching varies in that it refers to any group that may or may not be working toward common objectives within a broader group goal. In short, members of the group have their own individual goals. The group coaching sessions may have broader, shared themes, for instance, members of the group may be in a similar phase or timeframe in their lives, yet members of the group set individualized goals or objectives related to the session themes–they all have their individualized journeys. Furthermore, these individuals may or may not know one another before participating in the group coaching sessions. When a group is diverse, and its members are motivated to learn and improve their shared beliefs, group synergy can be significantly improved (Sawyer, 2012; Dolny, 2009). Group coaching raises an individual's self-awareness by enabling them to think out loud and listen to others' stories (Thornton, 2010) in an "intimate conversation space" (Britton, 2013, p. 117). A career coach working in a group coaching setting may help group members set individual goals connected to their professional motivations and then collectively facilitate the connection between group members to encourage and motivate one another to reach individual goals. It is helpful to take a deeper look at group career coaching.

Group Career Coaching

Careers ebb and flow with time, as do the needs, supports, and strategies required to manage those needs. Sometimes these needs call for individual support. Other times, individuals are needed who share the same challenges and walk the same journey committed to similar broad-based goals. At times individuals seek varying advice–a wider swath of resources and connections. These occasions call for group support, occasions where individual coaching, while effective, may not provide the most impactful support available or needed. Group career coaching can serve as this resource and support community. Group leaders may be coaches, facilitators, instructors, or teachers. Regardless of the title, there are many benefits of group career coaching universal to the clients and coach.

Benefits of Group Coaching: The Client

Group career coaching is ideal for clients committed to their career success who prefer to work in a group or whose career transition calls for a more group-focused strategy. Pyle and Hayden (2015) noted that as the relationship among group members develops, normalizing occurs in that individuals are less likely to see themselves as alone in their situation. Kemmis and McTaggart (2005) posited that collaboration offers the best space for reflection, and in the career exploration process, reflection is a common form of learning. Everyone has varied styles of learning and preferences of space in which they learn. Some people enjoy learning independently–they prefer the comfort and solitude it offers, the uninterrupted freedom to craft the learning experience on their terms. For others, a sense of community is necessary to stimulate creativity or motivate learning. When learning in isolation is not a satisfactory experience, working in a group allows individuals to gain knowledge, share experiences, and brainstorm through group association. "The leader can call upon and use the diverse and varied personalities within the group as part of the learning process" (Pyle & Hayden, 2015, p. 3). Benefits of group coaching to the client include:

- Being part of a community
- Exposure to differing perspectives and approaches
- Having the ability to expand their network
- Being with individuals that share similar topical interests
- Working with a trained group coach
- Working toward common yet individual goals as part of a structured, step-by-step program
- Reducing isolation that can accompany a transition
- Normalizing situations and dispelling fears by listening to others' stories

The elements of group peer pressure play to the coach and client's favor in that the clients tend to participate more readily. Group coaching aims not to reach consensus within the group setting but rather to listen to various voices and opinions.

Benefits of Group Coaching: The Coach

There are also many benefits to running group coaching sessions for a coach. According to Clutterbuck (2007), a group coach actively participates and collaborates with the other group members. Although some facilitation is needed, connecting with group members, sharing expertise, and engaging in content-based discussion help clients stay active and involved. From the coach's perspective, group coaching:

- Helps clients work toward common yet individual goals as part of a step-by-step process

- Offers the ability to reach more clients in a condensed timeframe
- Allows the coach to set clear facilitation timelines
- Provides increased accountability and commitment among members
- Offers better (e.g., monetary) value to clients
- Utilizes fewer resources than one-on-one coaching
- Often has less strain on the coach's schedule

The ability to see more clients simultaneously can increase and stabilize the coach's income. The more secure income is a benefit because income often varies regardless of whether the coach works for an organization or maintains a private practice as an independent coach. When facilitated skillfully, these are just some of the many benefits of group coaching.

Challenges with Group Coaching

While group coaching impacts each individual differently and provides countless benefits, it is not without challenges. However, the coach can mitigate these challenges with proper training and boundary-setting. Common group coaching challenges are as follows:

Untrained or Poorly Trained Coaches

There are specific skills needed to be a strong group facilitator. Being a content expert or an expert in the population participating in the group coaching session may not qualify the group coach. When coaches are poorly trained, group dynamics suffer.

Inexperience Handling Sensitive Topics

Group coaching entails a high level of social engagement and frequently delves into topics of a sensitive nature (Brown & Grant, 2010). When the conversation shifts to complex or intimate issues, participants may get anxious or uncomfortable. These discussions might cause friction in the group, or uncertainty can inhibit openness, resulting in a negative outcome if the coach does not handle the situation effectively.

Unclear or Lack of Goal Accountability

Another challenge with group coaching is establishing clear goals and taking action. It is difficult to determine if the group is making progress without setting and tracking specific goals and actions. Outcomes must be measured, just as they must be with individual coaching to ensure optimal performance.

Misguided Intentions

Although there is usually a financial benefit to group coaching, outcomes may suffer if this is the primary motivator for the coaching experience.

Ethical Considerations in Group Career Coaching

As with any coaching practice, ethical consideration is paramount. The National Career Development Association (NCDA) *Code of Ethics* (2015) (see Appendix E) or similar code can provide a detailed roadmap in ethical boundaries in working with clients in a variety of settings. Section A.8.a of the NCDA *Code of Ethics* explicitly states a coach's steps in facilitating work with groups. First, a career coach must screen candidates based on the criterion set for group participation. For instance, if the group is designed for participants searching for careers post-retirement, age would be a criterion for participation. Allowing individuals new to the workforce to participate may impede the group process as these members are not compatible with the goals set for the group. Allowing individuals incompatible with group goals could jeopardize the overall group experience and well-being of members.

In addition to pre-qualifying participants, informed consent is vital. NCDA's *Code of Ethics* (2015) states that providing details on the coach/client relationship is essential when working with clients in any setting. Section A.2 offers guidance on the importance of informed consent, the types of information to provide the client(s) (e.g., group purposes, goals, techniques, procedures, limitations, potential risks, and benefits of group services, the coach's qualifications as a career professional, and appropriate technology use), and confidentiality precautions taken by the coach. Communicating and maintaining confidentiality are essential when facilitating group coaching. If participants feel their information is protected and trust other group members and the facilitator, they will share more readily. The coach must outline a confidentiality clause in the informed consent form (see Appendix C) and review the confidentiality clause with candidates before group participation. A coach can ensure their own personal confidentiality but cannot ensure group members will honor the request to keep the group interaction confidential, and this point must be communicated (NCDA, 2015).

Another ethical consideration in configuring and facilitating groups is developmental and cultural sensitivity. Across all ethical codes, a call for and suggested guidelines that ensure cultural and developmental sensitivity can be found across all ethical codes. For example, NCDA's *Code of Ethics* (A.2.c., B.1.a., C.5., E.8.) states that clear, concise, and age-appropriate verbal and non-verbal communication must be used at all times by the coach and group members. Sensitivity issues may arise if group members do not see eye to eye on the subject. In addition, group members from varying cultures or backgrounds may have different understandings of the topical nature of the discussion, language barriers, or assessment interpretation questions. When in doubt, consult a code of ethics and, if needed, secure an interpreter or welcome a participant to invite one of their choosing if agreed upon by members of the group (NCDA, 2015).

The Group Coaching Process

Pre-Work

Just as in individual coaching sessions, coaching principles apply to group coaching. Before executing the group coaching session, the career coach wants to ensure the completion of all pre-work. When executing the group coaching session, the goal is to build trust and rapport. The coach and group members simultaneously build trust and rapport through verbal and non-verbal communication (see Chapter 2). Skillful facilitation by actively listening, asking powerful questions (see Appendix A), communicating effectively, planning and goal setting, creating awareness, deep listening, and action and accountability apply to group coaching (see Chapter 6). Before a coach begins facilitating a group, thorough and detailed pre-planning must occur. There are several boxes to check in the pre-planning process:

- consider and choose the most appropriate **group style** to deliver content
- consider the varying **learning styles** of group members when planning content and delivery of content
- **preparing content**, considering expertise and population.

Let us examine the pre-planning components individually.

Group Styles

There are various group styles: pairs, triads, learning teams, or large groups to consider. Each style has a separate and distinct function and should be considered depending on the learning objectives and desired outcomes. *Group pairs* (dyads) provide participants with a more intimate learning opportunity, increasing direct connection. This rapport-building allows group members to feel more comfortable, encouraging more sharing and self-disclosure. People who are less comfortable in larger groups but want broader connections beyond one-on-one coaching may prefer the group pairs style. However, members may not benefit from as vast or diverse input and could miss out on broader connections or networking opportunities due to the group's small size.

Triads are another style typically used in observation activities where two group members role-play while the third member observes and provides feedback. The group members rotate until everyone can assume all triad roles. Triads are ideal when group activity calls for skill development (e.g., interviewing skills) or practicing a technique (e.g., career coaching). Many group benefits apply to triads, as do working in pairs. Triads work best when group members have established a baseline or more intimate rapport with one another, so they feel comfortable giving feedback. Otherwise, there may be less self-disclosure or information sharing. Lack of self-disclosure is a challenge with triads, as many group activities involving triads require participants to be honest and open.

Learning teams (small groups) are reserved for activities that call for a less intimate environment and benefit from multiple perspectives and backgrounds. Law (1996) posited that small group work spans the boundaries between one-on-one interviewing and group work. Learning teams are small enough for individuals to stand out or contribute and encourage collaboration and camaraderie among group members, and the relationships established in the group often extend after group work is complete. Solving challenges or brainstorming solutions to scalable problems are excellent tasks for learning teams. However, learning teams often introduce a topic or concept for educational purposes, and thus, the group has less chance to build deeper connections with one another outside of the group instruction.

A final group style is *large group interaction*. Large group coaching is appropriate for single topic dissemination or when the topic needs to reach people in bulk. Seminars, workshops, conferences, and opportunities to celebrate achievements are examples of large group interactions. Large groups serve an essential and distinct purpose of disseminating information efficiently and in mass; however, self-disclosure and lengthy, deep conversations or connections are difficult to achieve. Less bonding will occur with the larger group, as one-on-one connections are difficult to establish. In addition, more dominant members may assert themselves as leaders and build smaller coalitions within the group, causing challenging facilitation dynamics (Ellis & Fisher, 1994). Therefore, consider the available group style options when planning group work. Considering the topic, learning objectives, and group work outcomes will help the coach choose the most appropriate style to deliver group support.

Learning Styles

According to current research, numerous factors influence learning: prior subject understanding, course content delivery, the volume of material provided and expected to retain, and learning preferences. Several learning preference models evaluate the ways individuals learn. Fleming (2019) and Fleming and Mills (1992) found a tangible and current way of assessing learning preferences by identifying four sensory modalities—visual, aural, read/write, and kinesthetic (VARK; vark-learn.com). Considering many learning styles when instructing is essential because learning preferences differ between individuals. For example, visual learners absorb material best through pictures, graphs, charts, visual aids, handouts and prefer to write to learn and retain information rather than hear information through a presentation. Visual learners appreciate handouts and other supplemental materials to complement other forms of content delivery in an educational setting. Aural learners prefer to hear content delivered to them and talk about and debate a topic for maximum learning. These individuals appreciate small group discussions and enjoy storytelling. They gravitate towards lectures, learn by reading aloud, and prefer listening to others through classroom lectures and audio delivery methods (e.g., podcasts). Reading/writing learners prefer essay work and enjoy content-heavy reading for knowledge purposes. During group instruction, these learners might highlight the book as they read or write in margins and take heavy notes. Like visual learners, they appreciate handouts and other supplemental materials to complement other forms of content delivery. Finally, kinesthetic/tactile learners enjoy and learn through touch and physical activity. Kinesthetic/tactile learners absorb information best in environments where the facilitator delivers content through ice breakers, activities, role play, building prototypes, and field trips. These learners prefer active learning group work.

Fleming designed the VARK learning preferences questionnaire to understand an individual's preferences for visual, aural, read/write, and kinesthetic learning modalities (Fleming, 2019). For coaches to address the diverse learning preferences, content must be delivered through various methods because no single method applies to all learning preferences (Lujan & DiCarlo, 2006; Schlairet et al., 2014). However, coaches can apply that awareness to curriculum design when they know their instructional and facilitation approaches and participant learning preferences. VARK is a simple theory to consider when planning group work to capture various learning styles.

Preparing Content Themes

In the world of career coaching, there are many content themes to choose from: navigating the job search, discovering the self, networking for job search success, and strength-based professional growth are a few themes that come to mind. Setting a content theme requires knowledge of labor market needs, what participants are interested in learning, and the coach's expertise. Facilitating a group coaching session based on the set theme takes a high degree of facilitation skills and confidence to embrace the unknown (Thornton, 2010).

It is essential to do homework to understand participants' goals. Before going into the group coaching session or workshop, the coach should brainstorm and design content themes, such as conducting an environmental scan of hot topics in the labor market or polling the participants (if known). The coach will want to think about their area of expertise, specifically current content themes, and plans to share if applicable. A few common career-related content themes include:

- **Labor market information:** workshops on researching occupations, employment options, educational requirements related to industry options, use of labor market tools and resources (e.g., O*NET).
- **Career portfolios/eRésumés:** the increased use of technology has sparked high interest in digital professional portfolios or eRésumés. Free or nominally offered web hosting services such as Wix.com allow easy development of professional websites geared towards a virtual representation of past accomplishments.
- **Job search process:** popular to career changers and job seekers are groups covering necessary career-related topics like building a résumé, interviewing techniques, workplace communication, and professional networking.
- **Self-exploration:** looking at skills, values, interests, strengths via informal and formal assessment administration (see Chapter 5) is a popular group activity.

Lesson Plans

Creating a lesson plan (see Appendix I) for the group coaching session or workshop can ensure the coach sets and meets learning objectives. A lesson plan typically contains the learning objectives and theme of the coaching session which are supported and executed through content, activities/methods, support materials, and logistics.

Once the coach decides on the theme to deliver during the group coaching session(s) or workshop, setting learning objectives, by beginning with the end in mind, is necessary. For example, the coach will question, "What content knowledge could the group apply to help further one of their professional goals?" Or, more specifically, "What are two strategies the participants could employ to further their goals after participating in the workshop?" The learning objectives will stem from answers to these questions.

The coach will need to ensure the learning objectives are concrete and quantifiable so they can be measured. Using action verbs is a reliable way to measure learning. For example, learning objectives associated with a workshop on networking using LinkedIn might read something like this: "At the end of this workshop, participants will have created and know how to maintain a professional LinkedIn profile. Participants will be able to describe the purpose of using LinkedIn for networking and list five ways to connect with contacts to build networking connections. Participants will know how the LinkedIn job search feature links to personal connections and how to use these connections when applying for positions through the job search function. Finally, participants will understand how to reach out to colleagues for professional recommendations through the LinkedIn endorsement feature."

Learning objectives should connect directly to the session topic and content. The coach should review learning objectives with the group at the beginning of the group session and answer any questions. There are various ways to assess whether the group coaching has met the set learning objectives. For example, a pre-post test for comprehension could be administered. In addition, participants could contribute to a group forum discussion to debrief on their learning experience. Minute questions at the end of the session are also an excellent exercise to test for learning.

In addition to learning objectives, a lesson plan includes content, activities/methods, support materials, and time. *Content* details how the lesson theme will be delivered during the group coaching session. For example, if the theme of the group coaching session is "résumé writing for the job search," the content might be the various types of résumé applicable to various industries (UX design, business, academia). *Activities* provide active learning for particular content. Examples of session activities during a résumé writing group coaching session might include icebreakers, skills card sorts, or small group idea generation. *Method* refers to how the coach will deliver the content, which might be in the form of a brief lecture, demonstration, video, group share, or a combination of methods. *Support materials* include any handouts or resources associated with the specific content block. Inform participants in advance if they must bring any support materials to the workshop (laptop, journal, copy of résumé). Additional things to consider may include the type of room set-up, teaching aids, props, or learning supplies needed. *Time* refers to the estimated time spent learning that specific content. Content blocks of time – or how the content is broken down into manageable learning buckets – typically range from 5-20 minutes. Table 11 shows an example of a lesson plan content block for a LinkedIn workshop.

Planning and Preparation

An effective coach takes time planning and preparing before executing group coaching. Learning content is thought out and planned well before the execution date. Creating an outline can help organize the content, which helps the coach attach learning objectives to content, consider varied learning styles when planning group activities, and organize materials and logistics to support the group coaching session. It is vital to conduct a run-through of the session beforehand, so it is necessary to plan group content and activities in advance.

Table 11
LinkedIn for Networking Lesson Plan

Method	Activity	Content	Support Materials	Time
Workshop	Discuss handout on the top 5 ways to use LinkedIn for networking	Instruct participants how to set up a professional profile and use the profile for networking.	Computer lab or personal laptops	20 min

Logistics

Logistical questions that need asking and answering will vary from session to session depending on the coaching theme or topic, event location, and group members. However, here are a few common questions to consider:

- How many participants are going to attend the group session? Will they register in advance? Will there be a drop-in policy? What is the minimum/maximum participation permitted?
- What will the participants expect from the session(s)? What expectations will the coach set for the participants before group attendance?
- Is there pre-work involved, and how will this be disseminated?
- What are the goals of the sessions? Have learning objectives been set? How will these be assessed?
- What is the duration and timeframe of each group session?
- Will the group meet in person (if so, where?), virtually, or through a hybrid model? Will sessions be recorded? (If yes, informed consent for recording is required.)
- Will there be an attendance fee? If yes, how will this fee be calculated (per session/program), and how will payments be made?
- Will learning materials be distributed? How will handouts meet standards for persons with disabilities (i.e., easy-to-read font style and size, available in print and virtual, closed caption if possible)?

Executing the Group Coaching Session

Being prompt is essential on the day of the group coaching or workshop event (in-person or online). Early arrival will provide time to test audio/visual equipment and check site logistics (e.g., location of restrooms, refreshments). The group coach should be the first on-site to greet participants, answer questions, make them feel comfortable, and dispel any participation nerves. First impressions make a difference, and communicating approachability from the start is key. Respect the audience by using all of the helping skills techniques.

Set Clear Group Expectations

Begin the group coaching session by setting clear expectations for working with the group and having the group set clear expectations for working together. The members should create established ground rules for group interaction to reflect the group's uniqueness and personality. Suggested ground rules should be discussed and agreed upon by all group members. Ground rules should be easy to remember and establish a foundation of rapport. Ground rules should also be as concrete and quantifiable as possible. For example, time is valued differently by people of different cultures, so setting a ground rule of "being on time" might need to be clearly stated as, "All group members will arrive by 9:00 am" or "Meeting will begin within five minutes of the established start time."

Go over the agenda for the group session, letting the group know what will be discussed within designated timelines, including any breaks. Answer questions enthusiastically and thoroughly. Remind the group that the coach's role is a facilitator, serving and leading the group. In this role, the career coach interacts with group members, observes interactions, acts as a point of contact, resolves conflicts if necessary, minimizes disruptions, helps members stay energized and engaged, and provides meaningful content. Remember that approachability is vital to building and maintaining rapport. Group members often feel vulnerable when participating in a group setting, but the content or nature of the group discussion could add a layer of sensitivity to the conversations. Modeling positive behavior will show group members the standard of care.

Explain Group Activities/Assignments

Clients may or may not have participated in group coaching recently. For some, it may have been years since their last group activity, workshop, or classroom learning experience. Therefore, it is essential to explain in writing and verbally all of the group activities and assignments related to the coaching early in the session. If the learning experience is lengthy and content-heavy, including a syllabus or other coaching materials, and review these materials with the group before beginning content delivery. Highlight due dates or session expectations and answer any questions posed by the group before moving on to the instructional portion of the coaching.

Group Dynamics

Whether the group session is workshop style, weekly drop-in, weekend seminar, or more intense, longer-term work, group dynamics should be considered as group members move from strangers to working colleagues. These shifts impact communication, instruction, and learning. Tuckman (1965) researched developmental stages that group members evolve through as they work together and become more familiar with themselves, each other, and the content of the group activity. Tuckman's four stages (1965), forming, storming, norming, and performing, were later revised to include a fifth stage, adjourning (Tuckman & Jensen, 1977).

Forming. During the first stage of group development – forming – group members are eager to begin. However, there is an underlying uncertainty associated with new relationships and tasks. As the group forms, cohesion sets in and can be stronger with voluntary groups (Hargie, 2011). The cohesiveness that develops during formation propels the group down a path determined by their feelings toward one another and their goals. As group members arrive and depart, the group cycles in and out of the formation stage, although there is less uncertainty when one or two new members join than when the group initially starts.

Many factors influence how the forming stage of group development plays out, and this initial interaction lays the foundation for later group dynamics. Personalities, skills, available resources, size of the group, and the group's purpose all set the tone of and climate within a group (Ellis & Fisher, 1994). Members are curious about the group structure and flow, the roles that members will assume, and the coach's expectations. Uncertainty related to expectations is reduced when a coach facilitates the group, setting agendas, goals, and expected group outcomes. Some level of structure is helpful, but too much can create resentment or a feeling of powerlessness among group members. The coach should be mindful of managing uncertainty to increase group cohesion and productivity.

Storming. Once group members settle into group coaching, stage two or storming takes over. During storming, group members begin questioning, even challenging the content and/or group coach. Participants establish roles within the group (e.g., dominating, quiet, argumentative), begin resisting some communicated messages, and are occasionally critical of other participants (Tuckman & Jensen, 1977). Discrepancies may be identified, leaving members feeling confused or incompetent. Storming can be difficult for coaches and clients because there may be uncomfortable discourse and uncertainty, raising questions about the program and facilitator. Although storming is a natural developmental progression of group work, a coach should expect some degree of resentment from members who want to take more of a leadership role, have interpersonal conflicts with the leader or other group members, or have difficulty being led. On the other hand, group discourse can be positive and productive in that it sparks deep discussion, engages members passionately, and typically raises issues not thought of initially.

Norming. As group members move through the learning process, and recognize their growth, norming occurs. The group accepts others' contributions and differences during this stage, leading to more stability, productivity, and cohesion. Norms are formed within-group and influenced by societal rules (e.g., tardiness, talking out of turn), which helps set the tone for what

COACH CORNER

Try to recall a previous small group facilitation or participation experience. Reflect on the group's developmental stages. Were all of the stages experienced? In what order? Did the group stay in some stages more than others?

group members ought to do and how they ought to behave (Ellis & Fisher, 1994). When group norms are challenged or imbalanced, the stage reverts to storming until communication patterns have been restored.

Performing. Increased group productivity leads to the fourth stage, performing. During performing, members gain confidence from their newfound growth and accomplishment, which opens the door to additional collaboration (Tuckman & Jensen, 1977). Relational aspects of group interaction during the performing stage are heavily task-focused. Ideally, group members begin to build synergy by pooling their talents, ideas, experiences, and resources, and, as with any of the group dynamics stages, reverting to a previous stage is possible. In performing, it is helpful to set short, attainable, conceivable, believable tasks for the group to ensure forward movement toward completion.

Adjourning. As the group ends its time together, a period of adjourning begins. Here, group members maintain a high level of rapport with one another and are excited for the possibilities of continuing networking connections post-session. There are feelings of anxiety and sadness as the session is nearing its end and satisfaction with accomplishments and excitement to transfer learned content to their job function. Some members may feel anxiety or uncertainty about how they will perform such functions without the support of the group or coach and whether they have learned enough to pay the knowledge forward (Tuckman & Jensen, 1977). To ensure maximum benefit from the adjourning stage and the close of the group coaching experience, the coach will want to facilitate structured reflection. Often, group members leave a group experience with new or more developed skills useful in future groups or individual contexts, so reflection is key to this post-participation application.

Facilitation Challenges

As the coach begins to execute the group coaching session facilitation, challenges may occur, such as absenteeism, inattention, low participation, acting out behaviors, and challenging participant dynamics. These challenges can be successfully navigated if considered in advance and planned for by keeping group facilitation notes, understanding one's strengths and challenges as a facilitator, receiving proper training in group facilitation before running a group session, continued growth and education as a group facilitator, and being honest regarding participant input. These challenges can be successfully navigated if considered in advance and planned for by keeping group facilitation notes, understanding one's strengths and challenges as a facilitator, receiving proper training in group facilitation before running a group session, seeking continued growth and education as a group facilitator, and accepting participant input. Any client evaluations collected should be taken seriously, as this also may improve group coaching.

It is also extremely important to ask and answer key questions, such as how to ensure participants will maintain accountability. There are three ways participants can check out of a group coaching session: mentally, emotionally, or physically. A mental check-out is when a participant is physically present in the virtual or in-person community space but fails to participate in the group work or does so unenthusiastically. Participants who mentally check out take little or no action and may not progress towards their goals.

An emotional check-out is when a group member feels they see little or no benefit from the group work. They are physically and (occasionally) mentally present, but emotionally, their enthusiasm for the group and the group's progress has waned. As a result, participants assume an "I don't care" attitude and disconnect from the program. Physical check-out results from a client mentally and emotionally detaching. This detachment shows itself in different forms. The participant may sporadically attend the group session or stop attending the group sessions altogether, essentially dropping out of the group. The client stops showing up and participating in the community space altogether. They officially "drop out" of the program.

To combat facilitation challenges, setting expectations for the group is vital. For example, what ground rules will be established for the group, such as actively listening, attendance, confidentiality, and respect, and how will these be communicated before the session? It is important to set expectations upfront regarding participation - this is one of the main jobs of a facilitator. Likewise, the facilitator will want to encourage people to share their experiences and ideas and urge those with relevant background information to share when appropriate. Finally, a facilitator should monitor for signs of disengagement. Do participants look bored, tired, or confused? Group members may need a break, or the coach may need to stop facilitating and check in with the group to ensure everyone is on the same page.

Post-Group Coaching Experience

Ending the group coaching experience is as important as delivering the session itself. The coach wants the group members' last impression of the session and the coach to be as strong as the first impression. To ensure the group coaching experience ends on solid footing and the coach is set up for continued development as a coach, here are a few things to consider:

1. **Group Journal:** Whether it is a one-time workshop or a lengthy group coaching experience, after each session, the coach will want to journal their progress as a coach, as well as the group's overall progress. What worked? What could have been improved? What was missing? These notes will be a roadmap to improving the next group coaching experience and a helpful way to debrief on progress as a coach.
2. **Post-Support:** The coach will also want to consider whether to provide a level of support outside of each session. This level of support might include post-workshop coaching, follow-up resources or topical content, virtual group discussion with other members facilitated by the group coach, or individual one-on-one coaching sessions with all group members. Deciding and planning post-support offerings before beginning the training ensures being ready to announce and provide details on this support as the training concludes.
3. **Evaluations:** During pre-planning, set learning objectives and a plan to assess growth in learning. It is time to measure learning growth and satisfaction with the overall group coaching experience. The goal as a group coach is to ensure the members receive the content and support that was promised.

Groups Facilitation Models

Online Group Coaching

Group coaching may be in a virtual or online format. This format has become increasingly popular to connect with colleagues, especially given the COVID pandemic, as it allows safety, flexibility, independence, and financial incentive. Platforms such as Zoom, Google Meet, Slack, Microsoft Teams, and others have and will continue to support coaching as a robust, safe, and convenient way to connect with clients in a group setting. In addition, costs are often lower and financially beneficial for both the client and the content creator, as room fees and travel time are less compared to in-person groups.

Cohort Model

A cohort model is used in many learning environments where participants benefit from learning together. Cohort members sign up in advance and generally start and finish on the same days. Members also generally move through coaching content simultaneously, increasing learning and comradery. As a coach, a cohort model provides an ideal way of piloting a program before investing resources and scaling. A cohort model does not require many clients to get the group coaching up and running. Participants of a cohort model typically see the coach as an expert in program content and expect interaction within the cohort itself with the coach as a facilitator. Monetarily, a cohort model carries a high price point as the group size is small and set, allowing for more interaction with the coach and other participants.

Program Model

A program model is more common for online coaching as the clients sign up when they want, the program is over a specified length, starting at any time, and clients follow a predefined schedule. This model can be more technically complicated to organize as the coach will have clients starting and ending at different times. Coaching is likely to include pre-recorded webinars and videos combined with one-to-many communications. However, if a coach has the right skills to set it up and is ready with a proven program and a potentially large audience, this is a scalable and potentially financially rewarding approach. There are typically rolling sign-ups. In terms of coach-client interaction, the content delivery involves heavily recorded webinars/podcasts or other scalable touchpoints. A program model assumes the coach has a high volume of clients and/or interest in the coaching program. In terms of price point, if one were charging, a program model would yield a lower price point per sign-up than a cohort model as the client-to-coach ratio is higher and participants have less one-on-one or small group interaction with other members.

Membership Model

A membership model runs on the same recurring schedule each year and combines many cohorts and program model benefits. Clients can start on multiple dates throughout the year, then work with others on the same schedule. While setting up involves some complexity, the membership model can be highly scalable online and will likely attract repeat customers returning for next-level coaching. In addition, membership models generally complement other coach offerings, such as a cohort model or one-on-one coaching program. Finally, the price point is less expensive, and there are no enrollment limitations in general.

Specialized Group Coaching Models

Group Interactive Narrative Approach (GINA)

The Group Interactive Narrative Approach (GINA) model is based on narrative life design (Savickas, 2012) using career story interviews and executed using Roger's (1961) person-centered counseling techniques. Together GINA uses high-quality interpersonal, collaborative interactions to develop group learning, heavily influenced by a constructivist approach that considers an individual's social interactions and experiences from personal and professional lives connecting, forming patterns, and holding meaning. The structure used to execute the GINA model (see Figure 14) is based on the G.R.O.W. coaching model (Whitmore, 2017; see Chapter 4). G.R.O.W. stands for goal, reality (current status or situation), options, and way forward or taking action steps to achieve one's goal(s). Used in a group coaching setting, coach and clients work together to actively create joint goals for the coaching session (concrete experiences), discuss each other's stories (reflective observation), and through the re-telling of stories and idea evaluation, help each other achieve their goals (abstract conceptualization). Re-telling stories, re-evaluating options, and reflecting on these options is a cyclical process (active experimentation). A small group model that sees the coach and group participants as co-facilitators, GINA effectively develops career management skills, dispelling the pressures related to career decision-making and transition through group understanding and idea generation via peer interactions (Meldrum, 2017).

The Collective Career Coaching Model

One interest in increasing group coaching is its potential to lessen passiveness and power imbalances across one-on-one coaching (Hooley et al., 2017). The collective career coaching model is a group approach that demonstrates the collective empowerment and social justice possibilities of group work anchored in critical pedagogy

Figure 14
The Group Interactive Narrative Approach (GINA)

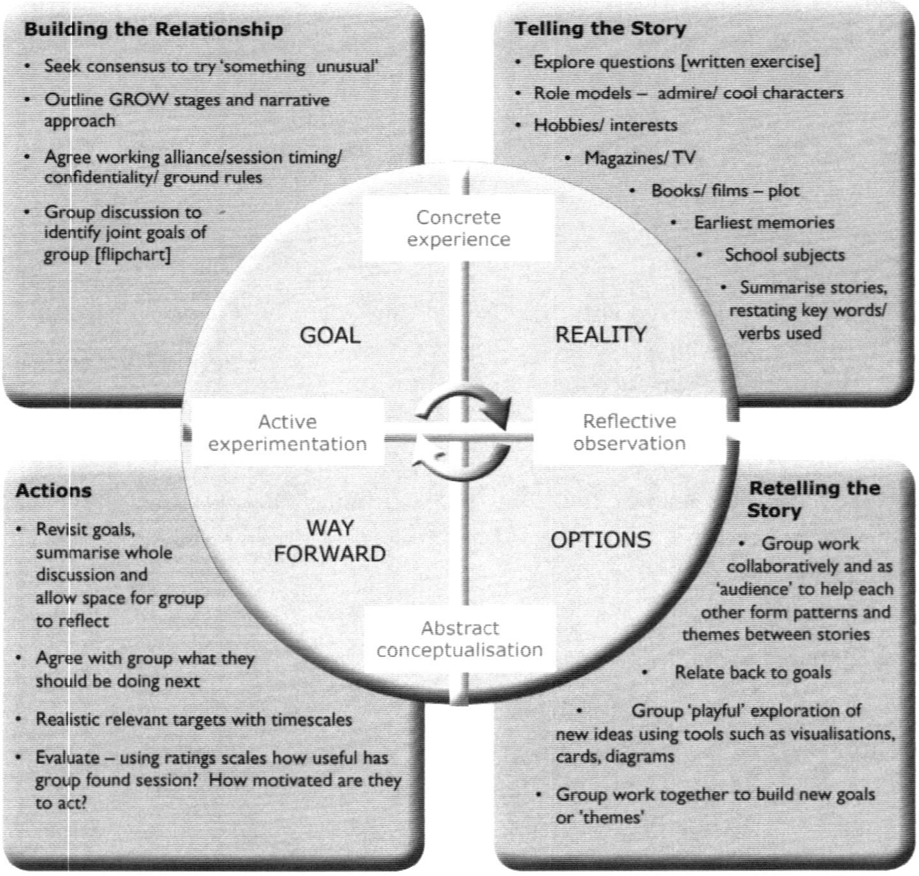

Adopted from "Group Guidance- Is It Time to Flock Together?" by S. C. Meldrum , 2017, *Journal of the National Institute for Career, 38*(1), pp. 36–43,

(Meldrum, 2021). Critical pedagogy as an approach can be a vehicle to help groups contextualize their learning into the wider community and socio-economic perspectives (Blustein, 1987), and the collective career coaching model can raise group awareness of social, political, and economic barriers and inequalities in career development (Meldrum, 2017; Westergaard, 2013).

Taking on a critical pedagogical lens in group work proposed emboldens a practitioner-student educative model, engaging group members in an active process of "collective dialogue, reflection, and action in order to learn to perceive social, political and economic contradictions and to take action against the oppressive elements of reality" (Freire, 1970, p. 60). Instead of being an expert, the career coach takes on the role of a facilitator, with the group members leading themselves toward a collection of meaningful interactions for a deeper understanding of their role in the world (Hooley et al., 2018). As a group coaching paradigm, collective career coaching can shift career coaching toward collective empowerment and the advancement of social justice. The collective career coaching model encompasses four stages (see Figure 15) geared towards reinventing the group's career development and life options (Meldrum, 2021).

Stage One

First, the coach and group members explore and agree on a joint vision for the session by sharing goals and desires. These goals and desires are revealed as the coach "gives the group space to identify, challenge and critique oppression through different activities and group discussions" (Meldrum, 2021, p. 218). These activities and discussions center around structural, societal, economic, and political topics.

Stage Two

The group is encouraged to reflect on themes arising from group members' shared stories and concerns. Stage two is entered when patterns and themes emerge from individuals' critical consciousness. For example, group members may realize barriers to their forward movement stem from their culture, geographical location, peer groups, or family. The activities awaken the group's critical consciousness and help them realize how identified barriers impact their progress, allowing them to create a collective action plan with other group members (Meldrum, 2021, p. 220).

Stage Three

From discussions in stage two, the group members feel empowered to change, which leads to exploring a range of options and taking steps toward reflective action in stage three. This transition may include addressing education, health, gender, change, or focusing on values, skills, beliefs, or interests.

Stage Four

There is no final stage of the model – it is arbitrary in that it is intended for the group to engage in a continuous learning cycle to include discussion, reflection, and action. This cycle aims to build up and awaken the learners to social, political, and economic inconsistencies to enable them to take collective action against oppression throughout their lifespan (Freire, 1970).

Career guidance (Kidd, 2006), coaching (Whitmore, 2017; Yates, 2013), and group guidance (Westergaard, 2009) models influence the structure of the collective career coaching approach. When a coach facilitates a collective career coaching approach, person-centered counseling techniques (Rogers, 1961) apply, and group work is grounded in narrative storytelling. The group approach is psychoeducational in delivery style (Corey, 2012), which is semi-structured, involves pre-planning, and has specific but fluid goals. A common goal brings the group together and provides learners with abundant opportunities to participate actively in the learning process at all times. Peer support, group learning, and coaching approaches offer more possibilities than one-on-one interaction (Meldrum, 2017; Westergaard, 2013). Participants who successfully and fully engaged in the group learning process receive long-term benefits related

Figure 15
The Collective Career Coaching Model

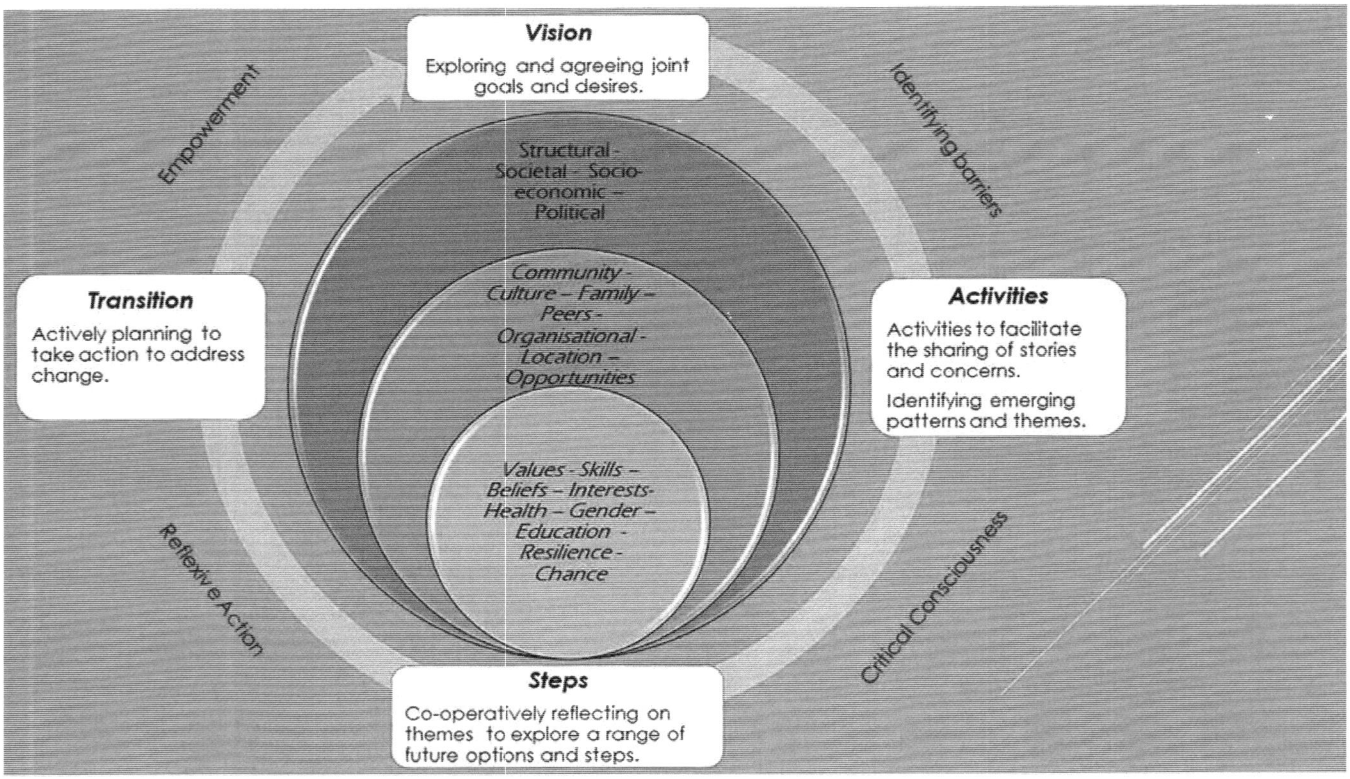

Adopted from "Group Career Coaching: A Critical Pedagogical Approach" by S. C. Meldrum ,2021, *The Journal for Specialists in Group Work*, 46(2), (pp. 214-225).

to one's career development journey.

Models such as the group interactive narrative approach and the collective career coaching model allow the group to support one another by creating meaningful exchanges through the deconstruction of stories and shared experiences. Group coaching models rely less on individual agency – rather, they celebrate and learn from the collective voice of participants. Therefore, it is necessary to support practice-based models for career development practitioners to employ in their daily work.

Combining Approaches

Csikszentmihalyi (1993) claimed that we must foster creativity to survive in today's unpredictable world. Career coaching regularly addresses unpredictability in the coaching process and navigating self and world-of-work exploration call for a fair amount of creativity (from coach and client). Rogers (1961) argued that reflection builds self-awareness, and Cox (2013) suggested that coaching provides the space and support required for such reflection. Kelly and Kelly (2013) suggested that one needs to be aware of one's creative potential and confidence to initiate any exploration process. Groups play a central role in helping individual members spark creativity; as new ideas emerge, new information is gathered (Hallowell, 2010; Sawyer, 2012).

There may be apparent differences between one-on-one and group coaching, but there are undoubtedly many overlaps, and there are times when it makes sense to combine the two approaches (Anderson et al., 2008). For example, a coach may navigate between group coaching and one-on-one coaching using the group setting to introduce broader topics or concepts, disseminate consistent information to all members, and engage in group share. After that, the coach may need to debrief with group members individually to gather more personalized reactions to the delivered content or coach each member through a plan of action related to the content. Another situation where a combined approach may be helpful is when a specific need arises or something is proving too personal to discuss in a group setting. A one-on-one intervention may be more appropriate. Therefore, coaching at a group level is most appropriate when its goal closely aligns with the attendees.

The Future of Group Coaching: A Call for Creating Conversations

The future of group career coaching involves a variety of settings in which creating conversations can be generated. Career development concepts have a place in life span development at all levels of growth and education when tailored to the population and setting (Super, 1975, 1990).

Early Career Education

Career exploration has a place in early education and can be facilitated widely through group coaching, especially at the secondary level. An option moving forward could be having students move through the school system, increasing their exposure to career coaching through group work as a curricular component. As their exposure increases, naturally and consistently, their career awareness grows.

Career Education in Counseling Programs

School counselors, academic advisors, and support professionals provide many career-related materials and experiences to students of all ages and stages. A wide swathe of schools across the country successfully offers coaching-related content and programming as part of the standard curriculum. As more and more schools realize the benefits of career education, the curriculum in counselor education programs at the graduate education level will need to be re-tooled in response.

Community Education

Community centers could utilize career coaches' expertise to facilitate regular workforce and other career-related conversations in cities and municipalities across the country. In addition, drop-in group sessions on career development topics could be open to all community members at reduced or no cost, supplemented by local businesses or town programming.

Harnessing Technology

Career coaching groups hosted on various social media platforms have been popular ways to connect in recent years. These connection modalities will only increase as coaches discover new ways to use technology to deliver career-related support. Here are a few ways that career coaches can use technology when working with groups:

1. Shared virtual group coaching: Many people enjoy meeting in a synchronous virtual environment, and video platforms such as Google Meet, Zoom, and Microsoft Teams allow such interaction. A coach can set up a large group or break-out interactions to suit curricular needs, group size, and time limits. Groups can connect from anywhere with internet access and a computer, screen device, or phone.
2. Curriculum: There does not seem to be a limit in using technology for group work when delivering learning content. Using some of the aforementioned platforms, a coach can assess group interaction and learning through forum discussions, 360 feedback, peer evaluations, and chat rooms. Group members can collaborate on projects using video, social media, website builders, web

applications, audio, and more and share these materials with the rest of the group.

3. Real Time Response: Applications such as Google Docs and Drop Box Forms invite group members from anywhere globally to provide documentation feedback to one another in real-time. These online collaboration spaces help participants track and record work development, and the coach can jump into the space at any time to offer guidance and feedback.

As the career coach works with varied technologies, their proficiency will grow, and their strategies for use will broaden. The coach will discover new and improved ways to assess group development, deepen group interactions, and increase collaborations. The coach can also use technology to seek feedback from group members on their performance as a facilitator. Technology allows anonymous input so participants feel they can speak freely and offer the most constructive feedback to improve the coach's practice (Brown et al., 2015).

Final Thoughts on Group Coaching

Group career coaching encourages knowledge building, cultural responsibility, and connectedness. Participants engage in a shared space designed for blended learning, where coach and client can benefit from diverse engagement, expression, representation, and collaboration. Various forms of technology can be introduced to modify in-person communications, gather facilitator feedback, design and deliver activities, and establish virtual short or longer-term collaboration spaces.

A group coaching model can benefit both client and coach. The client can benefit from reduced costs and a shared learning experience, and the coach can reach more people and utilize resources more efficiently. For these benefits to materialize, a coach should strive for buy-in and agreement over a standard set of broad-based facilitation goals in a group coaching environment and work to increase trust and intra-group communication early on. Career coaches doing group work should also have a clear vision and plan for offering a given program and define and communicate the value of that offering for themselves and their clients. In short, a coach should be clear on how to deliver a group coaching program and the value that offering group coaching brings to the participants.

Considering a move to a group coaching model may secure the coach's future and reach more clients, transforming their lives into those they wish to lead. However, resistance and lack of confidence to fully utilize group work has been challenging in expanding group coaching (Higgans & Westergaard, 2001). Clients may have concerns regarding consent, willingness to openly discuss personal feelings or issues in front of peers, existing tensions, or poor facilitation. Group coaching can be challenging for these reasons and others, requiring highly skilled coaches to effect permanent and positive change. Good, relatively safe group work relies on the effective screening of group members and trusts that clients will abide by certain ground rules, such as confidentiality and not engaging in intimate relationships with other clients (W. C. Briddick, personal communication, November 7, 2021). However, even with the best-made plans and screening, there is no guarantee that a group member will not violate one of the group's rules. That said, with skilled facilitation and preparation, group coaching can be a successful method of career coaching.

Knowledge Check

1. What are various ways career coaches can work effectively with groups?
2. How do learning styles affect group facilitation strategies?
3. What are group stages, and how does one navigate group dynamics?
4. What are the various ways a coach can improve their skills for delivering career services to groups?

K-W-L Model – What Have I Learned?

To conclude this chapter, revisit the K-W-L model to assess whether this chapter provided you with information to fill some of your knowledge gaps. Finally, reflect on what you ***learned*** from this chapter and how you can apply it to your coaching practice.

References

Anderson, M. C., Anderson, D. L., & Mayo, W. D. (2008). Team coaching helps a leadership team drive cultural change at Caterpillar. *Global Business and Organizational Excellence*, *27*(4), 40–50. https://doi.org/10.1002/joe.20212

Benson, J. (2019). *Working more creatively with groups* (4th ed.). Routledge.

Berg, J. M., Dutton, J. E., & Wrzesniewski, A. (2008). *What is job crafting and why does it matter?* The Center for Positive Organizational Scholarship, University of Michigan Ross School of Business.

Bloisi, W., Cook, C., W., & Hunsaker, P. L. (2003). *Management and organisational behaviour.* McGraw-Hill Education.

Blustein, D. L. (1987). Integrating career counseling and psychotherapy: A comprehensive treatment strategy. *Psychotherapy: Theory, Research, Practice, Training, 24*(4), 794–799. https://doi.org/10.1037/h0085781

Brown, B., Dressler, R., Eaton, S. E., & Jacobsen, M. (2015). Practicing what we teach: Using action research to learn about teaching action research. *Canadian Journal of Action Research, 16*(3), 61-78.

Britton, J. (2013). *From one to many: Best practices for team and group coaching.* Jossey Bass.

Brown, S. W., & Grant, A. M. (2010). From GROW to GROUP: Theoretical issues and a practical model for group coaching in organisations. *Coaching: An International Journal of Theory, Research and Practice, 3*(1), 30–45. http://doi.org/10.1080/17521880903559697

Clutterbuck, D. (2007). *Coaching the team at work.* Nicholas Brealey Publishing.

Cockerham, G. (2011). *Group coaching: A comprehensive blueprint.* iUniverse.

Corey, G. (2012). *Theory and practice of group counseling* (9th ed.). Cengage.

Cox, E. (2013). *Coaching understood: A pragmatic inquiry into the coaching process.* Sage.

Csikszentmihalyi, M. (1993). *The evolving self.* HarperCollins.

Dolny, H. (2009). *Team coaching: Artists at work: South African coaches share their theory and practice.* Penguin Books.

Ellis, D. G., & Fisher, B. A. (1994). *Small group decision making: Communication and the group process* (4th ed.). McGraw-Hill.

Fleming, N. D. (2019). *VARK: A guide to learning preferences.* VARK Learn Limited. https://vark-learn.com/

Fleming, N. D., & Mills, C. (1992). Not another inventory, rather a catalyst for reflection. *To improve the academy, 11,* 137-155.

Freire, P. (1970). *Pedagogy of the oppressed.* Bloomsbury.

Hallowell, E. M. (2010). What brain science tells us about how to excel. *Harvard Business Review, 88*(12). 123-129.

Hargie, O. (2011). *Skilled interpersonal interaction: Research, theory, and practice* (5th ed.). Routledge.

Higgins, R., & Westergaard, J. (2001). The role of group work in careers education and guidance programmes. *Career Research and Development NICEC Journal, 2,* 14–17.

Hooley, T., & Sultana, R. G. (2016). Career guidance for social justice. *Journal of the National Institute for Career Education and Counselling, 36*(1), 2-11. https://doi.org/10.20856/jnicec.3601

Hooley, T., Sultana, R. J., & Thomsen, R. (2017). The neoliberal challenge to career guidance: Mobilizing research, policy and practice around social justice. In T. Hooley, R. J. Sultana, & R. Thomsen (Eds.), *Career guidance for social justice: Contesting neoliberalism* (pp. 1–28). Routledge. https://doi.org/10.4324/9781315110516

Hooley, T., Sultana, R. J., & Thomsen, R. (2018). Representing problems, imagining solutions, emancipatory career guidance for the multitude. In T. Hooley, R. J. Sultana, & R. Thomsen (Eds.), *Career guidance for emancipation, reclaiming justice for the multitude* (pp. 1–14). Routledge. https://doi.org/10.4324/9781315110486

Kelly, D., & Kelly, T. (2013). *Creative confidence.* Penguin Random House Company.

Kemmis, S., & McTaggart, R. (2005). Participatory action research: Communicative action and the public sphere. In N. K. Denzin & Y. S. Lincoln, *The SAGE handbook of qualitative research* (3rd ed., 271-330). Sage Publications Inc.

Kidd, J. M. (2006). *Understanding career counselling: Theory, research and practice.* Sage.

Kolb, D. (1984). *Experiential learning: Experience as the source of learning and development.* Prentice-Hall.

Law, B. (1996). Career education in a curriculum. In A. G. Watt, B. Law, J. Killeen, J. Kidd, & R. Hawthorn (Eds.), *Rethinking career education and guidance: Theory, policy and practice.* Prentice-Hall.

Lujan, H. L., & DiCarlo, S. E. (2006). First-year medical students prefer multiple learning styles. *Advances in Physiology Education, 30*(1), 13–16. https://doi.org/10.1152/advan.00045.2005

Meldrum, S. C. (2017). Group guidance- is it time to flock together? *Journal of the National Institute for Career Education and Counselling, 38*(1), 36–43. https://doi.org/10.20856/jnicec.3806

Meldrum, S. (2021). Group career coaching – A critical pedagogical approach, *The Journal for Specialists in Group Work, 46*(2), 214-225. http://doi.org/10.1080/01933922.2021.1929619

National Career Development Association. (2015). *2015 NCDA code of ethics.* Author. https://www.ncda.org/aws/NCDA/asset_manager/get_file/3395

Pyle, K. R., & Hayden, S. C. W. (2015). *Group career counseling: Practices and principles* (2nd ed.). National Career Development Association.

Reid, H. (2016). *An introduction to career counselling and coaching*. Sage.

Rogers, C. (1961). *On becoming a person*. Houghton Mifflin.

Savickas, M. L. (2012). Life design: A paradigm for career intervention in the 21st century. *Journal of Counselling and Development, 90*(1), 13–19. https://doi.org/10.1111/j.1556-6676.2012.00002.x

Sawyer, R. K. (2012). *The science of human innovation: Explaining creativity.* Oxford University Press.

Schlairet, M. C., Green, R., & Benton, M. J. (2014). The flipped classroom: Strategies for an undergraduate nursing course. *Nurse Educator, 39*(6), 321–325. https://doi.org/10.1097/NNE.0000000000000096

Super, D. E. (1975). Career education and career guidance for the life span and for life roles. *Journal of Career Development, 2*(2), 27-42.

Super, D. E. (1990). A lifespan, life-space approach to career development. In D. Brown & L. Brooks (Eds.), *Career choice and development* (2nd ed., pp. 197–261). Jossey-Bass. https://doi.org/10.1016/0001-8791(80)90056-1

Thomsen, R. (2012). *Career guidance in communities.* Aarhus University Press.

Thornton, C. (2010). *Group and team coaching: The essential guide* (1st ed.). Routledge. https://doi.org/10.4324/9780203852385

Tuckman, B. W. (1965). Developmental sequence in small groups. *Psychological Bulletin, 63*(6), 384-399. https://doi.org/10.1037/h0022100

Tuckman, B., & Jensen, M. (1977). Stages of small-group development revisited. *Group and Organization Management, 2*, 419 - 427. https://doi.org/10.1177%2F105960117700200404

Westergaard, J. (2009). *Effective group work with young people.* McGraw Hill Education.

Westergarrd, J. (2013). Group work: Pleasure or pain? An effective guidance activity or a poor substitute for one-on-one interactions with young people. *International Journal for Education and Vocational Guidance, 13,* 173-186. https://doi.org/10.1007/s10775-013-9249-8

Whitmore, J. (2017). *Coaching for performance* (5th ed.). Nicolas Brealey Publishing.

Yates, J. (2013). *The career coaching handbook.* Routledge.

CHAPTER 8
The Growing Practice of Career Coaching and Future Directions

"Coaching works because it's all about you. When you connect with what you really want and why — and take action — magical things can happen."

– Emma Louise Elsey

"When it comes to designing the future of work, one size fits none" was a quote by Karen Mangia as the 2022 year began (Mangia, 2022, para. 1). The COVID-19 pandemic, which began in 2020, shifted both personal and professional lives in ways unimaginable by most. As a result, people are reprioritizing and redefining work, and it looks much different than it did pre-COVID. As the pandemic impacts career coaches worldwide, no one cannot predict the future of the coaching profession or the demands of the workforce. However, coaches know that individuals need support in times of transition, and now more than ever, support is needed.

Influential Themes

The following themes influence the practice of career coaching today and will continue to raise questions in the coming years:

Freedom

The universal term is freedom - individuals and organizations want more freedom to exercise their values, choose their work hours, pursue their goals, and design models that fit their lifestyle (Mangia, 2022). Employees will be looking for, and employers should have, more empathy and flexibility regarding work schedules. There will continue to be three groups of workers: (1) in-person, (2) remote, and (3) hybrid (in-person and remote). The desire for more workplace freedom is fundamental and universal, which raises questions such as, what is the client's preference, and is their preference realistic and attainable?

Wellbeing

There is an uber focus today on mental health and wellbeing. Employees will be expecting additional benefits, and employers should continue to support employees as people navigate the pandemic and beyond. Furthermore, wellbeing encompasses positivity – are clients experiencing life to the fullest? Are they practicing self-care? How are they balancing work and personal care in a way that energizes and feeds their goals?

Safety

Since our brains are cognitively wired to sense danger and protect ourselves, events that heighten our awareness for safety, such as a pandemic, lead us to question many of our rote practices. Based on this knowledge, questions to explore with clients include, "Are you feeling safe at work?" and "How are your experiences of safety and security driving your career decisions?" and "What threats are you 'avoiding' in your career decision-making?" (Hutchison, 2022).

Decision-Making

Wellness and safety have a substantial impact on decision-making and will continue to be an important theme in career transition. Helping people build strong decision-making skills is essential. In *Good to Great*, Collins (2001) asks the question: "What can we be the best at?" And equally important, "What can we not be the best at?" These are profound questions that coaches need to help clients answer. More important, coaches can help clients determine if they face instances where good enough will have to be good enough as part of their decision-making. Sometimes 100% is not possible, and trying to achieve this result leads to burnout and underperformance in one or more areas of life. Building strong decision-making skills is a needed skill that will serve clients in all aspects of their lives, now and in the future.

Developing Your Skills as a Coach

Career coaching as a discipline is rapidly evolving, and with it, the skillset and competency needs of today's career coaches. Acquiring new skills and honing them over time is iterative – assessing existing skills is necessary to see if new skills need to be acquired and sharpened. The Dreyfus model of skills development outlines stages of learning that address key factors for skill acquisition (Dreyfus, 1981, 2004; Dreyfus & Dreyfus, 1984, 1986), which can be useful to career coaches today. The model evaluates and supports the development of new skills as the learner relies less on abstract principles and more on concrete evidence, as well as aids in the reduction of professional attrition (Lewis, 1996). Dreyfus and Dreyfus (1986) described the path to competence as a theoretical continuum or learning process of skill attainment, moving through distinct stages from novice to expert without apparent thought (Dreyfus & Dreyfus, 1986). The Dreyfus model has five key stages: novice, advanced beginner, competent, proficient, and expert (Dreyfus, 2004), with expert being the highest level of skill demonstrated by fluid performance based on previous situations (see Figure 16). Each stage is described here.

Novice

A novice learner has little or no experience or background knowledge. As a result, they must adhere to a clear set of rules or guidelines and often need close supervision or instruction to complete tasks or learn the competency at hand. As a result, novice learners often have a detached commitment due to their cursory level of knowledge (Dreyfus & Dreyfus, 1986).

Advanced Beginner

Once the novice can exercise judgment and has learned the basic rules, progression to an advanced beginner is possible. Moving away from novice happens when the learner perceives similarity of concrete situations with previous examples of the same experience. Actions can now be based on the new situation and earlier context-free components (Dreyfus & Dreyfus, 1986). Although some tasks can be completed independently by the Advanced Beginner and with their judgment, most work is supervised or overseen. The individual needs to receive feedback when mistakes are made, which is necessary for learning.

Competent

During the competency stage, the learner shifts thoughts and actions from short to long-term goals. Competent individuals rely on past experiences to decide what is essential for future decision-making (Honken, 2013), occasionally leading to the individual becoming paralyzed by indecision. Situations arise where the individual does not feel the rules apply, is unclear which rules are applicable, or tends to overuse rules. Over time, they realize the futility of applying each rule in every situation.

Proficient

A proficient individual can select an appropriate course of action for any situation with confidence because, at this stage, the individual begins to utilize their emotional expertise from past experiences (Dreyfus, 2004). Reaching this stage requires many hours of deliberate practice as this knowledge base acts as a compass to guide the individual away from learning transitions that are rule-based to those that are situation-based (Honken, 2013). Risk-taking increases as the individual relies less on rules and an analytical decision-making mindset to get the job done (Benner, 2004).

Expert

In the expert stage of skills acquisition, a deep understanding of subject matter drives action (Dreyfus, 2004). The individual sees what needs to be done and the solution, which is readily available with little effort because at this level, the individual is fully immersed in understanding the situation, making decisions on how to proceed, and the outcome (Honken, 2013). To the outside observer, the performance of an expert appears effortless, yet, the expert must revert to an earlier stage if changes in their field of expertise necessitate new learning (Honken, 2013).

According to Dreyfus, individuals must progress through each stage of expertise and must draw on their experiences of solving problems in context to reach higher levels of expertise. They could not have arrived here without progressing through the previous stages of skill acquisition and accumulating experiences, and emotional involvement. The Dreyfus model assumes that competence evolves through time due to experience and mastery. However, according to Hall-Ellis and Grealy (2013), "rules and procedures do not simply move to the unconscious level; there is a discontinuity between the competent level and the proficient and expert levels" (p. 589). When experts adhere to rules and guidelines that they did as novices, their performance suffers. Each time individuals acquire a new skill, they start at the novice stage, where they need to learn the facts and the rules for determining action. Learning can occur formally (classroom) or through observation and self-instruction (workplace setting).

Figure 16
Model of Skills Acquisition

STAGE	CHARACTERISTICS
Novice	•Learning rules and routines •Low sense of control and responsibility •Experience and skills levels are developing
Advanced Beginner	•Ability to short-term plan; Lacks long-range planning •Situational perception is limited •Difficulty assigning levels of need to problems (miopic)
Competent	•Seeing and connecting similarities/differences •Developing strategic knowledge •Considering and setting longer term plans
Proficient	•Deep understanding of theories, rules, systems, processes •Big picture; Systems thinking •Addresses important issues; Ignores irrelevant details
Expert	•Futuristic thought; Vision •No longer relies on rules/guidelines •Works on decision-making intuition

Adapted from "The Five-Stage Model of Adult Skills Acquisition," by S. Dreyfus, 2004, *Bulletin of Science Technology & Society, 24*(3), p. 6.

Assessment of Skills within Each Stage

As individuals move from novice to expert, there are four categories by which each level of competency is assessed: components, perspective, decision, and commitment (Dreyfus, 2004; see Table 12). As a novice, perspectives of information and situations are more context free because the coach lacks an experiential base to competently change their perspective. They will stick to a proscribed script, follow a strict outline, and rely on textbook examples for reference. Tangible and prescribed application of information is necessary because of their knowledge level (Benner, 2004). Situational perspective is more easily obtained as the coach occupies an advanced-beginner to competent skills acquisition. Consider a career coach who conducts a small group coaching session to facilitate a values exploration activity. The coach's ease with executing this activity can vary depending on their skills acquisition level. The novice lacks a coherent sense of overall task need, treats each situation as if it were new, and looks for appropriate rules to follow. Recognition of relevant discrete facts, features, and rules for decision-making is clearly and objectively defined and adhered to (Dreyfus & Dreyfus, 1986).

As the career coach progresses through skill acquisition to expert level, they are totally immersed in fluid, efficient performance, recalling and drawing upon previously learned context without extensive thought. Flyvbjerg (2001) posited that experts operate based on knowledge of several thousand such cataloged concrete cases in their area of expertise. "When things are proceeding normally, experts don't solve problems and don't make decisions; they do what normally works" (Dreyfus & Dreyfus, 1986, p. 31). Responses are reactive rather than studied and premeditated (Chambers, 2012). The expert focuses more on their intuition than the calculations produced through reflection. (Flyvbjerg, 2001).

Application of the Skills Model to Career Coaching

In 2004, Benner applied Dreyfus's model of skills acquisition to the nursing profession, arguing that context and meaning inherent in situations strongly influence performance; therefore, "evaluation strategies used by educators and practitioners that relied on context-free principles and elements could not capture the knowledge embedded in the expert's actual practice" (p. 589). Like nursing, career coaching is more than a set of techniques, but a collection of work practices and "thinking-in-activity" (Hall-Ellis & Grealy, 2013, p. 590) where practice and activity are interchangeable. Thus, like nurses, career coaches must engage clients in exploration activities to derive meaningful contexts for understanding

Table 12
Levels of Expertise

	Novice	**Advanced Beginner**	**Competent**	**Proficient**	**Expert**
Components	Context free	Context free and situational	Context free and situational	Context free and situational	Context free and situational
Perspective	None	None	Chosen	Experienced	Experienced
Commitment	Detached	Detached	Detached understanding and deciding involved outcome	Involved understanding detached deciding	Involved
Decision	Analytic	Analytic	Analytic	Analytic	Intuitive

their actions (Kuutti, 1996).

The development of a career coach is an ongoing and lifelong process. Although career coaches are responsible for acquiring the skills and knowledge needed to be effective in their roles as guides, mentors, advisors, teachers, trainers, supervisors, and staff, those that manage career coaches must be aware of the level of expertise in different areas and be able to guide career coaches so that they can acquire higher levels of expertise.

Credentialing: What Is It and What Does It Mean?

Credentialing is the process of obtaining, verifying, and assessing a practitioner's qualifications to provide care or services in a specific industry or profession or for a specific organization through documented evidence of licensure, education, training, experience, or other qualifications (Diaz & Weaver, 2019). Examples of credentials are a certificate, letter, badge, or other official identification that confirms position or status. There is value in credentialing, and credentials hold varying values across industries.

At the time of this publication, a few credentialing, certificate, and certification options are available for career coaches. The National Career Development Association (NCDA) offers credentialing as a Certified Career Services Provider (CCSP) and the Certified Master of Career Services (CMCS) (www.ncdacredentialing.org). The Center for Credentialing and Education (CCE) offers the Global Career Development Facilitator (GCDF) and the Board Certified Coach (BCC) credential with a career coaching distinction (cce-global.org) and the Certified Professional Career Coach (CPCC; cpcc-careercoach.com) credential through the Professional Association of Résumé Writers & Career Coaches (PARWCC). These options provide direct competency development in career coaching. The National Association of Colleges and Employers (NACE; naceweb.org) also offers career coaching certificates and certification options. Additional certificate and credentialing options may become available in the years to come as the career coaching profession expands. Briddick stated

> This is a critical piece for Career Coaches. The title of "coach" is widely used, and it is important to consider the protection of the title of "Career Coach" as the profession evolves. It is a similar dilemma faced by counselors. There are admissions counselors, sales counselors, etc. It can be confusing for some people. Having licensure/certification and recognition by state credentialing bodies can help reduce confusion, protect the title, and strengthen credibility for the profession. (W. C. Briddick, personal communication, November 17, 2021)

Credentials are a mark of distinction for credential holders and a source of credibility for organizations and clients who employ the credential holder. Credentials are important because they protect the client, ensure industry compliance, and certify qualified and competent professionals (Diaz & Weaver, 2019). Holding a credential means one has completed the competency standards established by the designated credentialing body and complies with the legal requirement and conduct standards (Center for Credentialing and Education, 2010). Credential holders possess a high level of subject-matter expertise, although the competencies assessed by the credentialing body vary. In addition, ethical guidelines established by the credentialing body bind ethics and practice, which ensures the credential holder properly uses the occupational credential awarded and serves as a compass for the performance of services and occupational activities (Center for Credentialing and Education, 2010). Tables 13-15 are competency snapshots for each coaching credential. For a complete description of each competency, visit the respective organization's website that awards the credential.

Table 13
BCC Competency Overview

BCC Competencies	
COMPETENCY	**DESCRIPTION**
Approaches for Businesses and Organizations	These coaching work behaviors include organization roles, change processes, mentoring, and conflict management related to the coaching process
Approaches for Individuals	These coaching work behaviors pertain to specific skills aimed at facilitating the client's desired goals during the coaching process, and include monitoring client progress, decision making, and use of resources
Assessment	These coaching work behaviors assess coaching goals, client strengths, and specific issues concerning the coaching process
Fundamental Coaching Skills	These coaching work behaviors focus on the basic coaching alliance, helping skills, coaching plans, and other essential issues concerning the coaching process
Screening and Orientation	These coaching work behaviors focus on client motivation level, informed consent, coach and client roles, and general parameters for establishing the coaching process

Table 14
CCSP, CMCS, GCDF Competency Overview

CCSP, CMCS, GCDF Competencies	
Helping Skills	Basic career facilitating processes, including productive interpersonal relationships
Labor Market Information and Resources	Labor market and occupational information and trends
Assessment	Both formal and informal career development assessments, with emphasis on relating appropriate career development assessments to the population served
Diverse Populations	Studies covering the special needs of various groups, as well as how to adapt services to meet those needs
Ethical and Legal Issues	Studies on the Codes of Ethics and current legislative regulations
Career Development Models	Career development theories, models, and techniques as they apply to lifelong development, gender, age, and ethnic background
Employability Skills	Job search strategies/placement techniques, especially with groups
Training Clients and Peers	Preparing and developing materials for training programs and presentations
Program Management/Implementation	Studies covering career programs and their implementation and working as a liaison in collaborative relationships
Promotion and Public Relations	Marketing and promoting career development programs
Technology	Understanding and use of career development computer applications
Consultation	Accept suggestions for performance improvement from consultants and supervisors

Table 15
CPCC Competency Overview

CPCC	
The Career Coach	The Foundation of Career Coaching Understanding Career Seekers Diane's Whole Person Theory The Industry of Career Coaching – A Positive Profession Career Coach, Consultant, or Counselor? Coaching Competencies Intake Procedures
Meet the Client	Career Purpose Goal Development; Goals Setting Values Exercise Interests & Motivation Think Outside the Box Assessment Testing & Personality Client Scenarios
Career Coach Communications	The Core Career Coaching Competencies Stretching the Comfort Zone & Reaching for New Horizons Chief Motivational Officer Coaching Through Circumstances Career Coaching in Action
Written Materials	Intelligence Collection Circle of Influence & Effective Networking Professional Career Development Dialogues Powerful Value-based Résumés & Written Job Search Management Documents Brand Your Clients Endorsements & References Upon Request Résumés & Career History Analysis Sample Career Marketing Documents
Intelligence Testing	Traditional Job Search Methods, Social Media & Web 2.0 LinkedIn; Blogs Web 2.0 & Social Medial Tools for Career Coaches Digital Dirt and Online Reputation Management Electronic Résumés Intelligence Collection in Action: A Case Study
Script for Career Services	Interviewing Dynamics – Let's Dance (Screening Factors & Interview Management) Image Interviewing Strategies Communications & Decision-making Styles Mastering the Art of Salary Negotiating Put it All Together Congratulations–Your Client Got the Position!

Growing Career Coaching Competencies

Developing skills as a career coach is vitally important to your clients' career growth. The changing and challenging complexities of the world of work and the nature of support career coaches offer in helping clients navigate changing waters requires regularly assessing and honing skills and competencies. Many training options are available for career coaches, and although this monograph has provided several options for professional development, it is not a comprehensive training directory. The organizations listed here are a starting point to the coach's research; however, when looking for professional development options, it is wise to assess needs, research, and find the credentialing, certificate, and certification option that works best. The words credential, certificate, and certification appear in the literature interchangeably, yet, standards and outcomes vary from industry to industry. As a career coach, understanding what these terms mean and how they influence professional growth and the work performed with clients is necessary.

Self-Care

One of the significant challenges of being a career coach is that the coach constantly gives to others. Coaches are not just professionals – they are partners, friends, colleagues, parents, and neighbors. When coaches experience stress in one area of life, it naturally spills over to the others. Entirely focusing on attending to the client's needs can be tiresome even with the best support systems. Self-care, on the other hand, is an ethical obligation. One of the essential messages that career coaches convey to their clients is the importance of health and wellbeing as a career strategy. Again, self-care is an ethical practice; without it, coaches risk burnout, resulting in inadequate care for their clients.

Compassion Fatigue

The circumstances of the first two years of the COVID-19 pandemic have required coaches to develop and utilize various coping mechanisms to navigate complex career and mental health concerns while helping clients negotiate similar challenges. Compassion fatigue, also known as secondary traumatization, is a condition of tension and preoccupation caused by witnessing the suffering of others (Figley, 2002). Like others in the caregiving professions, career coaches are at high risk for compassion fatigue and burnout from working with individuals in high-stress environments and situations (Morse et al., 2012). Mathieu (2007) offered common signs of compassion fatigue, including but not limited to:

- Misplaced anger
- Dread of working with certain clients
- Diminished sense of career enjoyment
- Irritability
- Intrusive imagery or dissociation
- Low self-esteem
- Hypersensitivity or Insensitivity
- Insomnia
- Difficulty separating work life from personal life
- Workaholic
- Impaired ability to make decisions
- Problems with intimacy/persona relationships
- Depression
- Tardiness or frequent absences
- Anxiety
- Substance abuse (food, alcohol, drugs
- Exhaustion
- Hypervigilance
- Somatic symptoms (e.g., headaches)
- Reduced ability to feel sympathy and empathy

The NCDA *Code of Ethics* (2015) emphasizes the significance of self-awareness and self-care for professional coaches. The code states that career professionals should "engage in self-care activities to maintain and promote their emotional, physical, mental, and spiritual wellbeing to best meet their professional responsibilities" (p. 8). Dealing with clients' negative life experiences is an expected part of the career coach's job, but it may disregard personal health and wellbeing. If not diagnosed and managed, compassion fatigue can be detrimental to the coaching process or the coach.

Elements to Self-Care

The National Alliance on Mental Illness (NAMI) outlines six elements to self-care (see Figure 17), which comprise our overall wellness. Coaches and clients should know which areas might need more attention as life circumstances change and brainstorm ways to achieve wellness in these categories. Following Figure 17 are several in-the-moment self-care or coping strategies. Chapter 4 also provided a Three Good Things Exercise, a proven exercise to increase well-being and reduce stress.

Figure 17
Self-Care Elements

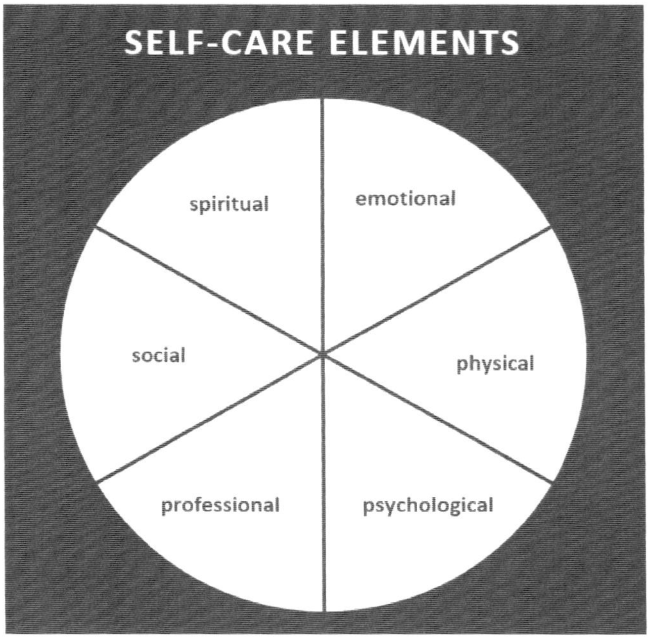

Coaches can employ many strategies and activities to help combat compassion fatigue. Below are a few in-the-moment options:

1. Stretch between working sessions
2. Take a short walk on breaks and at lunch
3. Deep breathing exercises
4. Use positive affirmations or inspirational quotes in your workspace
5. Surround yourself with humor (reading, colleagues, tv, social media)
6. Practice meditation or mindfulness
7. Practice healthy eating habits
8. Keep a gratitude journal and do minute reflections
9. Practice mini-yoga or Tai Chi sessions
10. Listen to music
11. Join a support group and connect with them at needed points during the day
12. Limit exposure to trauma and filter when possible
13. Regularly reach out to colleagues
14. Elicit an accountability partner to keep you focused on your goals and what is important
15. Limit your exposure to social media

To learn more about your level of compassion fatigue, take a compassion fatigue test at: https://proqol.org/proqol-measure

Embracing a Coaching Mindset

Being a successful career coach begins with embracing a coaching mindset and ends with the client gaining true independence and self-reliance in pursuing their goals from working with a coach. Every career coach has their coaching style and unique way to cultivate performance. As mentioned in Chapter 3, the process of coaching varies, and each coach utilizes techniques, strategies, and models differently based on their training, ethics, theoretical beliefs, and background. However, the

COACH CORNER

It is an exciting time to be a career coach! The industry is evolving and expanding with new knowledge, talent, and skill. As you advance in this profession, continue to reflect regularly – a practice that is crucial to your growth and career evolution.

desire to develop and grow one's abilities should be central to all career coaches. After all, lifelong learning as a daily practice is a message that career coaches communicate to job seekers and career changers. Career coaches must hold themselves to their client's expectations and standards: continued professional development and lifelong learning to maximize career success. Below are five areas to consider in maximizing one's career coaching success.

Top Five Tips for a Successful Coaching Mindset

Enhancing Awareness

Understanding one's skills and knowledge level is the essence of good coaching because it enables natural learning (Whitmore, 2017). Self-awareness cultivates skills and knowledge development. The method to establish and sustain the perfect frame of mind for performance consistently enhances awareness.

Learn Something New – Every. Single. Day

Peak performance happens when a coach frequently adds to their knowledge toolbox. For example, learning a new coaching technique or acquiring a new facilitation skill keeps the mind fresh and active. Whether reading the latest workforce hiring trends or following legislation related to social justice issues in the workplace – these topics help serve clients' needs and help the coach develop self-awareness and construct a barometer for desired growth areas.

Take Time

Jim Peacock, award-winning career coach and founder of Peak Careers, educates career coaches to take time to unplug. Jim is famous for going off the grid on monthly day-long retreats (Peacock, 2021), where he clears his mind of clutter and focuses on his professional goals and accomplishments. While technology has provided tremendous benefits to life and how coaches work with clients, the use of technology can be a distraction. Unplugging offers the focus needed to get back on our professional track.

Be Honest with Yourself

Coaching is hard work. Furthermore, as good as a coach may be, there will be bad days and mistakes. Many clients will feel supported during the coaching process, and most will reach their set goals. Coaches will form a strong working relationship with clients, and the coaching process will be enjoyable and rewarding. However, there will be missed connections with clients, clients who get stuck, and clients who are unable to get un-stuck under the coach's guidance despite the coach's most profound efforts. This is OK and normal. Coaching is powerful but is not always successful. There are many variables, any one of which can affect the outcome. Whether the client is unmotivated, cannot overcome their change barriers, or is not a good match with the coach, the important thing to remember is that all coaches have coaching difficulties. Building a solid network can help when situations arise, and if a referral is necessary, coaches can feel good that the client eventually received the needed support.

Visit and Re-Visit Positionality

Positionality is the relationship between self and roles to discipline, setting, and/or goals (Maxwell, 2013). A critical understanding of self and identity related to the world and specific coaching work is invaluable as a coach. Topics related to positionality to consider (see Chapter 6) are social identity/location (e.g., social class, race, culture, ethnicity, sexual orientation/identity, and other aspects of one's external or internal identity); assumptions that shape beliefs (setting/participants); biases and potential implications/influences; other aspects of identity and/or positionality to the client and the coach's role. It is vitally important to understand one's biases in order to do good work with the client.

Future Directions

In early 2022, news headlines across the country read, "America is in the midst of a great resignation" (Kamal, 2022; Mehta, 2022; Sherr, 2022; and others) or something similar, referencing a term coined by Anthony Klotz, professor of management Texas A & M. The great resignation, also known as the big quit, is an economic trend in which employees voluntarily resign from their jobs in large numbers, beginning in early 2021, primarily in the United States (Wikipedia, n.d.). In May 2021, Klotz predicted a mass exodus from the workforce in the coming months, much of the movement due to the COVID-19 impact on the workplace. The September 2021 Bureau of Labor Statistics' Job Openings and Labor Turnover (JOLT) Survey reported a record-high 4.4 million workers quit their jobs, followed by 4.2 million in October and 4.5 million in November of the same year–it appears he was not incorrect. At the time, that was 3% of the workforce. Moreover, the great resignation stretched into 2022 as a Harris Poll shows that 41% of Americans plan to search for new work (Niles, 2021).

The reasons clients enter, leave, and re-enter the workforce is always complicated and varied and driven by internal and external forces. Healthcare, labor-market fluctuations, self-employment, childcare, burnout, improved working conditions, and reprioritization of goals and values around work are a few of the many challenges associated with the great resignation. For career coaches, fluctuations in the workforce mean clients are on the move, and the coach's job is to support them during their journey. The following sentiment shared by Savickas in 2012 is keenly applicable nearly ten years later in a post-COVID work-world where fluctuations and instability remain the norm.

> As the form of work changes from stability to mobility to reflect the labor needs of post-traditional societies, so too must the form of career intervention change. The paradigms of guiding and preparing now must be supplemented with a new paradigm that fully addresses the life design needs of workers in information societies that have destandardized the life course. (Duarte, 2009 as cited in Savickas, 2012, p. 13)

The new career metaphor is no longer climbing up the ladder, nor is it jumping from one project to the next (Savickas et al., 2009); it is re-inventing oneself in an uncertain, complex workforce (Merisotis, 2021). As Harfoush posited, "We're in this really big period of flux right now where the pandemic has given people some options and forced people to stop and rest" (Sherr, 2022, para. 9), causing individuals and the workforce to redraw the boundaries of work. However, defining new workforce boundaries and change - as a whole - is uncertain. It is an individual journey, and it looks very different for each person.

In 2015 Ewenstein and colleagues reported that approximately 70% of all change fails and that when people are truly invested in change, it is 30% more likely to be sustained. Whether clients are forced into change or seek change voluntarily, many will need career-related support to navigate the change. As Jim Collins, author of *Good to Great and the Social Sectors* (2005), has stated:

> We have pockets of greatness in nearly every difficult environment.... Every institution has its unique set of irrational and difficult constraints, yet some make a leap while others facing the same environmental challenges do not. This is perhaps the single most important point in all of *Good to Great*. Greatness is not a function of circumstance. Greatness, it turns out, is largely a matter of conscious choice, and discipline. (p. 35-36)

The great resignation is a time of immense change for clients, yet much of the change centers around work culture and improving one's working conditions for a more satisfying life. This is a time of great opportunity. As career coaches, we can be ready to continue the journey, walking with our clients to make conscious choices, build capacity, and close the gap between present realities and future goals.

References

Benner, P. (2004). Using the Dreyfus model of skills acquisition to describe and interpret skill acquisition and clinical judgment in nursing practice and education. *Bulletin of Science Technology & Society, 24*(3), 188-199. https://DOI.org/10.1177/0270467604265061

Center for Credentialing and Education. (2010). *BCC code of ethics*. Author. https://www.cce-global.org/Assets/Ethics/BCCcodeofethics.pdf

Chambers, D. W. (2012). Dental education's involvement with dentists' learning in practice: Data and theory. *Journal of Dental Education, 76*, 107-117.

Collins, J. (2001). *Good to great*. Random House Business Books.

Collins, J. (2005). *Good to great and the social sectors*. HarperCollins.

Diaz, S., & Weaver, T. (2019). The credentialing, privileging, and enrollment process: What you don't know can hurt you! *American Medical Association*. https://www.ama-assn.org/system/files/2019-11/i19-credentialing-privileging-enrollment.pdf

Dreyfus, S. E. (1981). *Formal models vs. human situational understanding: Inherent limitations on the modelling of business expertise*. University of California, Berkeley, Office of Scientific Research.

Dreyfus, S. (2004). The five-stage model of adult skills acquisition. *Bulletin of Science Technology and Society, 24*(3), 177-179. https://doi.org/10.1177/0270467604264992

Dreyfus, H. L., & Dreyfus, S. E. (1984). Putting computers in their proper place: Analysis versus intuition in the classroom. *Teachers College Record, 85*(4), 578–601.

Dreyfus, H., & Dreyfus, S. (1986). *Mind over machine: The power of human intuition and expertise in the era of the computer*. Blackwell Publishers.

Ewenstein, B., Smith, W., & Sologar, A. (2015, July). Changing change management. *McKinsey Digital*. McKinsey & Company. https://www.mckinsey.com/~/media/mckinsey/featured%20insights/leading%20in%20the%2021st%20century/changing%20change%20management/changing_change_management.pdf?shouldIndex=false

Figley, C. R. (Ed.). (2002). Psychosocial stress series, no. 24. *Treating compassion fatigue*. Brunner-Routledge.

Flyvbjerg, B. (2001). *Making social science matter: Why social inquiry fails and how it can succeed again*. Cambridge University Press. http://doi.org/10.1017/CBO9780511810503

Hall-Ellis, S., & Grealy, D. S. (2013, November). The Dreyfus model of skills acquisition: A career development framework for succession planning and management in academic libraries. *College and Research Libraries, 74*(6), 587-603. https://doi.org/10.5860/crl12-349

Honken, N. (2013, June), *Dreyfus five-stage model of adult skills acquisition applied to engineering lifelong learning*. Paper presented at 2013 ASEE Annual Conference & Exposition, Atlanta, Georgia. https://doi.org/10.18260/1-2--19457

Hutchison, B. (2022). Knowing and not knowing: It's okay. *Career Development Network Newsletter Thriving in a New Career Landscape, 44*(1), 3.

Kamal, R. (2022). Quitting is just half the story: The truth behind the 'Great Resignation.' *The Guardian*. https://www.theguardian.com/business/2022/jan/04/great-resignation-quitting-us-unemployment-economy

Kuutti, K. (1996). Activity theory as a potential framework for human-computer interaction research. In B. A. Nardi (Ed.), *Context and consciousness: Activity theory and human-computer interaction* (pp. 17-44). MIT Press.

Lewis, J. (1996). *Reducing missionary attrition consultation*. All Nations College England.

Mangia, K. (2022). The great resignation & the future of work: Rajnish Sinha of TaskUs on how employers and employees are reworking work together. *Authority Magazine*. https://medium.com/authority-magazine/the-great-resignation-the-future-of-work-rajnish-sinha-of-task-us-on-how-employers-and-employees-89a0f07bed5b

Mathieu, F. (2018). *Running on empty: Compassion fatigue in health professionals.* https://www.caltrin.org/wp-content/uploads/2021/02/Mathieu-2018.pdf

Maxwell, J. A. (2013). *Qualitative research design: An interactive approach.* Sage.

Mehta, S. (2022). Going from the great resignation to 'the great retention' and other 2022 priorities. *Fast Company.* https://www.fastcompany.com/90707830/going-from-the-great-resignation-to-the-great-retention-and-other-2022-priorities

Merisotis, J. (2021). *Human work.* Rosetta Books.

Morse, G., Salyers, M. P., Rollins, A. L., Monroe-DeVita, M., & Pfahler, C. (2012). Burnout in mental health services: A review of the problem and its remediation. *Mental Health and Mental Health Services Research, 39*(5), 341–352.

National Career Development Association. (2015). *2015 NCDA code of ethics.* https://www.ncda.org/aws/NCDA/asset_manager/get_file/3395

Niles, S. G., (November 2021). Career development during a pandemic: Results of the NCDA Harris poll. National Career Development Association. https://www.ncda.org/aws/NCDA/asset_manager/get_file/631259?ver=2

Peacock, J. (2021). Thinking about starting a career coaching private practice? *Peak Careers.* https://peak-careers.com/?s=Thinking+about+starting+a+career+coaching+private+practice

Savickas, M. L. (2012). Life design: A paradigm for career intervention in the 21st century. *Journal of Counselling and Development, 90*(1), 13–19. https://doi.org/10.1111/j.1556-6676.2012.00002.x

Savickas, M. L., Nota, L., Rossier, J., Dauwalder, J., Duarte, M. E., Guichard, J., Soresi, S., Esbroeck, R., & van Vianen, A. E. M. (2009). Life designing: A paradigm for career construction in the 21st century. *Journal of Vocational Behavior, 75*(3), 239-250.

Sherr, I. (2022). The great resignation is changing work in America, and it's here to stay. *MSN News.* https://www.msn.com/en-us/news/technology/the-great-resignation-is-changing-work-in-america-and-experts-say-its-here-to-stay/ar-AASaZFp

U. S. Bureau of Labor Statistics. (2021). *Job openings and labor turnover survey.* Author. Retrieved September 30, 2021 from https://www.bls.gov/jlt/

Whitmore, J. (2017). *Coaching for performance* (5th ed.). Nicolas Brealey Publishing.

Wikipedia. (n.d.) Great resignation. Retrieved March 10, 2022 from https://en.wikipedia.org/wiki/Great_Resignation

Appendix A

SAMPLE: Powerful Coaching Questions

Goal-Setting

1. What are your desired goals? How will you know if you have achieved it? Why is what you desire to achieve important to you?
2. What does success represent to you? What have you attempted so far in your pursuit of achieving success?
3. What would you try now if you knew you could not fail? How can you make this something you are aiming towards, rather than something you are trying to move away from?
4. Is now the right time for you to make a commitment to achieving these goals?
5. What could you work on right now that would really put a smile on your face?
6. What will be different about your life once your goal has been achieved?
7. How do your goals align with your values? skills? interests?
8. Are all your goals S.M.A.R.T.?
   - **Specific:** *What exactly do you want to accomplish?*
   - **Measurable:** *How can you quantify this goal?*
   - **Achievable:** *Is this goal within your capabilities to achieve? Do you need to depend on others to achieve this goal?*
   - **Relevant:** *What are you willing to let go of to get this goal completed?*
   - **Time-bound:** *When will you start? What is your deadline?*

Change

9. When you have a need to change, what has worked for you in the past?
10. What values or strengths can you draw upon in making this change?
11. What is currently standing in the way of you getting out of your current situation?
12. What are you willing to do differently presently to get out of your situation?
13. What strategies might you use if you find yourself stuck accomplishing a task?
14. For your life to be perfect, what would you have to change?
15. What's one change you could make to your lifestyle that would give you more peace?
16. Imagine for a moment that your obstacle(s) are removed. How did you get to this point?
17. What could you stop doing that is preventing you from moving forward?

Supports

18. What type of personal or professional support do you possess?
19. Who can you declare has had a positive influence in your life and why?
20. Who can help hold you accountable for your growth?
21. Who could you connect with so achieving your goals becomes natural?

The Coach and the Coaching Session

22. What could we work on that would help you the most over the next few weeks?
23. What would be the most helpful thing for you to take away from this session?
24. What is the biggest change you are willing to commit to making in this session?
25. What would you like to get out of the next 30/45/60 minutes?
26. What kind of coach would you like me to be for you?
27. What will you need from me to be most successful in your [job search, career journey, etc.]?
28. What is one thing you will do immediately after our session today?
29. What is the most exciting part of working with a coach?
30. How will we evaluate the success of the coaching at the end of this session?
31. What will you do to continue your success post-coaching?

Adapted from International Coaching Federation. (2021). https://coachingfederation.org/

Appendix B

SAMPLE: Career Coaching Intake Form

Note to client: Please complete this form and send a copy of your most recent resume prior to your appointment to the contact email below.

Demographic Information:

Name: ____________________

Date: ____________________ Date of Birth: ____________Relationship Status: _____

Home/Mobile Phone: ____________________Is it ok to leave a message at this number? Y / N

Work Phone: ____________________Is it ok to leave a message at this number? Y / N

Email: ____________________Is it ok to email you? Y / N

Mailing Address: ____________________

Current occupational status: (i.e., F/T, P/T, self-employed, student, returning to work): ____________

Emergency Contact Name: ____________________

Emergency Contact Phone: ____________________Emergency Contact Relationship: _________

How were you referred? If online, which website? ____________________

Education/Training:

1. Briefly list the highest level of formal education obtained and any other relevant education, certifications, or specialized training:
2. What subjects have you most enjoyed studying?
3. What subjects have you least enjoyed studying?

Employment Information:

1. Current job title/employer: ____________________
2. Years in current position: ____________________
3. Are you having any difficulties/stressors in your current job? If so, please briefly describe those difficulties.

Career Information (please use as much room as needed):

1. What do you hope to accomplish from working with a career coach?
2. What are your current career goals? (Even if you are very uncertain, just fill in any thoughts that you might have.)
3. What would you most like to change about your current career?
4. What kinds of barriers could get in the way of meeting your career goals?
5. If you could do anything you wanted, what would it be?
6. Which 3-5 of these values are most important to you regarding your work?

____Achievement ____Environment ____Leadership ____Stability ____Enjoyment ____Creativity ____Money
____Moral Fulfillment ____Security ____Competition ____Helping others ____Status/recognition
____Intellectual Stimulation ____Variety ____Challenge/adventure ____Helping society ____Free time/leisure
____Self-Direction ____Authority ____Independence

7. List aspects of all your prior experience that you MOST enjoyed.

8. List aspects of all your prior experience that you LEAST enjoyed.

SKILLS:

1. What are the skill requirements for your next job?

2. What are the top three skills that you offer an employer?

3. What can you do easily that other people find difficult?

4. What is difficult for you that others seem to find easier?

HOBBIES:

How do you spend your leisure time?

Are there things that you would like to do with your leisure time that you are not able to do or have little time to enjoy?

FAMILY BACKGROUND:

What is/was your parents' career(s)?

In your opinion, were they satisfied with their career choice(s)?

What types of careers do other significant family members have (brothers, sisters, others who influenced you)?

Life Satisfaction Scale Instructions: Using a scale of 1 (least satisfied) to 10 (most satisfied), rate your satisfaction level with each of these life domains by placing an "X" in the box that corresponds to your rating.

	1	2	3	4	5	6	7	8	9	10
Career										
Community										
Family										
Friends										
Fun / Hobbies										
Home Environment										
Money										
Physical Health										
Partnership										
Spirituality										
TOTAL										

Comments on Life Satisfaction Scale:

PREVIOUS PROFESSIONAL ASSISTANCE:

1. Have you ever invested in professional career and/or personal development services?

2. What were the results of this support?

3. How were these results helpful?

Coach Name | Coach Phone Number | Coach Email Address

Appendix C

SAMPLE: Informed Consent

[coach business name / company name]

Informed Consent for Coaching Services

Coach:

Client:

Introduction

Please read this form carefully. You elect to participate in career coaching services provided by [coach name and/or company name]. Participation is voluntary, and you can cease participation at any time. Please ask any questions you may have before coaching begins. You will receive a copy of this consent form.

Benefits of Career Coaching

The International Coaching Federation (2021) defines **coaching** as an act of partnering with clients in a thought-provoking and creative process, inspiring them to maximize their personal and professional potential. The National Career Development Association's (2015) *Code of Ethics* section states A.1.b. "career planning" services are differentiated from "career counseling" services in the types of services provided to the client by the coach (A.1.b.). NCDA (2015) further explains that career planning services include:

> an active provision of information designed to help a client with a specific need, such as review of a résumé; assistance in networking strategies; identification of occupations based on values, interests, skills, prior work experience, and/or other characteristics; support in the job-seeking process; and assessment by means of paper-based and/or online inventories of interest, abilities, personality, work-related values, and/or other characteristics. (A.1.b.)

Delivery and Cost of Coaching

The following points regarding service are based on Section A of the NCDA (2015) *Code of Ethics* which establishes guidelines on services rendered, means of communication, fees, gifts for service, non-payment, and termination of service.

- *Disclosure of costs:* [The coach should establish a consistent price and disclose the total price of services before the coaching starts. Have agreements for services in writing approved by both parties before beginning the work. If a client cannot afford the cost of service, help to locate an appropriate alternative.]
- *Engagement and feedback boundaries:* [The coach should establish a clear feedback communication strategy and ensure the client understands delivery of engagement: number of sessions, delivery modality of service, length of engagement…].
- *Exit strategy:* [The coach should ensure clear next steps follow coaching, and determine how the coach and client will manage the transition.]

Privacy

Coaching records will be kept private. Coaches must appropriately document discussions throughout the working relationship, and in order to do so, informed consent is needed. Sessions will be documented to the best of the coach's ability and recollection, and information will be collected and recorded only when necessary and shared only when client permission is given or the law requires (NCDA, 2015). The ICF (2021) ethics code suggests coaches "maintain, store and dispose of any records, including electronic files and communications … in a manner that promotes confidentiality, security, and privacy, and complies with any applicable laws and agreements" (p. 5).

Contacts and Questions
[list coach's contact information here]

Statement of Consent
I have read this form (or have had it read to me). I have been encouraged to ask questions. I have received answers to my questions. I give my consent to participate in coaching. I have received (or will receive) a copy of this form. I understand the details outlined in this document and understand that I may cease coaching at any time without penalty.

Signature(s)/Date

Client Printed Name: ____

Client Signature: ____ Date: _______________

Appendix D

SAMPLE: Guided Imagery Exercise

Planning Your Future - Visualization Exercise

You may want to have a friend or career coach read the following imagery, or you may want to read through the exercise first and then imagine it on your own.

Find a quiet, calming place to close your eyes and relax as you imagine...

You are walking along a path...it could be in the woods, on a beach, in a valley...whichever is your favorite place in nature. As you walk along, feel the air around you...notice the smells...be conscious of the sounds...take note of any plants or vegetation around and what the path feels like under your feet...

Ahead you notice the path divides in two different directions. You take the first pathway that represents the first option you are considering. As you go down that path, experience that option. Try it on fully. How does it make you feel in your body...your heart...your mind? Notice everything inside you and outside you and what is happening...

Walk back to the fork in the path and try the other pathway that leads to your second option. Experience that option fully. How does it feel to experience this option?

Walk back again to the fork in the path. You suddenly see a third path that you had not been able to see before. You take the path and experience a solution you had not thought of before. What is it? What does it feel like?

Return back to the fork and then back down to where you originally started. You feel clear about something from these experiences. You take a deep breath, open your eyes, and come back to the present to write about your observations.

Write down your responses to the following questions:

1. What is your reaction to this exercise?
2. What feelings, thoughts or experiences did you have?
3. What did you realize about yourself and your plan that you did not realize before?
4. How have you or your goals changed as a result of this experience?
5. What goals would you like to set for yourself now?
6. If you are not ready to set a goal for yourself, what additional information do you need?
7. What are any barriers that are preventing you from setting a goal?
8. What can you do about these barriers?

Berkley Career Center. (2021). *Planning your future - Visualization exercise.* University of California Berkley. https://career.berkeley.edu/Plan/VisualizationExercise

Appendix E

National Career Development Association Code of Ethics

https://www.ncda.org/aws/NCDA/asset_manager/get_file/3395

Appendix F

American Counseling Association Code of Ethics

https://www.counseling.org/knowledge-center/ethics

Appendix G

International Coaching Federation Code of Ethics

https://coachingfederation.org/ethics/code-of-ethics

Appendix H

SAMPLE: Coaching Agreement

Client Name

Phone

Email

Summary of Client Needs:

Proposed Working Plan:

Components:

Package Details:

Cost:

Services Not Included:

<u>Engagement Letter</u>

Fees: Client fees are based upon the package agreed upon between coach and client. See fees section above for details. The quote is good for 30 days. 50% of fees must be paid at the time of signing the engagement agreement. The remaining balance is to be paid upon delivery of the last session as described above in the package.

Terms of Service: Client has 60 days from signing the contract to initiate utilization of service. Once initiation has begun, the client has set date (see above) to utilize the service. Client has the right to terminate the engagement at any time. Coach also has the right to terminate the engagement at any time, subject to giving the client a reasonable opportunity to arrange alternative assistance.

Understandings: Client understands that any estimate provided for fees and costs associated with this engagement letter is only an estimate based on uncertain factors, as to which information is incomplete and constantly changing, and that the actual fees and costs will be determined in accordance with the provisions of this letter and may vary from the estimate. The coach cannot make and has not made guarantees regarding the outcome of any matter. Any discussions the coach has with the client are limited to her[his] knowledge at the time.

Confidentiality and Code of Conduct: Communications between coach and client follow the NCDA *Code of Ethics*, which can be found on the coaching website. The coach will not share personal information or records of conversations without the client's consent. Exceptional circumstances may include legal or duty of care circumstances.

Statements of Account: The policy is to bill each client for full service at the beginning of the working relationship. Upon receipt of the signed contract, 50% of the total bill must be paid in full for service to begin. The remaining balance must be paid when the last service date is provided and/or termination date agreed upon by coach/client in this signed document.

If the above terms of our engagement are acceptable and agreed upon, please sign and return by email or US mail. If there are any questions about this letter, please call.

Looking forward to working with you!

Coach Name, Title

Accepted and Agreed:

By: ____ Date: ____________________

Maietta, H. N. (2022). *Career Coaching: Fundamentals, Applications, and Future Directions*. National Career Development Association.

Appendix I

SAMPLE: Lesson Plan

Emotional Intelligence (EI) Skills for the Workplace

Title of Lesson:	Emotional Intelligence Skills for the Workplace
Instructor Name:	
Total Time Required:	Full-day, 8 hours (~6 hours net without breaks)

Learning Objectives

As a result of this workshop, clients will be able to:

1. State the importance of emotional intelligence in life and in career
2. Describe the four basic aspects of emotional intelligence
3. Assess one's emotional intelligence levels according to the four aspects
4. Identify different strategies to develop emotional intelligence
5. List the basic skills of emotional intelligence in the workplace
6. Describe what low and high emotional intelligence looks like
7. Document a development action plan for one's emotional intelligence

Lesson Introduction

Method/Activity	Content Description	Support Materials	Duration
Ice breaker	Introduce yourself using a drawing highlighting your career, interests, hobbies, and/or talents	Poster Board/Paper Colored marker pens Double-sided tape	20 mins
Interactive lecture	Introduce the concepts of emotional intelligence and why it is important	PowerPoint slides Projector	30 mins

Main Lesson

Method/Activity	Content Description	Support Materials	Duration
Individual assessment	Complete an electronic 40-question individual assessment of EI	WiFi connection Mobile phones	45 mins
Small group discussion	Share assessment results with a small group and reflect. Provide feedback	Assessment Scores	20 mins
Assessment Debrief	Summarize findings from group discussions and answer any common questions or concerns	Flipchart Marker pens	15 mins

Large group discussion	Discuss different strategies for developing EI, and augment with own experiences	Flipchart Marker pens	20 mins
Interactive lecture	Introduce the common strategies for developing emotional intelligence	PowerPoint slides Projector	20 mins
Paired Exercise	Select and document 3 strategies to address critical areas of improvement in one's EI, offer ideas and feedback	Development template	20 mins
Interactive lecture	Introduce the basic skills contributing to the four emotional intelligence aspects	PowerPoint slides Projector	20 mins
Role Play	Discuss common scenarios of emotional intelligence skills in the workplace and role play potential responses	Scenario Handouts Chairs for Role play	30 mins
Small group discussion	Review roles plays and reflect on which ones had low or high emotional intelligence and why	Feedback Handouts, or Flipcharts and pens	15 mins
Group Debrief	Summarize findings from group discussions and answer any common questions or concerns	Flipchart Marker pens	15 mins

Modified from a lesson plan by Abdurrahman Q. AlQahtani, 2020

Appendix J

SAMPLE: Appreciative Inquiry Coaching Questions and Prompts

Disarm: In the *Disarm phase* or pre-cycle, the coach aims to create a welcoming environment that begins the rapport-building process. A few coaching suggestions might be:

1. Welcome clients personally with eye contact, kind facial expressions
2. Be mindful of verbal (words) and nonverbal communication (gestures)
3. Call client by name – consider offering client to use your first name
4. Begin the discussion with light, small talk to help your client feel comfortable
5. Use inclusive pronouns "We can explore your options together."
6. Give positive feedback. "That is good work – you are making excellent progress!"
7. Ask for feedback. "Do you have questions?" "What can I do to help?"

Discover: The coach begins the *Discovery phase* by asking positive, open-ended questions that help them gather information about the client's goals. A few coaching prompts might be:

8. Ask positive questions to learn more about the client "What worked this week?"
9. Explore the client's strengths, skills, accomplishments
10. Use non-verbal and verbal communication to help the client feel heard.
11. Ask behavioral based questions. "Tell me about a time when you enjoyed doing class projects or assignments. How did you feel? Why do you think you enjoyed it?"
12. "Tell me about a time when you experienced academic success. Why do you consider that a success? What did you do to make it successful? Who helped you?"
13. "What activities were you involved with in high school?"
14. "What do you like to do in your spare time?" "What books, movies, travel, hobbies, etc. interest you?"
15. "What accomplishment are you most proud of? Why?"
16. "Describe some life events that have made you into the person you are today?"
17. "Who are the most important role models in your life? Why?"

Dream: Once the coach and client have set goals, they can begin to brainstorm and map possibilities, which is key in the *Dream phase*. A few coaching suggestions might be:

18. Listen purposefully to what the client is trying to convey.
19. Make connections between information from the Discover phase and what is currently being shared. "What might be possible?"
20. Encourage clients to be open to the possibilities and remind them that there is more than one answer.

Design: The *Design phase* is a time to create a plan to materialize the client's dreams into reality. A few coaching prompts might be:

21. Explain technical information (assessment, occupational) in easy to understand language.
22. Avoid confusing acronyms.
23. Encourage inquiry and engagement from the student. "That's a good question."
24. Share options and discuss pros and cons of each option.
25. "What would that look like? Are there other options or versions of that option available?"
26. Make effective referrals.
27. Work together to set goals and specific sub-goals.

Deliver: Once the coach and client outline a plan of action; the client can act on their goal attainment in the *Deliver phase*. A few coaching prompts might be:

28. Review what you have accomplished in this session.
29. Review the client's responsibilities and the responsibilities and deadlines you have established.
30. Encourage the client to contact you with any problems or concerns.
31. Reiterate your confidence that the client can indeed accomplish the goals set forth.
32. Close up the conversation with optional follow-up questions:
    "Do you have any questions for me?" "Is there anything else that I should have asked you?"
33. "Thanks so much for coming. I really enjoyed meeting with you. Please don't hesitate to contact me if you have any questions."

Don't Settle: In the final phase, the coach supports the client as they execute their action plan, setting high expectations and check-points.

34. "Have high expectations for yourself."
35. "Set and meet daily goals."
36. "Celebrate progress and win's along the way."
37. "Use setbacks as growth opportunities."
38. "Document and share your progress with others."
39. "Don't just deliver but go to next degree—every time."

Modified from "119 Appreciative Inquiry Interview Questions and Examples," by Catherine Moore, 2021, *Positive Psychology*. https://positivepsychology.com/appreciative-inquiry-questions and "Appreciative Inquiry within the 5-Questions Model," by David L. Cooperrider, 2017, *Center for Appreciative Inquiry*. https://appreciativeinquiry.champlain.edu/wp-content/uploads/2017/10/appreciative-inquiry-within-the-5-question-model.pdf

Appendix K

SAMPLE: Standard Behavioral Interview Questions

Communication

Describe a time when you were able to effectively communicate difficult, sensitive, or unpleasant information.

What was the situation?

What steps did you take to ensure that your audience understood the information?

What was the outcome?

Describe a situation where you successfully persuaded others to do something or to see your point of view.

What was the situation?

What did you do?

What was the result?

Tell me about a time when you had to coach other leaders on presenting sensitive and complex information in a manner that could be easily understood.

What did you do?

What was the outcome?

What techniques did you teach the other leaders to use to confirm that the audience understood the information?

Interpersonal Skills

Tell me about a time when you had to coach other leaders on effectively "reading" others and guiding their actions by their understanding of the non-verbal cues.

What did you do?

What was the outcome?

Describe a time when you and your team members were dealing with a stressful work situation.

What was the situation?

How did you handle it?

What was the outcome?

Were you satisfied with the outcome, why or why not?

Tell me about a situation where you developed trust and respect with others throughout the organization.

What was the situation?

What steps did you take?

What was the result?

Were you satisfied with the result, why or why not?

Flexibility and Change

Give a specific example of how you have helped create an environment where different perspectives are valued, encouraged and supported.

What was the situation?

What did you do?

What was the outcome?

There are many internal and external factors that can impact an organization's key actions. Give me specific example of what you have done when the organization's priorities changed quickly.

What was the situation?

What did you do?

What was the outcome or result?

Sometimes it is essential to break out of the routine, standardized ways of doing things in order to accomplish the goals of the organization. Provide us with an example of a time when you identified that the organization needed to make a significant change, and tell us how you prepared the organization and the employees for that change.

How did you identify the need for change?

What were the impacts of the change?

What did you do?

Who did you involve in the change process?

What challenges did you face and how did you address them?

What was the result?

Were you satisfied with the result, why or why not?

Ethics and Integrity

Give me an example of a time when you created an environment of honesty, inclusion and respect for others.

What was the situation?

What did you do?

What challenges did you face?

How did you overcome these challenges?

What was the result?

Accountability and transparency are important values of an ethical leader. Give me a specific example of when you have demonstrated these values.

What was the situation?

What did you do?

What factors did you consider?

What was the outcome?

Modified from "Executive Behavioral Interview Guide," by HR Modernization Project, 2011, https://www.calhr.ca.gov/Documents/training-behavioral-interview-guide-executive-expanded.pdf

Another helpful source:

Society for Human Resource Management. (2016). A guide to conducting behavioral interviews with early career job candidates. https://www.shrm.org/LearningAndCareer/learning/Documents/Behavioral%20Interviewing%20Guide%20for%20Early%20Career%20Candidates.pdf

Appendix L

SAMPLE: G.R.O.W. Coaching Model

Step 1: Goal: The first step in the **G.R.O.W.** coaching model is defining the goal of the coaching trajectory. That includes the long term (the central theme of the trajectory) and the short term (the goal for every session). Goals need to be **S.M.A.R.T.**: Specific, Measurable, Achievable, Relevant, and Time-bound.

Example questions to identify the goal:

1. What's important to you when it comes to [theme]?
2. What will reaching the goal give you?
3. What do you want to achieve in [theme]?
4. How will you know you have reached your goal?
5. How will you know the problem has been solved?

Step 2: Reality: Step two of the **G.R.O.W.** coaching model is becoming aware of the client's actual situation. The coach's role is to stimulate self-evaluation with this client, and to identify the obstacles that have been holding the client back.

Example questions to discover the reality of one's client:

6. What is happening to you now?
7. What, when, with whom and how often?
8. What is the result of that?
9. Why is this theme a problem?
10. What are concrete examples of this problem?
11. What has been going wrong so far?
12. How do you manage to fail? Teach me how to do it.
13. What went well?
14. Is this always a problem or are there situations in which it isn't?
15. What are the defining factors? What can make the difference?
16. What have you done so far?

Step 3: Options: Step three of the **G.R.O.W.** coaching model generates ideas that can contribute to a solution. Try to start a creative brainstorming process without censure or conditionality. Generate solutions then structure to evaluate every option.

Example questions to generate options:

17. What else could you do?
18. What would you do if [obstacle] didn't stop you?
19. Imagine you already reached your goal. How did you do it?
20. What if this obstacle was not there anymore?
21. What else do you need to reach your goal? Where can you get it?
22. Which criteria will you use to evaluate this option?
23. What are the pros and cons of this option?

Step 4: Will: The fourth and last step of the **G.R.O.W.** coaching model is a concrete plan of action. Then the client's motivation to follow this plan is maximized.

Example questions to maximize the will:

24. What exactly will you do to reach your goal, and when?
25. Which of these options will you take?
26. What concrete step can you take now?
27. What steps come after?
28. Are all obstacles taken into account?
29. How will you overcome your obstacles?
30. How motivated are you, on a scale from 1 to 10, to go for this option?
31. What do you need to have a 10? Where can you get it?
32. How can your surroundings support you?
33. Will this plan get you to your goal?
34. Will it solve the underlying problem, too?

G.R.O.W. Worksheet

GOAL: What do you want?
REALITY: What is happening now?
OPTIONS: What can you do?
WILL: What will you do?

Adapted from "Coaching for Performance," by J. Whitmore, 2009, Nicholas Brealey Publishing.

INDEX

J

L

M

N

O

P

Q

R

S

T

V

W